PRAISE FOR *NURTURE FAITH*

"This book is an invitation to enter a world where biblical texts come alive and centuries-old characters speak truth and wisdom. It's an invitation to enter a world where God is active and faith is real. And then—and this is the volume's true strength—the book helps us realize this described world isn't some imagined destination; rather, it's the very place in which we live and breathe."

—GREG RAPIER, associate pastor, First Presbyterian Church of Delray Beach

"In this book, you will see evidence of the personal spirituality and literary talents of both the father and son. Doug and Nathanael Hood open up to the reader biblical treasures which are then faithfully applied to our personal needs and dreams. This book is not merely a collection of thoughts or essays. It is, instead, a journey in the direction of timeless truth."

—MICHAEL B. BROWN, former senior minister, Marble Collegiate Church

"For me personally, the daily devotional readings provided by *Nurture Faith* open a unique dimension to my quiet times of prayer, Bible study, and meditation. I feel like I have a colleague walking beside me, showing me wonderful discoveries along a shared journey, his comments and observations full of warmth, wit, humanity, and an authentic sense of wonder."

—RHYS L. WILLIAMS, Florida Atlantic University

"To the overall richness of this volume, Nathanael Hood, Doug's son, provides his own probing and thoughtful meditations. He opens new and often unexpected windows on scriptural passages, allowing us to see what we had not seen before and to reflect on these great texts in new and life-giving ways. Each one of his meditations is bold, clear, and provocative—a polished gem."

—THOMAS G. LONG, Candler School of Theology

"Nathanael Hood is an articulate writer and gifted storyteller, with the ability to unpack a scripture passage and expose its demand on the reader's life. His insightful messages often have a 'rest of the story' feel to them, whether taken from ancient history or current popular culture."

—DANIEL W. KLEIN, retired business executive

"These daily meditations strengthen my walk in the faith and help me to practice 'Christlikeness' daily as one of his followers."

—PEGGY SHUFORD, church member

Nurture Faith

Nurture Faith

Five-Minute Meditations to Strengthen
Your Walk with Christ

W. DOUGLAS HOOD JR.
NATHANAEL CAMERON HOOD

Foreword by Michael B. Brown

RESOURCE *Publications* · Eugene, Oregon

NURTURE FAITH
Five-Minute Meditations to Strengthen Your Walk with Christ

Copyright © 2022 W. Douglas Hood Jr. and Nathanael Cameron Hood. All rights reserved. Except for brief quotations in critical publications or reviews, no part of this book may be reproduced in any manner without prior written permission from the publisher. Write: Permissions, Wipf and Stock Publishers, 199 W. 8th Ave., Suite 3, Eugene, OR 97401.

Resource Publications
An Imprint of Wipf and Stock Publishers
199 W. 8th Ave., Suite 3
Eugene, OR 97401

www.wipfandstock.com

PAPERBACK ISBN: 978-1-6667-5111-6
HARDCOVER ISBN: 978-1-6667-5112-3
EBOOK ISBN: 978-1-6667-5113-0

08/11/22

All Scripture quotations, unless noted otherwise, are taken from the Common English Bible, copyright 2011. Used by permission. All rights reserved.

Where indicated, the Scripture quotations contained herein are from the New Revised Standard Version Bible, copyright 1989, by the Division of Christian Education of the National Council of the Churches of Christ in the U.S.A. Used by permission. All rights reserved.

Where indicated, Scripture quotations are from the *ESV® Bible (The Holy Bible, English Standard Version®)*, Copyright © 2001 by Crossway, a publishing ministry of Good News Publishers. Used by permission. All rights reserved.

Contents

Foreword by Michael B. Brown		xi
Preface		xiii
Acknowledgments		xv
Abbreviations		xvii
1	Ordinary Saints	1
2	Paul's Keynote Address	3
3	After the Flood . . . (Nathanael Hood)	5
4	Fruitful Disappointments	8
5	Victory On Our Knees	10
6	Love's Modesty	12
7	Longing for God	14
8	Happiness Begins Here	16
9	A Christian's Strength	18
10	When God Seems Distant	21
11	When God Laughs (Nathanael Hood)	23
12	Finding Hope in the Present Difficulty	26
13	The Continuing Work of the Resurrection	28
14	Diet Religion (Nathanael Hood)	30
15	Which Voice Shall I Follow?	33
16	Remembering Who We Are (Location: En-Gedi)	35
17	Plants of Steel	37
18	Defeated Lives (The Band's Visit)	39
19	The View from the Top (Location: Mount of Beatitudes)	41
20	When the Door Remains Closed	43
21	Leavening Faith (Nathanael Hood)	45
22	What We Can Know	47

23	Disillusioned at Christmas	49
24	Not Ashamed of Jesus (Location: Caesarea)	51
25	The Common Life Lived Uncommonly	53
26	The Mark of Christian Character	55
27	Living In the Present Tense	57
28	Tearing the Church Apart (Nathanael Hood)	59
29	A Real and Vital Faith	62
30	A Year of Faith and Hope	64
31	Doing What We Can (Location: Cana)	66
32	In the Crater of Calamity (Nathanael Hood)	68
33	What Makes People Good?	70
34	Nonconformist	72
35	The God Who Carries Us	74
36	The Promise of Something New (Location: Jerusalem) (Nathanael Hood)	76
37	Holy Moments	78
38	What We Might Be	80
39	The Two Popes (Nathanael Hood)	82
40	Ministry of Imagination	85
41	A Call to Prayer	87
42	Tears in a Bottle	89
43	When Faith Is Not Enough	91
44	When We Get God Wrong (Location: Capernaum) (Nathanael Hood)	93
45	Paying Attention to God	95
46	Unbeatable	97
47	The Fear of Insignificance	99
48	The Sound of God	101
49	A Cry of Desperation	103
50	Miracle in Bethany (Nathanael Hood)	105
51	Our Failure With Prayer	107
52	Ending Well	109
53	When Anger is a Virtue	111
54	A New Outlook	113
55	The Remarkable Power of Story	115
56	The Dust of Qumran (Location: Qumran)	117
57	God's Purpose. God's Call. God's Power	119
58	Conch Shell	121

59	When We Struggle (Location: Mount of Olives)	123
60	Vintage Sand Pails	125
61	How Shall We Rebuild? (Nathanael Hood)	127
62	Prescription for Unhealthy Anger	130
63	The God We Don't Expect (Nathanael Hood)	132
64	Thanksgiving Day in Bonaire	134
65	The Disciple's Rest	136
66	Fast Food Religion (Nathanael Hood)	138
67	Breakfast with Harry Emerson Fosdick	141
68	Weekend Tomb (Location: The Garden Tomb)	144
69	Throwing Away Self-Pity	146
70	Prayer and Responsibility	148
71	Christmas Begins with Wonder	150
72	Rethinking Sabbath (Nathanael Hood)	152
73	Living Positively with Our Handicaps	155
74	The Plain and Simple Gospel	157
75	Surrender (Nathanael Hood)	159
76	Speaking Wisely	161
77	The Great Wisdom of Prayer	163
78	Praying As Jesus Prayed	165
79	Where God Is Found (Nathanael Hood)	167
80	Hungry for God	170
81	Waiting to Understand	172
82	From Why to Where (Nathanael Hood)	175
83	Brush Strokes	178
84	A Life Unnoticed	180
85	Knowing God's Will	182
86	Success in the Spiritual Life	184
87	Religious Dropouts	186
88	Unfinished Discipleship	188
89	In the Silence We Hear, In the Stillness We See (Nathanael Hood)	190
90	Christ's Own Denial	193
91	Undefeated	195
92	When You Don't Know	197
93	Breaking and Remaking the Temple—Faith in a Time of Rioting (Nathanael Hood)	199

94	When God Says No	202
95	Never Alone	204
96	The Allure of a Defeated Life	206
97	Smash Your Statues, Drown Your Idols (Nathanael Hood)	208
98	A Life Trained By Christ	211
99	The Gift of Encouragement	213
100	Stuck Like Stockdale (Nathanael Hood)	215
101	Brokenness at Christmas	218
102	Instant Family	220
103	The Struggle to Doubt	222
104	Sandcastles	224
105	Ambition	226
106	Not Waiting for Happiness	228
107	A Multitude of Anna's (Nathanael Hood)	230
108	The Spirit of Christmas	233
109	How to be Miserable	235
110	Once Upon a Time in Denmark . . . (Nathanael Hood)	237
111	Dissatisfaction with the Ordinary	239
112	Maintaining Calm in the Tumult	241
113	Where Joy Is Found	243
114	Telling the Story Again	245
115	Determining Your Own Outcome	247
116	God's Hope for Us in the New Year	249
117	Disillusionment With God	251
118	How To Live by Faith	253
119	How Can I Find God?	255
120	Memory and God	257
121	A Very Strange Town (Nathanael Hood)	259
122	A Prescription for Living	262
123	Happy People	264
124	Don't Complain	266
125	The Deepest Form of Prayer	268
About the Authors		271
Bibliography		273

Foreword

DOUG HOOD IS AN insightful writer who brings solid biblical exegetical understanding to everything he composes. Additionally, he possesses a brilliant way of translating his scholarship into nurturing pastoral care and/or spiritual challenge that is accessible to everyone. In short, when you read his writings, you get an idea not merely of what the Bible says in general but, more personally, of what it says to us as communities and individuals of faith.

In Nathanael Hood, we see confirmation of the cliché that an apple does not fall far from the tree. I first came to know Nathanael when I served for a decade as Senior Minister at Marble Collegiate Church in New York City. He was in the journalism industry at the time and began attending our church primarily, I think, because of his dad's friendship with my predecessor, the late Dr. Arthur Caliandro. From time to time, Nathanael and I would meet for coffee and conversation. It didn't take long for me to be impressed by his keen intellect and strong gifts for writing. The more I read his spiritual/biblical compositions, the more convinced I became that his obvious gifts were indicators of a Divine Calling, which would one day bear fruit for the Church at-large.

In this book, you will see evidence of the personal spirituality and literary talents of both the father and the son. Doug and Nathanael Hood open up to the reader biblical treasures which are then faithfully applied to our personal needs and dreams. This book is not merely a collection of thoughts or essays. It is, instead, a journey in the direction of timeless truth.

Having transitioned for the most part from pulpit to classroom, this is the very sort of book I hope my students will read. Their textbooks give them information. This, however, will give them inspiration, guidance, and hope.

DR. MICHAEL B. BROWN
Former Senior Minister, Marble Collegiate Church, New York, New York
Instructor of Biblical Studies, High Point University
Adjunct Instructor in DMin Studies, New Brunswick Theological School

Preface

MANY PEOPLE TODAY HAVE pretty much reduced their Christianity to an admiration of Jesus. This is an easy response, a natural response. This response requires no effort. Yet, admiration alone is insufficient for a meaningful relationship. Admiration alone fails to take Jesus seriously. It is no different from any other relationship. Tell your spouse or close friend that you admire them and an appreciative smile comes your way. Yet, if you stop there, stop with words of admiration, the relationship does not grow. Relationships that matter requires effort, they require time listening to the other and learning all that you can about them. It is then those relationships deepen beyond admiration to something so much richer. This is taking someone seriously because he/she matters to you.

In her deeply profound and poignant book, *Small Victories: Spotting Improbable Moments of Grace*, Anne Lamott shares the brokenness of growing up in a home with a mother and father who were so unhappy together. Dinners were largely silent, eye contact avoided, with an occasional clipped comment thrown at another. What happened that turned parents, once deeply in love with one another, into cheerless people who occupied the same house? Lamott writes that the better question is what did not happen. "They were not able to take their pleasures, their love of their children, out to the next concentric circle, where something bigger awaited."[1]

That is a helpful insight for looking at the faith of many today. They quietly move through the rhythms of Christian practice, attending worship as regularly as they can, attending an occasional dinner and teaching at the church, and completing an *Estimate of Giving Card* each year that demonstrates their financial support for the church. Yet, they fail to take their faith to the next concentric circle. Interest in learning more of Christ, of leaning deeply into a relationship with Jesus fades. The result is that the joy of faith also fades. The practice of faith simply becomes one more responsibility demanding attention among so many other life responsibilities.

---

1. Lamont, *Small Victories*, 99.

The great Christian thinker and author, C. S. Lewis said that often it is not teaching that we require. Occasionally what we need is a reminder of what we already know. In this collection of meditations, my son, Nathanael, and I hope to remind you of what you already know—that we belong to a God that seeks a relationship with us. God is not content with our admiration. God desires a relationship that is eager to know more and to experience more of God's power, love, and strength for the challenges that we must confront each day. Intentional time each day engaging God's word in the Bible provides fresh inspiration and increases our desire to reach the next concentric circle in our relationship with God.

W. Douglas Hood Jr.

Acknowledgments

FRED CRADDOCK ONCE COMMENTED to me that creativity doesn't take place in a vacuum and that great preachers read the sermons of great preachers. Through this practice our own grasp of scripture is deepened, our understanding of effective communication is broadened, and the use of illustrative material triggers the remembrance of our own stories that are useful for faithful preaching, teaching, and writing. My own devotional practice has been nourished by the work of many great preachers, some of another generation and others who continue to proclaim with considerable impact—"impact" defined by Saint Augustine as the ability to teach, to delight, and to persuade. Of a former generation, I am particularly grateful for the work of Henry Sloane Coffin, J.H. Jowett, and Harry Emerson Fosdick. Today, I remain a student of the continuing ministry of Thomas G. Long, Will Willimon, Barbara Brown Taylor, Thomas K. Tewell, and Michael B. Brown.

I am confident that Craddock would agree that faith formation requires more than a persuasive sermon. The formation of a vital faith is best completed in faith communities. I am grateful for the communities of faith that have formed me and taught me how to be a pastor and communicator of God's redemptive story. That includes the Trinity Presbyterian Church, Meridian, Mississippi—for they welcomed me for fifteen months as a seminary intern and, with the patient wisdom of their pastor, Fred C. (Rusty) Douglas, taught me the value of presence and listening for effective ministry. I am grateful for the community of First Presbyterian Church of Columbus, Georgia which provided me with my first call of ministry as an Associate Pastor, and for the McLeod Memorial Presbyterian Church of Bartow, Florida, who welcomed me as their pastor following my ministry in Columbus. Both of these congregations were gracious with my stumbles and continued to form me for stronger ministry. For the congregations of Woodhaven Presbyterian Church of Irving, Texas, and the Lenape Valley Presbyterian Church of New Britain, Pennsylvania, I am grateful for the opportunity to build strength upon strength as a communicator both in the pulpit and in writing. Each continued to challenge me, stretch my understanding of ministry, and encourage continued professional development. And finally, in my present call as the Senior Pastor of First Presbyterian Church of Delray Beach, Florida, I have been given the good fortune of working alongside other pastors whose own imaginative practice of ministry strengthens my own. Greg Rapier, my present colleague in ministry, is one of the finest pastors practicing ministry today and I am grateful to him for his kind words prepared for this book. Clearly, this book is a product of a shared journey with multiple communities that have loved my family and me.

Manuscript preparation requires strong administrative ability, attention to detail, and a careful eye. I thank Nancy Fine, the Business Administrator of the church and a close friend, for her work on this book. Nancy has offered wise counsel on the selection of meditations assembled here, proofed the manuscript multiple times, corrected mistakes, and checked references for accuracy. This book is the stronger because of her.

I deeply appreciate Rob Tanner and his wife, Joan, spiritual leaders of the church. Both dear friends, Rob chaired the pastor search committee that invited me to this present ministry. Each of them remains encouragers of my ministry and continually nudges me toward greater effectiveness. John C. (Skip) and Leslie Randolph, Ken and Vandy Janson, and Al and Elaine Hulse are close friends who have enriched my family and me in uncommon ways. Shared meals, vacations, and family celebrations of birthdays and anniversaries have woven each of you richly into the fabric of our family life.

Most importantly, I deeply appreciate my family, my wife Grace, and my two children, Nathanael, and Rachael. On my desk is a family picture of the four of us. Each morning I look at that picture and recall the words from the 2017 movie, The Greatest Showman, starring Hugh Jackman: "All I ever want, all I ever need, is right here in front of me." Each of you continues to cause me delight and immeasurable joy.

Abbreviations

AD	Anno Domini
BC	Before Christ
BCE	Before the common era
CE	Common Era
CEB	Common English Bible
ESV	English Standard Version Bible
NET	New English Translation Bible
NRSV	New Revised Standard Version Bible

1

Ordinary Saints

"'Whoever is faithful with little is also faithful with much, and the one who is dishonest with little is also dishonest with much.'"

Luke 16:10

There are people who live daily in the grip of a vast inferiority complex. Always ready to do some great thing, contribute on a grand scale, and produce extraordinary changes or innovations they fail to value the small and ordinary. With an insufficient view of less imposing matters of life, they settle into a pattern of mediocrity. Worse, failure to appreciate the importance of common occasions and tasks their lives tumble into defeat and despair. Their take on a life well lived is in variance with the view of God, "Whoever is faithful with little is also faithful with much." God does not despise the common, ordinary, and small. On one particular occasion, Jesus celebrates the power of faith that is as small as a mustard seed.

Generally, the failure to value the common and small is located in the ignorance of the real significance of events, which we think we understand. Recently, a pastor received a note from someone in a former church who wrote of how their life was turned by some single word of compassion and hope given at a time of desperation and fear. The pastor struggled to remember the occasion, an incident that seemed so small and trivial as to scarcely warrant the pastor's notice. On the other hand, many of us can recount high and stirring occasions, which, at the time, appeared to have occupied a large stage in the unfolding drama of the day only now leaving no trace of importance in their memory.

One personal experience suggests that there may be more value and honor and reward in attending to the daily small and ordinary occasions than one great event. When my daughter, Rachael, was very young she spoke of a friend from school. Seated at the family dinner table, Rachael shared that Cathy's father was taking her to Hawaii that summer for vacation. My wife and I glanced at one another, bracing for our daughter's certain disappointment when we had to share that we simply could not afford a vacation as nice. But Rachael continued, "But I have a family that loves me and that is all I need." That should have been enough for me but I probed deeper. "Doesn't Cathy's parents love her?" I asked. "Maybe. But Cathy's dad works long hours. She never sees her dad. You help me every day with my homework and read to me at bedtime. I prefer that."

Jesus is asking that we reappraise the value of living honorably in the ordinary and small things of life. Not all of us will occupy a leading role in a Broadway play, serve on a prestigious board, or appear on the cover of a magazine for some extraordinary achievement. As a young disciple, Jesus tells us that we all begin "first the stalk, then the head, then the full head of grain." (Mark 4:28) It is the very nature of growth that we have a humble beginning. The character of a disciple is developed by attention to the small things as growth occurs. The disciple that accepts—and loves—the duties of the common, daily walk with Christ shines brightly not because they purpose to shine, but because they are filled with the light of Christ. It is then that what may appear small and ordinary grows dignified and sacred in our sight.

Heavenly Father, fill me with your Spirit and guide me toward excellence and dignity in all the small things before me this day. Amen.

2

Paul's Keynote Address

"Love never fails."

1 CORINTHIANS 13:8A

ONE OF MY MOST dramatic experiences occurred one evening during a semester of study in Coventry, England. I gathered with other students to attend a performance of Handel's *Messiah* in Coventry Cathedral. Hung from the chancel wall of that cathedral is a large tapestry that depicts Jesus seated in power over all creation, his two hands held up as if to communicate a blessing. We listened to the beautiful music from that oratorio, aware that we were being grasped by its message about the way the world ought to live, that we are to follow the way of Jesus and his example of love. As the Hallelujah Chorus began, the lights of the cathedral were dimmed, and then extinguished altogether, leaving a bright spotlight on the tapestry—a bright light on the seated Jesus offering his blessing to the world.

I was overcome with emotion. I stood to exit the cathedral to keep my tears private. As I turned my back on the chancel and turned my back on the seated Jesus now lit up in the darkness, the visual impact almost brought me to my knees. The light on the tapestry was reflected on the all-glass façade of the cathedral. Just outside that cathedral, which was constructed following the Second World War, are the ruins of the original cathedral destroyed in the war. The visual impact that I experienced was Jesus seated in power, hands raised with a blessing, juxtaposed over the brokenness and devastation of the world. Since that evening I have often reflected on what it would mean if the world were to give itself completely over to the love of Jesus Christ.

This chapter of Paul's first letter to the Corinthian Church, chapter 13, is regarded as his keynote address—Paul's great oratorio of love. Like the twenty-third Psalm, this is one of those passages of our Bible that is so saturated with imagery, beauty, and power that the substance of our faith reveals itself in uncommon ways. While it daunts the reader it also fascinates and challenges. For in this hymn of love, Paul does more than assert the supremacy of love. Here, Paul declares that it is love that gives every other gift its value. He names many of the treasured gifts of the Christian faith—the gift of tongues, the gift of prophecy, a sturdy faith that can move mountains, and generosity beyond compare and boldly states that they amount to nothing without love.

Paul turns the searchlight onto our lives. In our Christian walk, in our corporate worship, do we have love for one another? He helps us examine ourselves deeply and honestly. Are we patient with one another? Are we kind? Do we practice humility rather than arrogance? Do we put aside irritability and complaints and the insistence on our own way and consider the well-being of others? Have we developed the capacity to think beyond ourselves to consider what may be best for the larger faith community? Paul is relentless. He pushes the question further. Do we still behave like a child who protests much when things are not going our way or have we matured in the faith and placed away childish things? This is how Paul concludes his keynote address. And the question lingers for each one of us to answer, have we love for one another?

Forgive my childish impulses, Oh God, and direct my attention once again to Christ's example of love. Amen.

3

After the Flood . . . (Nathanael Hood)

"Noah, a farmer, made a new start and planted a vineyard. He drank some of the wine, became drunk, and took off his clothes in his tent. Ham, Canaan's father, saw his father naked and told his two brothers who were outside. Shem and Japheth took a robe, threw it over their shoulders, walked backward, and covered their naked father without looking at him because they turned away. When Noah woke up from his wine, he discovered what his youngest son had done to him. He said, "Cursed be Canaan: the lowest servant he will be for his brothers."'

GENESIS 9:20–25

DOES ANYONE ELSE THINK it odd that the story of Noah and the Flood is one of the first Bible stories we tend to teach our children? Far from the stories of Jesus healing the sick, Moses leading the Hebrews out of Egypt, or Jonah sitting in the belly of a whale, the story of the Flood is one of apocalypse—the world ends! Countless men, women, children, and animals drown! Yet Noah is a mainstay of Sunday Schools everywhere. On a certain level, it's understandable why: in addition to being one of the most dramatic and suspenseful stories in the Old Testament, it's a useful tool for teaching the importance of living kind, righteous lives like Noah and trusting in God the way his family did while on the Ark. The story of the Flood is also an easy way to teach children how God always keeps God's promises—you can point to a rainbow as proof! So, we clean up the story, sidestepping the human suffering and focusing on the happy ending.

But there's another part of the Noah story that nobody really tries to sanitize because nobody really tries to discuss it anymore: the Curse of Ham. After the Flood, after the world has dried up and the animals have returned to the earth, Noah and his family begin building a new home. Noah abandons his previous responsibilities as shipbuilder and sea captain and becomes a farmer, a toiler of the land. One of the first things he does as an ex-sailor is to plant a vineyard, make wine from the grapes, and get blackout drunk. So drunk, in fact, that he ends history's first bender passed out and naked. When his son Ham finds him, he tells his other two brothers about their father's sorry state. These two brothers then take a garment, hold it between them, and walk back into their father's tent to clothe his nakedness without seeing it. After waking and learning what his sons did, Noah curses Ham. Or more specifically, Ham's son—Noah's own grandson— Canaan. Turning then to the two sons who covered his nakedness, he praised them and doomed his grandson Canaan to their perpetual slavery. The story of Noah then ends.

What exactly did Ham do to justify this perpetual slavery of his ancestors? The answer is . . . we're not sure. There's a long history of Jewish and Christian scholars trying to reverse engineer Ham's supposed transgression, some saying it was sinful in Biblical times for sons to see their fathers naked, others identifying absent details and suggesting he castrated his father. But personally, I don't think there *was* a rational reason for Noah's curse, because I don't think Noah was acting rationally. I think Noah was traumatized, and in his trauma lashed out at Ham over a trifling matter in a way that would hurt him the most, by hurting his son. Think back to the realities of the flood—the suffering, the death—and consider that Noah witnessed it all firsthand. Do you think he ever looked out on the flooded world and trembled at the thought of the waters never receding? Do you think he ever wondered if he deserved to survive at all?

I've been thinking about Noah, trauma, and survivor's guilt a lot lately. In a way, we've all lived through our own Flood recently in the shape of Covid-19. What was Noah's family living on the Ark but a literal quarantine? Covid might not be flooding cities, but millions have died from it. In its own way, the resulting societal trauma has been just as devastating. I've seen friends and loved ones—good, kind, generous people—transform into hungover Noah's, desperate to relieve their trauma by ripping and tearing into bystanders and fellow congregants over things as simple as mask mandates. By the grace of God, this pandemic will blow over one day. And once these floodwaters recede, what next? Will we try to reconcile with those we've hurt? Will we try to repair our broken communities, re-knit our divided congregations, and revive our lost friendships? The stakes are too high not to try, lest we—just like Noah—doom ourselves and our loved ones to perpetual slavery of hate and resentment.

Lord, forgive us our selfishness and ugliness. Help us to always see your sacred image in others and treat them with love and compassion. Guide us in our trauma and hold us in your arms until the floodwaters recede and the rebuilding begins. Amen.

4

Fruitful Disappointments

"I'll visit you when I go to Spain. I hope to see you while I'm passing through. And I hope you will send me on my way there, after I have first been reenergized by some time in your company."

Romans 15:24

I ONCE KNEW A woman whose romance had gone on the rocks. She made a grand announcement to her work colleagues that she was never going to permit herself to fall in love again. "You only get hurt," she said. I was a young graduate student struggling in the romance department myself so I remained silent. Fortunately, an older and wiser woman who was our supervisor made the observation, "If you deal with each disappointment that way, you don't live." I don't recall how many work associates were present at that moment but each of us became silent as those few words sunk deep into our hearts. The supervisor continued, "Reassess that relationship. Take something useful from it. Make it fruitful for the next."

The Apostle Paul wanted to go to Spain. He had his heart set on it. Paul's zeal for preaching the Gospel of Jesus Christ compelled him to reach the outermost rim of the world. What Paul got was a prison cell in Rome. Like my work colleague, Paul was disappointed. Life's unexpected turns and twists never permitted Paul to take that journey to Spain. That one historical fact dispels the notion that those who follow Christ are never disappointed, and never experience disruptions in their own life journey. Paul wanted

Spain. Paul got a prison cell. How Paul responded is instructive for us. Paul used that time in prison to reassess God's claim upon him, Paul wrestled something useful from his disappointment. Imprisonment provided quiet time to penetrate deeply into the mysteries of Christ.

Psychologists tell us that suicide, addictions, and some forms of nervous breakdowns are evidence that people are ill-equipped to manage disappointment. Loss and disappointment, regardless of the magnitude, deprive us of our ability to think and act beyond ourselves. Our focus on disappointment becomes so sharp that we are unable to see what remains that is positive in our lives. Consequently, loss and disappointment shrink our life to the exact size of our desire that is unmet. Popular speaker and author, John Maxwell, encourages us along a different path—encourages us to embrace failure and disappointments, extracting from them lessons that result in us "failing forward." It is then those mistakes, failures, and disappointments become stepping-stones to something so much more.

Few people have the opportunity to live life on the basis of their first choice—whether that be a choice in career, a spouse that "checks all the boxes," or some other longing. Paul wanted to go to Spain. He got a prison cell. A large majority of us will find that life moves in directions that are not of our choosing. That is precisely when the Christian faith tells us that we should get something out of every experience, every new direction, even out of disappointment. The bulk of the New Testament is letters written by Paul—many of them written while in prison! After twenty-some years as an iterant preacher, Paul gets a prison cell. At last, Paul found the quiet time to think deeply about what he had learned of Jesus Christ and pour those thoughts out in a written form. That would be Paul's greatest contribution to the Christian Church.

Forgive me, O Lord, when disappointment reduces my vision to see what you are doing in my life. Direct my gaze away from myself to a larger story. Amen.

5

Victory On Our Knees

"I live on high, in holiness, and also with the crushed and the lowly, reviving the spirit of the lowly, reviving the heart of those who have been crushed."

Isaiah 57:15

Recently Grace and I spent a weekend in the Florida Keys with two dear friends. In addition to sharing meals together, shopping, stimulating conversation about our families, and an evening of bicycling, the four of us summoned the courage to try something we had never done before—paddleboarding. The popularity of the sport seems to be growing exponentially in South Florida, particularly the Keys. It looked fun and appeared to be a sport that would be easy for beginners. It was not. Paddleboarding challenges both core strength and balance and beginners spend more time falling from the board than standing. My wife, Grace, perhaps an exception; other people asked me how long she had been paddleboarding

After several attempts at standing—and failing—Grace said to me to begin on my knees, "you have more control on your knees." Hearing my wife's words, my friend commented, "I hear a sermon in there somewhere!" Naturally, I was frustrated that I was unable to master paddleboarding immediately. But then, where would have been the satisfaction in that? Satisfaction with life is often preceded by considerable effort and discipline. So it is with our Christian faith. We must experience failure on our own before we can value God's presence and strength that enables us to stand. The pinnacle of joy and satisfaction in our faith is our communion with the Risen Christ. That communion begins on our knees in prayer—our demonstration that we can't do life apart from God.

To be a Christian is to follow Jesus. And his own life was no leap from the cradle in Bethlehem to the victory of Easter morning. Victory implies something was defeated. Between birth and resurrection, Jesus lived deeply. It was a life that knew suffering, betrayal, and abandonment. We experience with Jesus the victory and joy of the Resurrection because we know all too well his hell of loneliness and pain. It was a hell that Jesus defeated because he spent so much of his life on his knees. Grace is absolutely right, "You have more control on your knees."

The central question that confronts many today is where is God in the darkness of the present world—the darkness that seems to defeat a hope for tomorrow? Isaiah declares that our God lives with the crushed and the lowly. God is not only present in our darkness; God is at work, "reviving the spirit of the lowly, reviving the heart of those who have been crushed." God did so for Jesus. God will do so for us. What is needed is that we wait for God's victory on our knees.

Holy Spirit, stir me and ready me for inspiration when the verdict of the day seems to suggest there remains little hope. Amen.

6

Love's Modesty

"Love is patient, love is kind, it isn't jealous, it doesn't brag, it isn't arrogant."

1 Corinthians 13:4

It is reported that Abraham Lincoln once made a speech before a huge audience and was greeted with loud and long applause. As he was leaving the podium, a man said, "That was a great speech Mr. President; listen to how they enjoyed what you said!" Lincoln, in his usual self-deprecating manner, responded, "I am kept humble by the fact that the crowd would be twice as large if I were to be hanged."[1] Always modest, never vaulting himself or puffed up, Abraham Lincoln cared little for his own reputation. He did not need to. His love for his country and his desire for useful service characterized by empathy, humility, and respect for opposing opinions made him as large as the monument erected in his honor in Washington, D.C.

"Love," the apostle Paul writes, doesn't brag, nor is it arrogant. These two qualities of love are closely related to each other. "Doesn't brag" refers to outward conduct and behavior; "isn't arrogant" refers to an inward disposition. Together they characterize someone who is modest, ready to stoop to serve. We think again of Jesus on that dark night that he was betrayed. On their way to the Upper Room, the disciples disputed as to whom of them was the greatest. Each of them presented arguments for their own claim to

---

1. Cobb, "Real Life, Real People," 108.

the highest honor. The result was that when they arrived in the Upper Room and took their seats, not one of them would stoop to the humble service of foot washing. So, Jesus rose from the table, took a towel and a basin, and began to wash the disciple's feet.

The church in Corinth is experiencing quarrelsome behavior that is dividing the faith community. Various members are elevating themselves, declaring possession of the greater spiritual gifts. The one who has the gift of tongues believed they exercised a gift beyond compare, especially over the more plain and practical gift of prophecy. The same manner of boasting and argument infused the discourse over any number of spiritual gifts. Rather than placing each gift at the disposal of the community, to bless and build, competitiveness became the order of the day. The result of all the boasting was friction and strife. The cure for all that, writes the apostle Paul, is love— a love that has no mark of brag, or swank, or swagger. Genuine love, love that builds the community of faith is modest.

Love never seeks to assert its superiority. The love that Paul desires for the Corinthian Church is one that serves, seeking the welfare of others. That love takes no notice of the worthiness of another. Nor does it seek acknowledgment. Only one concern is present—to serve another in a manner that eases the strain and burden of life. It is a love that is captured by the belief that God continues to be at work in the lives of individuals, reconciling them to God and changing them into something so much more than they presently are. As this demonstration of love takes possession of our souls, what is ugly, bitter, and broken in our lives is diminished. What increases in our hearts is patience and love that knows no jealousy and celebrates the gladness of another.

Envy grows into hate and hate is demonstrated in strife and discord. Forgive all my impulses that diminish the value of another. Increase love in my heart today, a love that thinks of another's needs before my own. In the name of Jesus, I pray. Amen.

7

Longing for God

"Just like a deer that craves streams of water, my whole being craves you, God."

PSALM 42:1

THE PHILOSOPHER BLAISE PASCAL once wrote that each one of us is born with a God-shaped hole in our hearts.[1] Naturally, Pascal was not speaking of a literal hole such as a square hole. The hole he speaks of is an empty space, a deep longing or hunger. We often attempt to fill this empty space with other things or pursuits. Perhaps we seek a relationship that will satisfy this longing, or acquire some material reward such as a new car or country club membership. Each of these may satisfy for a period. Cracker Jacks at dinnertime will satisfy hunger for a little while. But the satisfaction will be short-lived. After all, if the empty space implanted in our hearts is for God, any substitute will simply leave empty spaces all around it. Our hearts remain empty.

This Scripture from Psalms speaks of deer that crave streams of water. What the original readers of this passage know is that many aqueducts in the Holy Land were built with a mesh-like covering to prevent trash from clogging the water supply. Thirsty deer could hear the streams of water, they could see the streams of water, but they could not drink from those streams. The mesh covering that prevented trash from entering the water

---

1. Pascal, *Pensees*, 48.

also prevented the deer access to the water. So, the longing to quench their thirst remained. What is important for the reader to understand is that before the deer "listened for" and "moved toward" the sound of streams of water, there was first a thirst.

As the deer experienced thirst, often we experience a spiritual thirst, a spiritual yearning for something more. Sometimes that thirst is noticed when we see others living a deeply satisfying relationship with Jesus. There is simply something about their faith that is missing in our own experience. Other times we simply become tired of acquiring more and more and finding that all of it fails to satisfy our deepest hungers. The emptiness remains. And most of us will try almost anything to fill that emptiness only to be disappointed time and time again. That is because they fail to recognize that only the pursuit of a deep relationship with Jesus through regular prayer and study of Jesus' teachings can ever satisfy that emptiness.

During my sophomore year of college, I had the opportunity to spend the fall semester of study in London. To complete a class assignment, I traveled to Liverpool for a weekend of research. Arriving in the early evening of a Friday—London to Liverpool—by train, I immediately looked for an inexpensive opportunity for dinner. Just as I began to enjoy the fish and chips I had ordered to go, eating while standing along a sidewalk, I realized I had lost my father's professional Nikon camera he had trusted to my care. I lost my appetite, threw away a largely uneaten meal, and went off searching for the camera. Ultimately my search led me to a homeless man, the Cathedral of Christ the King, and Father Murphy, who had my camera. Returning the camera to me, Father Murphy looked deep into my eyes and asked, "Are you hungry?" At that moment I sensed that the question was intended for something much deeper than my stomach.

Father, help me today to correctly identify those longings that only you can fill. Amen.

8

Happiness Begins Here

"Therefore, you should treat people in the same way that you want people to treat you; this is the Law and the Prophets."

MATTHEW 7:12

RECENTLY I FOUND SOMETHING on Facebook that may interest you. "'I suffered, therefore you must suffer, too' is such an odd mindset to carry through life. I hear it all the time when people defend unpaid internships, awful entry-level jobs, student debt, etc. Whatever happened to wanting the next generation to have it better than you did?" I don't recall the source of these words. I simply took a screenshot of them to share. What would be fascinating is to listen to how these words land upon the mind and hearts of others. My guess—and this is a guess—is that our response to these words will demonstrate whether we live by an ethic of fairness or an ethic of generosity. My contention is that those who live by an ethic of generosity are the happiest.

There is much that is unfair in life. It is unfair that an apple is a better diet choice than a blueberry muffin. It is unfair that some have a greater fluency with languages than others. More deeply, it is unfair that some children must struggle with cancer and other illness while—fortunately—a vast number of children will mature into adulthood with health. This week I read in the news about an airline employee who noticed a pregnant woman experiencing considerable discomfort while waiting to board her flight. The airline employee asked the person at the head of the line if he would graciously permit the pregnant women to board first. His response was, "Tell her to wait in line like everyone else!" Upon hearing this, another man near the front of the line invited the woman to take his place.

What is remarkable in this story is that the man who gave up his place in line walked to the rear. Apparently, he sought to avoid anyone else behind him making an argument of unfairness. Who does that? Perhaps he would answer that this decision—the decision to put others first—makes the world a little more pleasant, a little brighter, and increases his own happiness that he can make that happen. There is an incredible force that is unleashed in the world by such a generosity of spirit, a force of such immense warmth that it is life-giving to others. It reminds me of a professor in my graduate studies that said that when the people of God fear scarcity, fear that there is not enough "good stuff" to go around, we become mean people, struggling with others for our fair share.

There are destructive forces that are loose in the world, forces of anger, fear, resentment, and jealousy. Additionally, misfortune falls upon every one of us from time to time. Car accidents, natural disasters, and theft are ubiquitous. Amy Morin writes, "We all experience pain and sorrow in life. And although sadness is a normal, healthy emotion, dwelling on your sorrow and misfortune is self-destructive."[1] Matthew's Gospel offers an alternative. Focus less on yourself and focus more on adding value to others. Treat others, as you would like to be treated. Such daily deposits into the lives of other people, strengthening them and encouraging them is one of the world's oldest and best rules. Practice this rule regularly in your life and you will discover that it is golden.

Forgive my preoccupation with my wants and desires, O Lord, and direct my attention to the needs of others, loving them as I want to be loved. Amen.

---

1. Morin, *13 Things*, 18.

9

A Christian's Strength

"I can endure all these things through the power of the one who gives me strength."

PHILIPPIANS 4:13

WHAT IS SO REMARKABLE about these words is that they are spoken by a man in chains. Paul is a prisoner in Rome. In a life dedicated to serving Christ, Paul has endured much—shipwreck, ridicule, hunger, and excruciating poverty. Now he sits in a Roman prison and writes that whatever the circumstances, Paul has learned the secret of inner strength and contentment. Perhaps even more remarkable, Paul lays aside his own needs and concerns to write a deeply personal letter to the Philippians to encourage them in their faith. Despite his imprisonment and impending trial, Paul's one desire is to share with the church in Philippi that joy and strength do not come from outward circumstances but from an intimate relationship with Jesus. That power is so tremendous and so available that Paul feels he can face anything knowing that nothing can diminish his spirit. His spirit was invulnerable. Paul wants the Philippians to utilize that same power.

The interesting thing about the New Testament is that we find that same power animating most of the early Christians. A profession of faith in Jesus usually pushed people to the margins of their communities. Families were torn apart—mothers and daughters, fathers and sons no longer in relationship with one another because one or the other decided to become a follower of Jesus. Worship services were conducted in secret and often disrupted by Jewish leaders eager to destroy the Jesus movement. The worst tortures that could be imagined were invented and performed to discourage participation in the new Christian faith. There was every reason for ignoring the swelling growth of the Christian Church, keeping your head down, and simply avoiding trouble. Yet, for all the compelling reasons to remain separate from those following Jesus, men and women who risked believing in Jesus made one dominating impression wherever they went, the impression of uncommon power.

That power has not been withdrawn. It is not a closely guarded secret. Where men and women continue to take Christ's attitude of loving others and serving others that same power is unmistakable. What is troubling is that few would say that the church today impresses the world with the same power as it once did. Somehow those who claim discipleship to Jesus Christ show little evidence of a changed life, a life of uncommon power. Absent in many Christians today is a sense of adequacy for meeting challenges and adversity. Membership and attendance decline of the Christian church has been tracked and documented for many years now. This has resulted in the publication of resources to perfect the church's hospitality, increase the vitality of its worship, and harness the power of technology. However valuable these may be, the most urgent need is for followers of Jesus Christ to get back to that power that is possessed by the daily nurture of a personal fellowship with Jesus.

Return for a moment to the first two words above, "I can." Some years ago, I was working with a personal trainer, Michael Bishop. One particular day he had me on my back, bench pressing what seemed to be an incredible weight for me. After pushing the bar above my head several times, I did a controlled drop of the bar to my chest. I was depleted. I delivered an eye message to him to remove the bar from my chest. I will never forget his response, "That's not my bar. You place it back on the upright supports." Then he did what his training taught him to do. He placed his hands around the bar with my own. That was simply to ensure that I didn't hurt myself. But the lifting belonged to me. I pushed with everything in me; I summoned all the power I could to lift the bar back onto the supports. As my strength began to fail, he matched the loss of my strength with his own until the bar had returned to rest on the support. Paul writes, "I can, through the power who gives me strength." If you are depressed or in trouble, say, "I can in him" and you will find God's strength comes alongside your own. If you struggle with passions or addictions that frighten you, or if you feel that you are losing your grip on life, say, "I can in him" and you will discover an unseen hand on the bar with your own, matching your strength. The Christian's strength begins with, "I can."

Lord Jesus, may I trust in your unseen hand and your uncommon power for the challenges I face this day. Amen.

10

When God Seems Distant

"I'm convinced that nothing can separate us from God's love in Christ Jesus our Lord."

ROMANS 8:38A

TOMMY LASORDA, FORMER MANAGER of the Los Angeles Dodgers, tells about an experience he had in church. One Sunday he was in Cincinnati for a ball game against the Reds. That morning he went to early morning Mass and happened to see the Red's manager there. They were old friends and sat beside each other during Mass. Afterward, the Red's manager said, "Tommy, I'll see you at the ballpark. I'm going to hang around a little." Lasorda said that when he reached the door, he glanced back over his shoulder. He noticed that his friend was praying at the altar and lighting a candle. He said, "I thought about that for a few moments. Then, since we needed a win very badly, I doubled back and blew out his candle."[1] Though misguided, what a powerful demonstration of faith in God's presence and activity!

Countless people today long for that deep confidence in God's presence and activity in their lives. God seems distant to them. They plod through each day, fearful, anxious, and burdened with uncertainty. Some may remember once having a close relationship with God but that was a long time ago. Prayers seem to never rise higher than the ceiling—and that is when we even feel like praying! The good news is that this is not an uncommon

---

1. Bouknight, *The Authoritative Word*, 30.

experience in the Christian faith. Just as people can grow apart in relationships with one another, so we can drift away from God. As Thomas Tewell once said to me, the difference is that in human relationships, both parties contribute to the distance. But, in a relationship with God, the reality is that we drift away from God. God never drifts away from us.

In those moments when God seems distant, what are we to do? Perhaps an experience I had this past week will help. My daughter, Rachael, is in Norway—a studio photographer for the Holland America Cruise Lines. It's not uncommon for Rachael to work twelve and fourteen-hour days. Wi-Fi is limited and with her long hours, it is difficult to "connect" with her by telephone or by other means in real-time. Just this week, Rachael reached out to me via Facebook Messenger. She said that for a limited time she was available to receive a phone call from me and that she really would like me to call. Immediately, I moved something that was already on my calendar to another time and placed the call. Do you see what happened? Suddenly, my greatest desire was to speak with my daughter. To do so, I had to make the time.

We reconnect with God the same way. We move beyond our desire to be close to God and carve out time from our busy lives to simply be still in God's presence. We open the Bible and read expectantly, asking God to speak powerfully through the words that we read on the page. We learn from our reading more about God, about God's good desires for us, and we learn what God requires of us. We spend time together with God. And we listen; we listen deeply in the silence following our reading to the hunches, the promptings, and the direction we sense from God. As we respond positively, the distance we once felt from God begins to close.

Thank you, O God, for your love that continuously surrounds me. Amen.

11

When God Laughs (Nathanael Hood)

"Immediately after he saw the vision, we prepared to leave for the province of Macedonia, concluding that God had called us to proclaim the good news to them."

ACTS 16:10

OH, TO TRAVEL TO Phrygia, the land of music, wine, and horsemen! Nerve center of trade and commerce since time immemorial. Mythic land of King Midas and the goddess Cybele. Oh, to preach in Galatia, the birthplace of the warlike Hittites and conquered home of the Celtic Gauls! The ancient cradle of ironworking. The land of Gomer and the dwarfish god Telesphorus. To spread the Gospel of Christ in these lands would have been a boon to the newborn church, and that's exactly where the Apostle Paul intended to go in the year forty-nine AD as he set out on his second missionary journey. He'd already evangelized in Athens, Corinth, and Ephesus, and now the early church father wanted to travel further east into Asia Minor. However, each time Paul and his companions tried, the Holy Spirit pushed them back. Frustrated, Paul then tried to enter Bithynia in the north of modern Anatolia. Yet once more the Holy Spirit refused. Disheartened and disappointed, Paul retreated back to Troas where one night he had an extraordinary vision: a man of Macedonia pleading for him to come and help them.

Macedonia was, of course, in the opposite direction of the lands Paul was determined to visit, especially after his disastrous previous attempts in

Europe. And Paul was not a man of flimsy convictions. He was a man with the fire of Jeremiah and the recklessness of Ezekiel, willing to risk life and limb, temperament and sanity for his ministry. His letters are filled with equal parts compassion and invective, cherishing his followers as children one minute before pronouncing them idiots the next. His temper could run away from him, much as it did in First Corinthians where in a fit of pique, he thanked God, ignoring the Corinthian Church before pausing and meekly adding that on second thought he'd actually baptized many of them. His anger could kill—did he not help lynch Saint Stephen? His outrage could cripple—did he not blind Bar-Jesus? His audacity could astonish—did he not preach to King Agrippa in chains? His was a dogged single-mindedness of purpose that could brook no delay, suffer no misstep, tolerate no foolishness.

And yet, look at the first word of verse ten: "immediately." Without any doubt or hesitation, Paul refocused his ministry, altered his plans, and reoriented his fervor for God. He set out at once eastwards towards Macedonia and Europe. The rest, as they say, is history. Shortly afterward he would plant the seeds of the European church, capturing not just the hearts of the people but the minds of the intelligentsia and the respect of the ruling authorities. The early church fathers would encounter the great thinkers of Greece through which they legitimized the faith in the eyes of the learned: Justin of Caesarea reconciled Christian theology with Plato while Tertullian did the same with Aristotle and Clement of Alexandria with Stoicism. And in Rome, the imperialist authorities who'd invaded the ancestral home of Judaism were forced once and for all to confront the specter of this new religious movement from Palestine, one which denied their pantheon of cruel, capricious gods in favor of a single deity that preached compassion, tolerance, and love. In time this strange faith would be accepted by the same imperial household that made a martyr of Paul and so many early Christians; for better or worse, the teachings of Jesus and the authority of his church would be the law of the land that could humble kings and emperors.

How many of us have struggled in life towards goals we knew in our hearts we needed only to have them denied? There's a saying that whenever man plans God laughs, and if the Acts of the Apostles are any indication this is not a flaw in the divine plan but an essential feature—we are simply incapable of controlling the full trajectories of our lives. One is tempted to think of Ulysses S. Grant who at thirty-eight worked at his father's leather goods business and at forty-seven was elected President of the United States. Or consider Oprah Gail Winfrey who worked her way up from desperate Mississippi poverty to becoming the first black multi-billionaire and global philanthropist. Of course, very few of us are ultimately called to become presidents or multibillionaires . . . or era-defining evangelists. Most of us will be called to live simple, quiet lives and undistinguished toil and service. But these are no less vital and precious in the eyes of the Almighty. We all fit into the tapestry of creation with every piece in its place. If we are to find happiness and contentment in our lives, perhaps we should stop asking when we'll find our Phrygia and Galatia and ask if we've already found our Macedonia.

Lord Jesus, as I look back on my life's journey, I see twists and turns I would never have planned that provided numerous blessings. Help me to trust you and your continued direction in my life. Amen.

12

Finding Hope in the Present Difficulty

"But not only that! We even take pride in our problems, because we know that trouble produces endurance, endurance produces character, and character produces hope. This hope doesn't put us to shame, because the love of God has been poured out in our hearts through the Holy Spirit, who has been given to us."

Romans 5:3–5

Covid-19 has produced among us a mood of calamity, discouragement, and despair. A vast structure of optimism that social distancing, wearing facemasks, and the summer heat would defeat the virus is quickly becoming dismantled. The epicenter of our nation's infection has simply moved from the City of New York to encompass California, Arizona, Texas, and Florida. Any sense that the ravages of this virus would soon "disappear" has now dissipated. Dr. Anthony Fauci just recently expressed optimism that we may defeat this virus in as "little" as twelve to eighteen months. We have a long battle ahead in our nation. Who today escapes the problem of wanting hope, but on every side seeing the collapse of hope?

If today, then, we are to grasp hope, we must rethink our way of getting it. These words from Paul's letter to the Roman Church provide help: "we know that trouble produces endurance, endurance produces character, and character produces hope." What is striking in these few words is that Paul's navigation to the place of hope is in another way than the route we have grown accustomed to. An easy-going optimism is a road we have traveled well. Only, that route now disappoints.

What Paul speaks of may be heard more clearly in the guidance I received early from my personal trainer, Bill Dorton. As Bill constructed a personalized training program for my particular needs, he summed up what would be involved: He would place before me multiple challenges that would resist my effort. Through my effort, I would build strength upon strength to meet the resistance. Over time, the meeting of that challenge of the opposing resistance would develop muscle, burn fat, and body tone would appear. Once I began to notice the change in my body—both in strength and in physical tone—I would increasingly grow hopeful of a better quality of life. I don't know if Bill was aware that he was taking a page from Paul's playbook: "trouble produces endurance, endurance produces character, and character produces hope."

Optimism can be cheap. To recline and engage in wishful thinking for better days simply results in defeat. Paul calls us to meet the present trouble as someone in physical training meets the resistance of the weights in a gym. Yet, notice, that we are not alone. Paul concludes his thoughts on the matter by declaring that the Holy Spirit has been given to us. As I train in a gym with the guidance, strength, and encouragement of my trainer, so God comes alongside us in the Holy Spirit. When our own strength is insufficient, the Holy Spirit joins our grip on the training bar. When we grow discouraged, the Holy Spirit whispers encouragement. And when we are in trouble, the Holy Spirit reminds us that we are not alone. Because "the love of God has been poured out in our hearts" we are not beaten. Our victory remains just ahead.

God, grant me strength today where my own is insufficient. Grasp my heart with the certain hope that my future is located in your care for me. Amen.

13

The Continuing Work of the Resurrection

> *"May the God of peace, who brought back the great shepherd of the sheep, our Lord Jesus, from the dead by the blood of the eternal covenant, equip you with every good thing to do his will, by developing in us what pleases him through Jesus Christ. To him be the glory forever and always. Amen."*
>
> Hebrews 13:20, 21

THE FIRST CHRISTIANS NEVER preached the resurrection simply as a once-and-done miracle, as Jesus' defeat of death and his return to his disciples. They always proclaimed the resurrection as the work of a living God that continues to work in the lives of women and men in each generation. The same creative energy that raised Jesus from the tomb remains available for each of us, not only to raise us to a new life following our death but grants us a divine purpose to pursue and equips us with the talent and strength to accomplish it. As the author of Hebrews states, God is continually "developing in us what pleases him through Jesus Christ." We are God's continuing work of the resurrection.

What this announces is that there is no present darkness that can extinguish the light of the resurrection, no despair that isn't answered with sudden hope. The celebration of Easter is more expansive than the remembrance of new breath filling the nostrils of Jesus one morning two thousand years ago. The celebration of Easter is claiming God's active presence today that calls to us, equips us, and sends us into a broken world to complete God's redemptive purposes. Once estranged from God by our rebellious nature, God wrestles with us until we once again embody and reflect God's perfect love and makes us apprentices with God redeeming and restoring all of creation.

Frederic Henry is the protagonist in Ernest Hemingway's novel, *A Farewell to Arms*. An American ambulance driver in Italy in 1915, Frederic wrestles with belief and doubt in a living, active God. During one poignant conversation with a Roman Catholic priest, Frederic questions what it means to love—to love God or anyone. The answer sparkles on the page, "When you love you wish to do things for. You wish to sacrifice for. You wish to serve."[1] Easter is an invitation to look closely again at God's love for us— demonstrated on the cross of Jesus—that we might return that love with a "wish to do things for, to sacrifice for, to serve." Our own immediate resurrection is from the death of selfishness to a life of selflessness and generosity.

These are tumultuous days. Covid-19 haunts each of us as we tremble in our quarantine spaces. We fear that the power of darkness may ultimately defeat our dreams. Doubt paralyzes and frantically we seek hope from any quarter. However, Easter reminds us that God has already faced evil at its worst, met its challenge, and destroyed its claim on us. Life never again has to be lived in helplessness, maimed, impoverished, and defeated. That is why the author of Hebrews is able to say, with a sturdy conviction, "To him be the glory forever and always. Amen."

Lord, I long for hope in uncertainty, and confidence in a time of anxiety. Help me today to sense your nearness that I might not be overcome by despair and live life more abundantly. Amen.

---

1. Hemingway, *A Farewell to Arms*, 68.

14

Diet Religion (Nathanael Hood)

"At this, many of his disciples turned away and no longer accompanied him."

JOHN 6:66

WHEN I WAS A grad student in New York City, I lived down in the Bowery in lower Manhattan. Walking back from class I'd frequently find myself strolling through Greenwich Village, that perennial home to New York's strange, artistic, and eccentric. On warm muggy nights, amateur psychics would seemingly sprout up from the pavement, setting up shop outside cafes and trendy restaurants with signs offering fortune telling for a meager $15. Some offered palm readings, others astrology charts, but the most popular service of these armchair clairvoyants was tarot card readings. For the price of a good pastrami sandwich a few blocks over at Katz's Deli, they claimed they could use their cards to predict your fate. Heavy with the weight of an ancient esotericism, they would sigh and moan with the flick of a wrist, this card predicting a successful career change, this one the failure of a promising relationship.

Ask these psychics how they learned their craft and they would twinkle an eye and say that it takes years of study and practice. What they probably won't tell you is that you can google "learn tarot" right now on your phone and get links to countless sites and YouTube videos promising to teach initiates how to read them in just a few hours. It turns out reading tarot cards is much easier and less mystical than originally advertised. And while many will claim that tarot cards originated in the courts of ancient Egyptians, in reality, the first tarot card decks appeared in fifteenth-century Europe, not as divining tools but as playing cards. It would take around two more centuries for them to gain widespread use among fortunetellers, and even then, mostly only in French and English-speaking areas. Go to other parts of Northern, Central, or Southern Europe and you'll find people still using them as they were originally intended: as simple playing cards.

But have you ever tried telling anyone who believes in the power of tarot cards that they're pure charlatanism? That their art is only a few centuries old and would be laughed at by the people that created them? The polite ones will hem and haw excuses. The impolite ones will scream at you for "violating their beliefs." Tarot cards and other forms of New Age quackery have weeded their way into the lives of millions and the emotional dependence they engender is tantamount to brainwashing. It makes sense why: they provide the benefits of religion with none of religion's demands. They give the customer a sense of cosmic purpose, personal direction, and even community, but without the insistence of moral improvement, personal reflection, and acts of charity towards the poor and disenfranchised. Have you ever heard of a palm reader telling customers to seek counseling for anger management? A salesperson for essential oils to volunteer at a soup kitchen? The answer is no. And the reason is that all of these things are, quite literally, diet religion.

We see the perils of diet religion even in the time of Jesus. Think of the rich man in Mark who asked Jesus what he must do to inherit eternal life and left after being told to sell his possessions and give the money to the poor. Perhaps this man was hoping for a dose of diet religion. Or what of the lawyer in Luke who asked Jesus who was his neighbor and was told his bitter enemy the Samaritans. Was this man seeking a diet religion answer full of reassurance? And then there's the sixth chapter of John where Jesus chastised and offended the multitudes who sought him for his miracles of loaves and fish and not the Bread of Life. The Scriptures literally record his disciples complaining that the message of his ministry was "too harsh" before abandoning him. They too were seeking diet religion. Real religion—the true Gospel of Christ—is demanding and difficult. It requires the complete transformation of one's life. It takes a lifetime to learn with no guarantee of mastery. We come to church, we come to Jesus, for something greater than fortune cookie platitudes. We come for rebirth. But if that's not what you want, then I know several people in Manhattan who for a modest fee would be happy to help.

Gracious God, I give you control of my life today. Forgive me for my half-hearted discipleship and make me a worthy instrument for your redemptive work in this community. Amen.

15

Which Voice Shall I Follow?

"Again the Lord called Samuel, so Samuel got up, went to Eli, and said, 'I'm here. You called me?'"

1 Samuel 3:6

Here is a startling story of a young boy named Samuel who had trouble sleeping one night because of a voice that spoke to him from the darkness. Most of us know that story—a voice that comes to us in the darkness at that moment when we want nothing more than to sleep. The volume of the voice is usually immense. It is a clamorous tongue that disturbs the mind and stirs physical restlessness as we lay upon the mattress. For some, the voice that speaks addresses our personal finances, most often when our financial resources are running low and our commitments are racing in the opposite direction. For others, the voice reminds us of estranged relationships but offers no solutions for healing. Other voices that bombard the mind's ear simply wish to generate anger at this or that political party and the absolute stupidity—or cruelty—of this or that policy out of Washington. Solutions rarely show up in the darkness of the bedroom. Neither does sound sleep.

Here, young Samuel is lying down in the Lord's temple. We know it is the night hour because fifteen verses later we are informed, "Samuel lay there until morning." But Samuel will not sleep that night. Before his mind drifts off to restful sleep, Samuel hears a voice. It is the Lord's voice but Samuel doesn't know that—not in the beginning. He believes the voice belongs to his mentor, Eli. Three times Samuel hears the voice and three times Samuel disturbs Eli to inquire what it is Eli wants. It is the third time that Eli grows suspicious that this is more than Samuel's imagination. Nor is Samuel simply hearing the whistle of the wind. Samuel is instructed to make an inquiry if he hears the voice again; to say, "Speak, Lord. Your servant is listening." And the voice does return.

This is precisely the point that Samuel makes a rather dramatic shift from simply jumping from his bed at the sound of a voice to careful listening. Samuel restrains his natural impulse to a quick response and practices alert and intentional discernment of the content of the voice that speaks. There is much all of us can learn from this simple act—pausing long enough to sincerely listen to the voice we hear, particularly if that voice is unsettling to us. What would happen in our nation if Republicans and Democrats were to exercise restraint from the vitriolic impulse they have for one another? Imagine the surprise if Evangelicals and liberals in the Christian church ever truly listened to one another. What might any of us discover in the darkness of the night if we calmly listened to all that unsettles us—personal finances, relationship difficulties, or concern for the health of those we love—and then, rather uncommonly, invited another voice to the conversation, "Speak, Lord. Your servant is listening."

At any moment of the day or night, there are voices that clamor for our attention. Some voices long for an impulsive response from us, usually a response that multiplies anger and hurt and fears among those we know and love. Perhaps a voice asks from us indignation and puerile criticism of another point of view. The only contribution that voice makes is increased brokenness in an already broken world. Do not trust these voices. But Samuel's story shows us another way. Eli counsels Samuel to "listen" rather than "jump" at the sound of the voice. If we listen and listen with humility and civility and respect, what we will discover is that the voices that clamor for an impulsive response will scatter and one will remain. It will be the loveliest voice of all. It will be a voice that asks for patience and love. Trust that voice. Ponder it. Respond to it. It will be then that you have in your heart neither doubt nor fear.

Remind me to follow the example of Samuel—to listen carefully and respond faithfully with humility and love. Amen.

16

Remembering Who We Are
(Location: En-Gedi)

> *"'Look! Today your own eyes have seen that the Lord handed you over to me in the cave. But I refused to kill you. I spared you, saying, "I won't lift a hand against my master because he is the Lord's anointed."'"*
>
> 1 SAMUEL 24:10

EN IS A HEBREW word meaning, "spring," while Gedi means, "young goat" or "kid." Placed together, the meaning of the name for this location is, "spring of a kid." Many springs are found throughout this area but only two are freshwater, the others providing water that is tainted with salt or Sulphur. The En-Gedi is one of the freshwater springs and is still visible today, flowing up from beneath a rock more than four hundred feet above the Dead Sea. This spring of freshwater, flowing down a cliff into a pool before finally emptying into the Dead Sea, is made all the more spectacular by its contrast with the drab, dry desert that surrounds it. During his years as a fugitive, David hid in one of the numerous caves among the cliffs that surround this spring.

Except for a green oasis immediately surrounding the En-Gedi, the barren mountains and plains that extend out from this spring have been called Israel's "bad lands"—a place of such desolation that it feels abandoned, even by God. Less than an hour's drive from Jerusalem, my initial response, upon my first trip here, was that this was the most inhospitable place on earth, a lonely place, a desperate place. Appropriate then, that David sought refuge here while on the run from King Saul who sought David's life. Hiding in one of the numerous caves that dot the mountains that surround this spring, David's future was uncertain. He was a wanted man and King Saul commanded a powerful army with one determined mission, the death of David.

Absorbing all the desolation, loneliness, and fear of this land into his own body and spirit, David received a gift from God's hand. During Saul's pursuit, he went into one of these dark caves to use the restroom, the very cave where David was in hiding. The good news for David, and one common to our own experience, is that David's eyes had adjusted to the darkness of the cave as David looked toward the bright entrance. Saul entering the cave could see nothing, including the man he was pursuing sitting right in front of him. Here was David's chance to strike first, to kill the man who sought his own life.

David did not. Rather, David snuck up on him and cut off a corner of Saul's robe while Saul was relieving himself. After Saul left the cave, David also went out of the cave and yelled after Saul, "My master the king!" Saul looked back, and David bowed low out of respect. Then David showed Saul the piece of the cloth that he had cut from Saul's robe. This was to demonstrate that David could have chosen to kill Saul and did not. David would not respond to Saul in fear and hatred, even though Saul sought David's life. David offers Saul his reason, "You are the Lord's anointed." Even in fear of his own life, David remembers who he is; David is a man who has given his life to one purpose, the service and glory of almighty God.

Heavenly Father, help me to remember that, in the midst of great difficulties, each can be overcome because of your strength and wisdom available to those you call your own. Amen.

17

Plants of Steel

"I can endure all these things through the power of the one who gives me strength."

PHILIPPIANS 4:13

THE GARDEN CENTER OF Home Depot features a selection of plants ideal for home or office called, "Plants of Steel." They are plants that seem to thrive in apparent adversity. Where other plants would wilt for lack of water and sunshine these plants enjoy optimal vitality from neglect. I have purchased several of these plants and it is fascinating to watch them flourish in spite of—or because of—my inattention to their care. They seem to have a preference for hardship.

These plants offer encouragement for spiritual life. Difficult circumstances, though never sought, can provide growth. Such growth is clear in the lived experience of the apostle Paul. In this letter to the Church of Philippi, Paul is in captivity in Rome. His supreme mission of preaching the Gospel of Christ appears to be at an end. No longer does Paul have the stimulus of travel, the joy of enriching itineraries, or the delight of preaching the good news over the broad landscape of Asia and Greece. That open road has been narrowed to the walls of a prison cell. Yet, there is an absence of gloom in Paul's writing. Throughout this letter of Philippian,s there is present incomparable strength and beauty.

Paul's imprisonment does not usher in a season of gloom. Rather, what Paul experiences is a time of spiritual graces. He writes of losing everything for Christ only to realize that what he lost has no value compared to what he has gained in a relationship with Jesus. Within prison walls, Paul realizes the broad range and wealth of his spiritual inheritance. While some of his friends referred to his misery, Paul writes of his joy. Though some regretted his poverty, Paul boasts of possessing all that he needs. What appears to be a season of winter for Paul is transformed into an opportunity to be clothed in a fleece robe of strength and hopefulness.

Some today become very poor in difficulty and adversity. When in the natural rhythm of life they reach desert places or what may feel like an endless winter of the soul, they live without any cheer. Sourness and fretfulness encompass them as the prison walls surrounded Paul. All of life becomes a menagerie of unpleasant things. Worse, they feel left alone. Paul's incredible witness is that this doesn't have to be their story. Paul writes letters from prison not to share his misery with a sympathetic ear. He writes to invest in others. Investments in other people, in the ministry of our Lord, scatter the gloom, brighten the place of our dwelling and preserve the leaf of our soul from withering. We become plants of steel! More, we will know such joy that the desert of the soul shall rejoice and blossom like a rose.

In the winter of the soul, help me to seek the face of Jesus, to invest in others, and experience uncommon strength and joy. In the certain name of my Lord, Jesus Christ, I pray. Amen.

18

Defeated Lives (The Band's Visit)

"'Aren't two sparrows sold for a small coin? But not one of them will fall to the ground without your Father knowing about it already. Don't be afraid. You are worth more than many sparrows.'"

Matthew 10:29, 31

The Band's Visit, currently on Broadway, has won several major awards including Best Musical at the seventy-second Tony Awards. Music and lyrics by David Yazbek and book by Itamar Moses, the musical is based on the 2007 Israel film of the same title. More a play than a musical, *The Band's Visit* is a ninety-minute narrative of a single night in the small, isolated Israel desert town, Bet Hatikva. The Alexandria Ceremonial Police Orchestra—an eight-member ensemble—has accepted an invitation to perform in the cultural center of Petah Tikvah. Difficulty with accents results in bus tickets to the wrong Israeli town. The next bus out of town—and to the band's intended destination—is not until the next morning. A charismatic woman named Dina, the owner of the local café, offers the band a meal and a place to stay for the night.

The musical opens silently with words projected on a bare wall: "Some time ago, some musicians from Egypt came to our town. You probably didn't hear about it. It wasn't very important." Those few words powerfully inform the audience that they are now invited into the lives of people who feel defeated; people who long for any sense that they are noticed and that their lives matter. With the arrival of the band from Egypt, a deep journey into brokenness begins—the brokenness of the residents of Bet Hatikva and the brokenness of the members of the band. Dina speaks to the prevailing mood of insignificance that has settled deep into the consciousness of their small town when she addresses the band: "They (Petah Tikvah) have art and culture and music. Here we have my café and apartments." The citizens of Bet Hatikva long for significance, for the presence of meaning to their meager, small lives.

Here, in this teaching from Matthew's Gospel, Jesus demonstrates a firm grasp of the fear of living lives that are seemingly unimportant. Though the larger conversation that surrounds this teaching addresses the conflict and persecution the disciples can expect as they do the work of Christ, it does present the view that nothing in the world went unnoticed by Jesus even something as small as a sparrow falling from the sky. And, *"You are worth more than many sparrows."* Few of us set out to be common. Most of us strive for excellence in our chosen endeavor, to outstrip our competitors, and receive the recognition that we have added uncommon value to the world. Ambition is, of course, an admirable quality. But, as Christians, we should never lose sight that, as children of God, we are all without distinction in God's eyes.

Perhaps the most powerful dynamic of the musical, *The Band's Visit* is how circumstances bring people together who hold a low appraisal of themselves. Thrust together for a night, they listen deeply to one another's brokenness and care unreservedly for each other. Within that embracing environment of love, healing bubbles forth for each person. People who led defeated lives discover that the simple act of listening, caring, and loving profoundly changes the life of another. That is the Christian source of inspiration—that each person, regardless of social rank or stature or achievement, can be used mightily to make a difference in someone's life. It is this that provides a more balanced self-appraisal. The musical ends with Dina stepping to center stage, facing the audience intently, and saying, "Some time ago, some musicians from Egypt came to our town. You probably didn't hear about it. It wasn't very important." Don't believe that for one moment.

Gracious God, emboldened me to choose hope rather than hopelessness, confidence in your power rather than despair, and the capacity to experience the value of self rather than uselessness. In the certain name of the one who gave his own life for me, Jesus Christ. Amen.

19

The View from the Top
(Location: Mount of Beatitudes)

"But the gate that leads to life is narrow and the road difficult, so few people find it."

MATTHEW 7:14

MOST PEOPLE TRAVEL THE broad road. This is the road that is motivated by a desire to please people; the road that seeks the approval of others. Values are forged from observing behaviors that seem popular. When questioned about an unwise decision, those who travel this road answer simply, "Everyone else was doing it." Traveling along this road may bustle with energy but misses the life we were appointed by God to live.

The narrow road is a little lonelier. This is the road of true disciples. Those who travel this road may be sensitive to what others think of them. They may desire to be loved and appreciated like those who travel any road. But ultimately, it is God's approval that shapes the large and little decisions of life. Thomas Tewell once shared a story of a woman in his New York City congregation who meets friends at the end of the day for drinks. When the friends order another round, she excuses herself and says she has to be going. "Where are you going?" her friends asked. Without apology, she answers that she is attending an evening Bible study at her church. When pressed why she goes to church, she simply answers, "It makes a difference in the way I live my life."

Many who travel to the Holy Land include in their spiritual pilgrimage a climb up the Mount of Beatitudes, the location where Jesus delivered his great Sermon on the Mount. There they find great views over the Sea of Galilee and many of the sites associated with Jesus' ministry. The serenity of this beautiful place, however, may be slightly unhelpful for travelers seeking an authentic spiritual journey. The splendor of the setting may suggest that Jesus' words were calm and soothing—conjuring images of a worship service back home with beautiful music, an inspiring sermon, and a lovely Sunday brunch following church. In fact, Jesus' sermon was radical, demanding, and countercultural. They were hard words to hear for many who had gathered that day. Jesus was calling people to a new way of life. Those who chose to follow would be few.

The road up the mountain attracts the casual tourist, of course. But for anyone on a spiritual pilgrimage, the road is difficult and few will find it. It is a road that demands that priorities be reordered, habits changed and room made in busy lives for God. It isn't a road for the faint-hearted or for those who still care more about what others think of them than obedience to God. But for those who make it to the top, the view is out of this world.

With your wisdom, O God, direct my steps up the mountain of authentic discipleship. Strengthen my resolve by the unmistakable embrace of your love for me. In Christ's name, I pray, Amen.

20

When the Door Remains Closed

"Meanwhile, Peter remained outside, knocking at the gate."
ACTS 12:16A

HERE IS A STORY for everyone; a story of someone who tried and failed, but refused to give up. Peter was one of Jesus' disciples. At a critical hour, he failed Jesus by denying him three times. But Jesus never failed Peter. Following Jesus' resurrection, his continued embrace and love for Peter launched Peter into a preaching ministry of considerable zeal and devotion. Up and down the countryside, Peter gave witness to the power of the risen Christ to change lives. Peter's primary exhibit for his testimony was his own life. Soon he found himself enmeshed by hostile forces and, finally, preached himself into prison.

Prayers were made for Peter by the Christian communities that he started and were now growing, as a result of his preaching. One night an angel came to Peter, placed the prison guard into a deep sleep, released the chains from Peter's hands, and opened the prison doors. An important detail of this miracle story is that the angel instructed Peter to place on his sandals. The angel was able to place the guard into a slumber, release Peter's hands from the chains that held him, and open the prison doors. Yet, the angel holds Peter responsible for placing on his own shoes. Apparent in this small detail is that God will always do what we cannot do, but God will not do for us what we can do. Peter was capable of placing upon his feet his shoes.

Peter, now freed from prison, goes out into the dark, hiding in the thickness of the night from Roman soldiers, and makes his way to a home where he hoped to be received and cared for. When Peter knocked at the outer gate, a female servant went to answer. Recognizing Peter, and overcome with surprise and joy, the servant runs back into the house with the grand announcement of Peter's release. Yet, in her amazement and delight, she forgets to open the gate and let Peter into the residence. *"Meanwhile, Peter remained outside, knocking at the gate."*

Peter does not shrug his shoulders and walk back into the night, commenting, "It's no use." Peter continues to knock. Peter is resilient. He will not give in or give up. Through his persistence, Peter reveals the grandeur of his trust in God's continuing presence and care. Many of us will stand—at some moment in our life—before a closed door. The closed-door may be a job opportunity that never materializes, a romantic relationship that is never found, or an illness that lingers—health seemly more and more elusive. Before that closed door, life asks, "Will you continue to trust God in the face of bitterness and disappointment?" Peter stands before a closed-door unafraid, determined to see it through. His strength is located in God's fidelity, demonstrated in his past. That same strength is available to us when we stand before a door that is closed.

I open my heart and my soul to your Spirit, O God, that I may receive again your encouragement and strength. Amen.

21

Leavening Faith (Nathanael Hood)

> *"And again he said, 'To what shall I compare the kingdom of God? It is like leaven that a woman took and hid in three measures of flour, until it was all leavened.'"*
>
> LUKE 13:20, 21 (ESV)

FOR THE FIRST SEVERAL months of the Covid-19 pandemic, I lived in a part of Brooklyn near one of the worst viral hotspots in the entire country. Not too far from my apartment were hospitals that had to bring refrigerated trucks in to store the bodies of pandemic victims because they were literally running out of space to put them. The entire city shut down and was ordered to shelter in place. These were some of the hardest months of my life, not only because I knew I was risking it every time I went out for essentials like groceries and medicine, but because I found myself unemployed after barely a week of quarantine. With no job and nowhere to go other than my phone for distraction, time began to lose its meaning. Every day and every week was just like the one before. With no end in sight, my emotions began spinning out of control.

But then my roommate made a suggestion: let's make a sourdough starter. To make one, all you need is flour and water. You soak some flour, let it sit somewhere stuffy overnight, add more flour and water the next day, and repeat the process until you have a richly sour and runny paste you can use as leaven to make bread with. It sounds easy, but it isn't. Any number of things can wreck a starter: using the wrong amount of water or flour, exposing it to too much oxygen, exposing it to too *little* oxygen, letting it get too hot or too cold, not "feeding" it with fresh flour on schedule, and many more. The point is, that making a starter required a level of attention and discipline that cut through the fog of my boredom and despair. It gave me a purpose to set my alarm every morning.

One of the most controversial of Jesus' parables is when he compares the Kingdom of God to yeast—or more accurately sourdough starter in the text's original cultural context. In addition to being one of Jesus' shortest parables, it's also one of his most obscure. Scholars have spent millennia trying to parse out what exactly he meant. Some argue it means that a little faith can transform an individual life or whole community. Others suggest that we Christians are the yeast and we're called to "leaven" the world around us. And still, others point out that in typical fashion Jesus inverts something perceived as negative in ancient Israel—while crucial to baking, leaven was frequently viewed back then as something potentially putrid and rotten—into something positive that inherits the Kingdom.

But as someone who has now dabbled in amateur baking, I see this parable differently. Note that "three measures" of flour in ancient Israel would be roughly equivalent to forty to sixty pounds. Whoever this woman is, she's preparing a feast. But before she can feed the masses, she must first make enough leaven, a process that must've taken literal weeks, if not months, of patient, diligent work. Our walk with God is no different. It too takes tireless commitment and effort for it to properly ferment into something we can use. Regular worship, Bible study, and personal reflection . . . are all tools we can use to work the flour of our faith into the living water of God (John 4:10). Only then, after the work has been done, can we find a faith we can use to leaven both ourselves and others. And the results, like my first sourdough loaf in Brooklyn, will be delicious.

Precious Lord, fill our lives with the leaven of your righteousness so we might have faith to feed both ourselves and others. In your name, we pray. Amen.

22

What We Can Know

"If an army camps against me, my heart won't be afraid. If war comes up against me, I will continue to trust in this."

PSALM 27:3

FOR SOME, THE GREATEST struggle of faith is uncertainty. One man spoke to me following worship recently and commented, "I find this Jesus you speak of very attractive. And I have no doubt that living as Jesus taught will positively impact a life. My difficulty is this, what can we know for sure?" The writer of these words in Psalm 27 records an ancient answer to this question that remains very present for some people: "What can we know for sure?" Here, the author makes an honest assessment of the world—a world that is fearful of hostile armies and war—and affirms that, nonetheless, trust in God will abound. Anyone would be grateful that this author is so confident in the presence and power of almighty God. Yet, the question remains, "How shall we find that same confidence?"

Gene E. Bartlett is helpful.[1] First is the consistent witness that God is a loving God. Naturally, this unwavering witness through the ages fails to prove the existence of God. Simply, it asserts agreement that if there is a God, that God is a loving God. Yet, an honest and fair reading of the Bible demands some attention to the cultural norms that shaped the day when these words were written. In the day of Scripture, the notion of "father"

---

1. Bartlett, "Some Things We Know," 96.

was much deeper and richer than our present use of the designation. More than a biological identification, "father" was one who had authority and commanded respect. Unquestioning obedience and honor were expected. So when Jesus addressed God as "Father," Jesus was making a theological claim—obedience was expected before proof was received. And throughout the ages, as men and women struggled imperfectly to obey God, the consistent experience was love, acceptance, and forgiveness. A common experience through thousands of years of struggling to live faithfully does, at the minimum, hint at the possibility of God's existence.

Second is the conviction that men and women are responsible creatures. We may shirk responsibility at various times in our lives but none of us can escape the conviction that, ultimately, we are personally responsible for the direction our lives will take. We have the capacity to decide to move in one direction or another, to love or to withhold love. Each person senses the freedom to make decisions that will impact their lives positively or negatively. Except in those cases where there exists some mental deficiently or handicap, the common experience is that there is a tug in those decisions to move positively for the benefit of others and oneself. From where does that tug come; the tug toward kindness, goodness, and mercy?

The third is the common experience that good is more powerful than evil. So pervasive is this thought that it is woven throughout the pages of science fiction. Look at the popular movie franchise, *Star Wars*. Anyone familiar with it has had the words, "May the force be with you" engraved upon their minds—"the force" is a force for good. Bartlett observes on this one point that in the long sweep of history, there is evidence after evidence that good beats evil at every turn. How is that so? For Gene Bartlett and countless Christians, the answer cannot be a coincidence. Behind the consistent witness of being deeply loved, behind every conviction of personal responsibility, and behind every experience that good is a greater force than evil is the notion that present is a common source. For many millions of people through the pages of Scripture to the present day, that source is God. "What can we know for sure?" The answer is these three things. And they all point to something much deeper.

O God, I offer today a simple prayer—that in my own moments of uncertainty I may experience something that cannot be explained by your work in the world. Amen.

23

Disillusioned at Christmas

"They asked, 'Where is the newborn king of the Jews? We've seen his star in the east, and we've come to honor him.'"

MATTHEW 2:2

SPEED BUMPS ARE INTENTIONAL obstructions along routes traveled by motorized vehicles to slow drivers down. They indicate the need for caution, that something unusual is present and requires particular attention for safe navigation forward. Ignore the speed bump and the driver will experience a jolt and, perhaps, minor damage to their vehicle. Matthew's Gospel has placed a speed bump into the Christmas narrative. If ignored—or not noticed—the reader will miss a greater truth that Matthew wishes to convey. Rather than hurrying to the end of the story, Matthew wants the reader to make a rich discovery as the story unfolds: The magi made much of their journey to Bethlehem without the light of the star.

Notice the speed bump: the magi enter the City of Jerusalem and make inquiry as to where the "newborn king of the Jews" is born. They began their journey to find the baby when they saw a star in the east but now the light of that star is unseen. Now they must ask for directions. Consulting with the chief priests and legal experts, King Herod learns that the Christ was to be born in Bethlehem. Herod then sends the magi on their way in that direction. Only when they come to Bethlehem do they see the light of the star again. This is why the magi "were filled with joy," Matthew tells us. They were on the right road and the promise of that star was about to be realized. Finding the child with Mary, his mother, the magi fell to their knees, honored him, and presented their gifts.

Matthew is writing to a particular people who are on the cusp of disillusionment and abandoning their faith. The decision to follow Christ has resulted in estrangement from those family members who don't believe in Jesus. More, followers of Jesus are no longer welcomed in Jewish worship. Divided from their loved ones and unwelcomed in the faith community, it is easy to question if they are on the right road. The easy path would be to admit a mistake in following Jesus, abandon the Christian movement, and return to the embrace of family and cherished worship. The light that began their faith in Jesus has dimmed considerably and now they are traveling in the dark.

So it may be with our faith. Oftentimes we do not experience the power, the light, the vitality of the faith we once experienced. Difficulties overwhelm us, the road becomes dark, and we are disillusioned. The path that was once clear is now an unknown way. Matthew wants us to remain confident in the promise. Circumstances may require that we stop, reassess our route, and seek guidance as the magi did in Jerusalem. But then, start out once again. There is much in the world—and in our lives—that we cannot change. It's not our task to repair the brokenness all around us. What we can and must do, says Matthew, is to speak of the promise of "the newborn king" that comes in the midst of that brokenness, kneel before him in worship, present our gifts, and trust that it will be enough

When I am disillusioned and the road is dark, direct my steps to Bethlehem, that place where I might see the star of your promise once again. Amen.

24

Not Ashamed of Jesus
(Location: Caesarea)

"Agrippa said to Paul, 'You may speak for yourself.' So Paul gestured with his hand and began his defense."

ACTS 26:1

ALONG THE COAST OF the Mediterranean Sea, between Tel Aviv and Haifa, rises the restored city of Caesarea, built by Herod the Great in twenty BC and named in honor of the Roman emperor Caesar Augustus. Caesarea served as the Roman capital for the province of Judea for nearly six hundred years and was the official residence of its governors, including Pontius Pilate who sentenced Jesus to death. It is here that several major events in the formative years of the Christian church took place including the baptism, by Paul, of a Roman military officer named Cornelius (see Acts 10:1–8).

For two years, the apostle Paul was imprisoned in Caesarea for preaching Jesus Christ and Christ's resurrection from the dead. During his imprisonment, King Agrippa and the king's sister, Bernice, came to Caesarea. During a conversation with Porcius Festus, the current governor of Caesarea, King Agrippa and Bernice learned of this man, Paul, and that he was being held there in that city as a prisoner. Fascinated with the story of Paul, his preaching and teaching, and Paul's imprisonment, Agrippa said to Festus, "I want to hear the man myself." The very next day, King Agrippa and Bernice entered the auditorium of Caesarea with considerable fanfare, and Paul was brought from his prison cell to address the King and honored guest.

Recently I sat in what remains of that auditorium, a place that can still seat hundreds, and imagined the apostle Paul standing in chains before the King and the city's most prominent men. Asked to speak, Paul "gestured with his hand and began his defense." In that day, the hand gesture was a common movement to quiet the audience and signal the beginning of an important speech. In that single movement of his hand, Paul delivered a bold sermon. Though he stood before a King, himself a prisoner in chains, Paul had the audacity to say, with that hand movement, "Listen, and be silent, for I have something of deep importance to say." Paul was not ashamed of the Gospel of Jesus Christ.

For whatever reason, I have entered a place in my life where I sense things more deeply than ever before; I am easily brought to a place of tears. Seated in that ancient auditorium, looking down at an empty stage, a place that was once occupied by Paul in chains, I pictured him making that hand gesture and I had to hide my tears from my colleagues. Paul thought nothing of his present humiliation, a prisoner in chains, and placed all his energy into one thing, the message of Jesus and Jesus' power to change lives.

It is a fact that we live in a world, not unlike the world of Christ, a world of difficulty and all manner of trouble, hardship, and discouragement. May Paul's courage and trust in the power of the Gospel embolden me to face anything today and all of my tomorrows. Amen.

25

The Common Life Lived Uncommonly

"To one he gave five valuable coins, and to another he gave two, and to another he gave one."

MATTHEW 25:15

IT IS NATURAL TO strive for greatness, for recognition, and for making a large contribution. Each one of us is endowed with some talent, some gift, and ability and the business of life is to discover what it is. Once discovered, that talent is developed and polished much like a rough, natural diamond that is placed in the hands of a jeweler. No one really wants to be common. Every normal young person has dreams and aspirations and strives to get on with life, climb the success ladder and, pass others in their walk of life.

This is admirable, of course, if the motivation is wholesome and the desire is directed toward worthy ends. But our Lord's parable of the valuable coins is a reminder that there is a limit on each one of us. Some may be endowed with greater ability but everyone has some limit on their capacity for achievement. Five-star generals do not win battles by themselves. Without apology, Jesus teaches that talent and ability are unevenly distributed. Some people will be exceptionally talented and have the potential for greater accomplishment than others. Some are uncommonly gifted and many of us are simply common.

The question then becomes, will we do our best with what we have? Will we focus our efforts on maximum contribution, to the welfare of others, or will we begin to whine and recline because we cannot shine? Unreasonable expectations and demands upon ourselves result in chronic unhappiness and diminish not only our lives but also the lives of those who love us. There are far more ordinary doctors, lawyers, and persons in the service sector and administrative roles than exceptional ones. Yet, each has the capacity to make an important contribution each day to their families, friends, and community.

The simple and practical course to follow is to make a realistic appraisal of our capacity and gifts. This may mean for many the discarding of delusions of grandeur, acknowledging and accepting that in the Lord's distribution of gifts we may have received only one or two talents and that God's expectation of us is the same as those who received five talents. The acid test of character is whether we have discovered what talent we have and then, having discovered it, placed it to maximum use. That is when the common life is lived uncommonly.

Guide me, O God, to recognize how you have uniquely gifted me for participating in your great work in the world. Then grant me the courage and wisdom to use them in such a manner that lives are impacted with the love of Jesus Christ. Amen.

26

The Mark of Christian Character

"We love because God first loved us."

1 John 4:19

There is a delightful—and poignant—cartoon currently circulating on Facebook. Jesus is teaching his disciples on the side of a mountain. Jesus teaches, "Love one another." The disciples begin to question Jesus. "What if people don't agree with our interpretation of Scripture? What do we do if someone doesn't share our political ideology or agree with us on the important issues of the day?" Jesus continues, "Let me try again. Love one another." Located in this cartoon is a powerful message for us all. Something has happened in our public discourse. Once, people could disagree politically, debate the pressing issues of the day, and then share a meal and laughter together. I miss that day, now largely gone. If you are honest, you miss it as well.

Recently, I sat in my office with someone who is both an elder of this church and a dear friend. He is a Republican and I am a Democrat. He has my highest admiration. Considerable wisdom and a kind and generous spirit mark his leadership on the church board. Occasionally we discuss with each other our differences in our political vision for our nation. The operative word here is, "discuss." Civility, respect, and humility saturate our conversations. Both of us acknowledge that we could be wrong on any issue. Most importantly, we listen deeply to each other. We listen with anticipation that we may have our own thoughts made more expansive by a different viewpoint.

We also share a lament. We are saddened by how little kindness we now see among those who disagree. One political party vilifies another party. Democrats are Socialist and Republicans lack compassion. People fear expressing any opinion lest they become caught up in verbal warfare. Worse, it is common today to question someone's fidelity to the Christian faith if there is a failure to think as we think. Again, we are a nation divided by itself. Hurtful rhetoric often becomes hate crimes. Imagine what has happened in our nation. Some believe that killing those who are different is a responsible course. Jesus continues, "Let me try again. Love one another."

Perhaps that is where we must begin. We begin by celebrating that, as Christians, what holds us together is our common confession that Jesus Christ is Lord. Bound together by faith in Jesus Christ, we recognize that none of us has grasped the whole truth. The Apostle Paul, speaking of faith in his first letter to the Corinthian Church, says that what we now understand is like looking in a dark mirror. We can see something, but not everything. Some things remain out of focus. "Love one another," teaches Jesus. That includes our enemies, those who persecute us, and those who disagree with us. Those are the words of Jesus. Obedience is the mark of Christian character.

Strive with me today, O Lord, and defeat those hostilities in my heart toward others who I disagree with. Increase my love for you and for others. Amen.

27

Living In the Present Tense

"'Therefore, stop worrying about tomorrow, because tomorrow will worry about itself. Each day has enough trouble of its own.'"

MATTHEW 6:34

IT IS THE PRACTICE of the Eskimos never to carry the day's evil experiences, its troubles, and its quarrels, over into the next day. Two Eskimo hunters might become engaged in a violent dispute over the division of the game which they had taken, and heated words might even bring them to blows, but once the sun had set and they had retired to sleep, all memory of the quarrel would be erased from their spirits, and the next day they would greet each other as brothers. If you were to exclaim in surprise: "But I thought you were enemies. You were fighting yesterday!" they would answer: "Ah, but that was yesterday and we live only today."[1] That is living in the present tense!

Mark Twain, with his characteristic humor, once commented that he has suffered many things most of which never happened.[2] Doctors tell us that much of our anxiety, which often results in physical, emotional, and spiritual unease, is located in tomorrow, a preoccupation with fears of the future. Consequently, our fears of tomorrow rob us of the opportunity to live fully and abundantly today. Naturally, wise and reasonable decisions

---

1. Williams, "Living Today Forever," 106.
2. Widely attributed to Mark Twain but no substantive evidence currently available of origin.

and personal behavior must shepherd us in the present day. Careless spending today will result in debt tomorrow. A word carelessly spoken or a relationship betrayed may negatively impact all of our tomorrows. Not all of us have been nurtured in the Eskimo culture!

Jesus' invitation in this teaching is to locate our hearts in God. Worry and anxiety are all about trying to avoid something, about trying to get away from something. The strain of worry is indicative that we don't trust the future. Jesus asks that we approach life from another perspective. Rather than fleeing what we fear most, Jesus asks that we run toward God. As Augustine once said, "Our hearts are restless until they rest in thee."[3] Jesus asks that we live in the present tense, free from the regrets of yesterday and the fears of tomorrow. That is possible after we have accepted God's forgiveness for the past and trust in God's care for the future.

Thomas Long writes that there is a kind of worry about the coming day that is normal, even healthy. "Tomorrow's chemistry test or job interview is bound to provide concern, and this command 'stop worrying about tomorrow' is not an invitation to finesse the exam or to waltz into the interview unprepared. Rather, it speaks to the deeper, more basic fear that something is out there in the future that can destroy our basic worth as a human being, something finally stronger than God's care, some silent killer shark swimming toward us from the future."[4] Jesus asks that we cling to God in such a manner that we can affirm that whatever tomorrow brings, it also brings God.

Lord Jesus, stir my heart to greater trust in your care. Guide each of my steps today so that my tomorrow may be faced with courage. Amen.

---

3. Long, *Matthew*, 76.
4. Long, *Matthew*, 76.

28

Tearing the Church Apart (Nathanael Hood)

"After a few days, Jesus went back to Capernaum, and people heard that he was at home. So many gathered that there was no longer space, not even near the door. Jesus was speaking the word to them. Some people arrived, and four of them were bringing to him a man who was paralyzed. They couldn't carry him through the crowd, so they tore off part of the roof above where Jesus was. When they had made an opening, they lowered the mat on which the paralyzed man was lying. When Jesus saw their faith, he said to the paralytic, 'Child, your sins are forgiven!'"

MARK 2:1–5

WHEN I FIRST ARRIVED as a student at Princeton Seminary, one of the first buildings I visited was Miller Chapel, the school's communal worship space used for daily services and seminary events. Fronted by six beautiful Doric columns, the chapel is a jewel of early nineteenth-century Greek Revival architecture. Generations of students and teachers have prayed and worshipped together within its walls, and despite being surrounded by colonial-era monuments and battlefields, few buildings in the Princeton area truly exude the same weight of history. Standing there, I was struck by its sacredness and beauty—it is a holy, beautiful space, worthy of admiration and preservation. Then I imagined it being torn to the ground.

Horrific to imagine, isn't it? Yet we see something not too different happening in the second chapter of the Gospel of Mark. Of all the Bible's healing miracles, this story of Jesus healing the paralytic is one of the most cherished in part because it's one of the most dramatic. It reads almost like a proto-heist movie: four friends come together, sneak on top of the building where Jesus is preaching, break inside, and lower their paralyzed friend down to Jesus, not unlike Tom Cruise in *Mission Impossible*. It's also dramatic because this was one of the only times in Mark where Jesus publicly reveals himself as the Son of God. For most of Mark, Jesus tells those he heals to tell no one of his power, but here he heals the paralytic and declares his sins forgiven in front of a massive crowd. Dramatic, indeed.

But there's a detail in this story that's lost on modern audiences: the paralytic's four friends essentially destroyed the house Jesus was in. First-century Palestinian roofs were two feet thick and contained layers of timber, tree branches, and dirt. This is what the paralytic's four friends dug through—and the original Greek text confirms that they didn't remove the roof, they didn't lift the roof, they *dug through* the roof. By the end, the house's insides would've been covered with debris. Additionally, first-century Christians would've drawn parallels between this house hosting a rabbi and the secret house churches they were forced to hide in while under Roman occupation. This house was a church. And for whatever reason, these men were denied entry. Jesus had established a reputation in Galilee by then as a healer, and his audience knew he could heal the paralytic—they knew that by letting him through he could get his life back. But shockingly, they didn't. For whatever reason, these five men didn't *belong* in that congregation. They were kept outside, away from the Messiah, away from the healing grace of God. And what was Jesus' reaction to these outsiders fighting back and destroying his "church?" He saw their faith, and he found it good.

If there's something in this text that we as Christians should take away that we traditionally haven't, it's that God blesses those who disrupt the church with their faith. God blesses outsiders who demand inclusion with God's people and scream "I am here!" And who are these people? Who has the church traditionally closed the door on? Immigrants and refugees? The disfigured and the homeless? Yes, all these and more. Maybe it *would* be better if we smashed every chapel and church, every pulpit and sanctuary that denies the unwanted, that rebukes the sinner, that ignores the helpless. As Mark 2 reveals, it's only when such churches—such roofs—are destroyed that the true Gospel of Christ can be revealed. Only then will God see us—all of us—and say "Your sins are forgiven—now take your mat and walk."

Precious God, remind us that the church can only be the church when its doors are open for all your children, no matter their background. Help us live lives of holy disruption and sanctified destruction so all peoples might know your grace. Amen.

29

A Real and Vital Faith

"Happy are people who have pure hearts, because they will see God."
MATTHEW 5:8

JESUS TEACHES, "HAPPY ARE people who have pure hearts, because they will see God." The "pure heart" is a faith that is "backed up by convictions, whose outward deeds match their inner commitments."[1] What Jesus is saying is that those who have "pure hearts" will have a faith that is real and vital. It is a faith experienced in the deep recesses of the heart, a faith that influences every moment of our lives. Such a faith confronts the God of the Holy Bible as an inescapable reality. Vagueness and doubt dissipate, senses become alert as though biting into something hot and spicy, and confidently we know that God is right in the midst of the present moment.

This is not a faith that simply believes in God or has opinions about God. The church has multitudes of people who do that. It is one thing to recite the creeds of the church and utter words of belief, as almost all of us do. It is quite another thing to say, "God is in this place! I feel God's presence." That experience is like taking notice of a beautiful piece of art, imagination stirred by the rich use of colors or the complexity of brush strokes, or standing on a beach watching a sunrise as if you had never seen one before. No one argues with a beautiful piece of art or with a sunrise. It is simply experienced.

1. Long, *Matthew*, 50.

The critical difference is awareness. Consider a conversation I had some years ago in Pasadena, California. During my graduate studies there, I commented to a resident what a joy it is to wake each morning, pour a cup of coffee, and enjoy the beautiful mountain range. At that comment, my friend looked up at the mountains, with no discernable emotion, and said, "After living here for a while, you no longer notice them." My friend acknowledged the presence of the mountains but they were not real to him. He had lost his capacity to notice them and have them move him deeply by the beauty that they generously shared day after day. His heart was not pure. Rather, his heart, muddied by the multitude of the small and large things that occupied his thoughts, fell numb.

Anything real to us results in emotional vividness. If such emotion is absent, we may question if we are paying attention, eyes wide open expecting the unexpected and anticipating wonder. Belief can be a profound matter, even courageous when such a statement of belief may result in marginalization or persecution. However, often our beliefs lie at the surface of our lives, very present but lacking any meaningful impact on us. Perhaps attention to responsibility, fulfilling daily tasks, or simply cynicism and exhaustion from the daily grind has narrowed our focus. Experiencing the uncommon in the ordinary requires a pure heart, that is, a heart released on occasion from the urgent tasks always before us, and open to the nuances of the present moment. It is what the Bible speaks of as stillness before God. Such a heart sees God in a child playing, in nature, in ordinary situations, and in opportunities to be useful to others.

Almighty God, stir my faith. Grant it bold expression. Save me from timidity that expects little from you. Amen.

30

A Year of Faith and Hope

"So what are we going to say about these things? If God is for us, who is against us?"

ROMANS 8:31

IT IS ALWAYS POSSIBLE to dwell on the bright as well as the dark side of life. Yet, for many people, they are inclined to direct their attention to what may go wrong, to anticipate the bitter rather than the sweet, the tears rather than the smiles, and the difficulties rather than the opportunities that may lie in the New Year that stretches out before them. This way of looking at things is probably nothing more than a carryover from how their parents approached life from year to year. Perhaps this is a view fashioned by disappointments and struggles over many years. But it remains a choice that anyone can make—quieting the voice of negativity and grasping the promise of faith that God is for us as we cross from one year to the next.

This is not to be blindly idealistic. People of faith know as much about real trouble as any non-believer, perhaps much more, in fact. Those who don't have faith often need a distraction to push through each day, some measure of artificial stimulation. Having no faith or hope they look to escape from the real challenges that confront every one of us. Alcohol, recreational drugs, or acquiring things of luxury and comfort divert attention from life's challenges and disappointments. Conversely, people of faith are genuine realists. They acknowledge and face real misfortune and then look right through the trouble to something beyond—they see hope in the promises of their faith. That is the real difference.

It should be clear that the Bible never asks that we turn away from the facts, that we deceive ourselves in order to be a people of faith. As Christians, we are aware of our own capacity for greed, cruelty, and selfishness. We know that those who would trample over us care little about our faith and that disillusionment lurks around every moment of every day. Such has always been the case and always will be. Emerson said: "He has not learned the lesson of life who does not every day surmount a fear."[1] But, in faith, we can look into the dense fog of the New Year without too much uneasiness because God moves forward alongside us, a God that is always struggling with us, always bringing good out of evil.

Life can be a struggle. Not every cloud will have a silver lining and not every wrong will be righted in this life. Ambitions may continue to remain unfulfilled and broken relationships may never be repaired. But that does not diminish the promise of faith that God is for us. Who believed that every round of disappointment, meanness, and heartbreak is the whole story? Life also consists of laughter, moments of happiness, and serendipitous occasions of surprise and delight. Each struggle to be experienced above the loud clamor of negativity. Our own free agency allows us to choose the tone that we attach to our lives. Perhaps all we need in the New Year is to be reminded that if God is for us, who is against us?

In this New Year, let us not forget, O Lord, that we are more than conquerors in the love, presence, and power of our Lord, Jesus Christ. Amen.

---

1. Emerson, *The Complete Works*, 276.

31

Doing What We Can (Location: Cana)

"His mother told the servants, 'Do whatever he tells you.'"

JOHN 2:5

JESUS' FIRST MIRACLE WAS in Cana, on the occasion of a wedding celebration. David A. Redding, a Presbyterian pastor, declares that this one miracle is a masterpiece to love.[1] Jesus makes an unforgettable impression that he knew how to laugh and have a good time. Though it goes without saying that moments of grief need God's help, says Redding, this miracle demonstrates that gladness needs it, too. What is dominant in this story is not the miracle or the wine, but Christ's presence. Jesus showed up when people were celebrating and having a good time. This says a great deal about Jesus. Jesus came to live with people and to love them—both in the midst of sorrow and loss, as well as in times of gladness and celebration.

From this miracle we make another discovery about Christ; Christ has both the power and desire to help people, even ordinary people like you and me. It is important that the wedding couple is never identified by name. Their name is irrelevant. They are, perhaps, ordinary people like us, busy celebrating their wedding with family and friends when something embarrassing happens—they simply run out of wine before the celebration has concluded. So, Jesus' own mother comes to him and asks for his help. It is the most basic pattern of prayer; simply asking God for help.

1. Redding, *The Miracles of Christ*, 3.

Naturally, Jesus does help. Jesus performs the first miracle of his ministry. But to read this story swiftly, without careful attention to how John, the evangelist, tells the story, is to miss a most powerful dynamic of how Jesus works miracles. Notice, that Jesus never touches the six stone water jars mentioned in the story. Jesus turns to servants and asks that they do the work of filling them with water. Notice again, that Jesus doesn't draw water from the six jars. Jesus never touches the water at all. Jesus simply asks the servants to draw some water and deliver it to the headwaiter and they do. When the headwaiter tastes what has been drawn from the jars he comments that it is the finest wine of the celebration! The miracle of Jesus, the miracle of turning water into wine, follows when others first do what they can.

When there is a need or a problem in our lives, Jesus is concerned and stands ready to help. But this story teaches us that we are expected to participate in our own miracle. Before Jesus fed the thousands, Andrew, one of Jesus' disciples, first brought a little boy, with his lunch, to Jesus. Before a sick woman was healed, she touched the hem of Jesus' garment. Before a blind man could see, he obeyed the command of Christ to go and wash his face in a pool. To receive a miracle from Christ, each one of us must do what we can. No person's situation is so bad that they can't do something. But it is after we have done what we can, that Jesus does what he needs to do. It is then that miracles happen.

I thank you, O God, for the vibrant life with which you have surrounded me. Revitalize me when I am overwhelmed. Show me what I can do and grant me the patience to leave everything else to your power. Amen.

32

In the Crater of Calamity (Nathanael Hood)

"But now, says the Lord—the one who created you, Jacob, the one who formed you, Israel: Don't fear, for I have redeemed you; I have called you by name; you are mine. When you pass through the waters, I will be with you; when through the rivers, they won't sweep over you. When you walk through the fire, you won't be scorched and flame won't burn you. I am the Lord your God, the holy one of Israel, your savior."

ISAIAH 43:1–3A

THE FALL OF JERUSALEM in the sixth century BCE was the literal end of the world for the Jewish people. This is no turn of phrase—for the ancient Judeans, it was an eschatological cataclysm. They were the Chosen People of the one true God, the God who led them out of bondage in Egypt to the Promised Land. This God was no abstract, metaphorical force, but a God physically present with them in their wanderings through the wilderness, physically present in his direct communications with his prophets and kings, and physically present within their sacred temple, a temple built to his specific measurements and design. Yet despite his presence, King Nebuchadnezzar of Babylon had laid waste to the city, looted their temple, and dragged the survivors into slavery. Even their kings, descendants of the divinely appointed line of David and Solomon, were humiliated and destroyed: Jehoiakim died during Jerusalem's besiegement, Jeconiah was driven into exile, and Zedekiah was blinded, taken to Babylon, and imprisoned until his death.

The world had ended. And yet God had not abandoned them. It is here in the Book of Isaiah that we encounter this passage, one of the purest messages of hope and love in the entire Old Testament. You have been broken, God says, but I have created you. You have sinned and been punished, but I shall redeem you. You have been enslaved, yet you are mine. You have been cursed and spat upon, beaten and destroyed, yet you are precious in my eyes. You have been scattered to the winds, but I shall bring you home.

It is important to remember that the Book of Isaiah was not written all at once by the same authors. Scholars believe that only the first half, roughly chapters 1–39, can be directly attributed to the ancient prophet, a man who'd predicted the fall of Jerusalem about a hundred years earlier. Scholars believe that this passage of hope and restoration was added by an anonymous author written during the Jewish captivity in Babylon. For this author, the disbelieving horror of Jerusalem's destruction was still fresh and powerful. We cannot imagine the surreality of having one's entire worldview and culture shattered by a conquering army. And yet, even in this time, the writer felt hope.

If it took a century for Isaiah's prophecy of destruction to come true, it would take another sixty for his prophecy of restoration. In 539 BCE, the Persian king Cyrus the Great permitted the Jews to return to their homeland. Two years later, under the instruction of the prophets Ezra and Nehemiah, the Jews rebuilt the walls and sacred temple of Jerusalem. And for another half millennium, they stood tall and mighty until falling before a new conqueror: Imperial Rome. Once more the Jews despaired. And once more God responded that he had not abandoned them. For this time he would send the greatest gift of hope mankind would ever know—a Son. A Son who would announce the destruction of death, a Son who would preach a life everlasting, a Son who would reveal a new world without end. And even in our darkest hour, this Son would remind us that we need not despair. The victory has been won. The world might fall, but God will not.

In a world as conflicted and violent as ours, keep my eyes open to your continued presence and work. In Christ's name. Amen.

33

What Makes People Good?

"But examine everything carefully and hang on to what is good."
1 Thessalonians 5:21

THE YEAR 2017 CELEBRATED the bicentennial birthday of Henry David Thoreau. In a splendid new biography published to mark this occasion, *Henry David Thoreau: A Life*, Laura Dassow Walls, a professor of English literature at the University of Notre Dame, offers an account of one evening, after young Henry had been sent to bed by his mother, was found awake long after, staring out the bedroom window. She asked her son, "Why, Henry dear, why don't you go to sleep?" "Mother," said he, "I have been looking through the stars to see if I couldn't see God behind them."[1] Thoreau reminds us that a journey of faith begins by "looking." For Christians, we look for God by paying attention to the person of Jesus Christ.

In his first letter to the church in Thessalonica, Paul offers instruction for a journey of faith. Paul's beginning point is an invitation to "goodness." Though goodness is difficult to define—and Paul makes no attempt to do so here—it is wonderfully easy to recognize. Often, simple goodness is observable on first contact with another. Paul asks that followers of Jesus "examine everything" and take notice of goodness wherever it may be found. If we believe that goodness is of paramount importance, as does Paul, it is obvious that we should do all we can to learn how it is achieved. That

---

1. Walls, *Henry David Thoreau*, 43.

begins, suggests Paul, when one takes notice of everyone and everything that is good and places ourselves in contact with it wherever it is found. The disciples became "good" men chiefly as a result of their acquaintance with Christ. That is because the soul grows by what it touches.

After bringing ourselves into steady contact with those of good character, Paul instructs the church to, "hang on to what is good." What Paul speaks of here is the discipline to identify and break down any barrier that hinders the soul from being positively influenced by those of good character. When people fail to respond to goodness it is because they are not sufficiently aware of impediments that block personal transformation or they fail to discipline their own behavior in the manner of good people. Behind any positive change is a period of "practice" and "self-mastery" over a period of time. "Hang on to what is good," says Paul. Grip it until the moment arrives that it grips you.

Some years ago, on a Celebrity cruise with my wife, I watched in wonder at a demonstration of glassblowing—through Celebrity's collaboration with The Corning Museum of Glass. Artists, with what seemed to be little effort, created beautiful colored glass pieces, one after another. After dazzling the passengers with their craft, they shared that "mastery" in their craft took ten thousand hours of practice. Each piece of glassware they produced took an incredibly brief period of time to produce. But, what could not be seen was the long, disciplined time of practice and mastery that made that speed possible. We tend to not notice, or we forget, what preceded anything done successfully. In the same manner, goodness is difficult. But Paul shows us the way. Place ourselves in direct contact with what is good and hang onto it until we profit from it.

Father, I cannot solve all of the world's problems, nor help everyone who reaches out to me. What I ask is that I may treat everyone with kindness, thoughtfulness, and respect even as I point to your Son, Jesus Christ as the one who can do all things. Amen.

34

Nonconformist

"Don't be conformed to the patterns of this world, but be transformed by the renewing of your minds so that you can figure out what God's will is—what is good and pleasing and mature."

Romans 12:2

STAND UP TO CANCER is a division of the Entertainment Industry Foundation, a non-profit committed to mobilizing people and financial resources toward new treatments for those battling cancer in the U.S. and Canada. Their current marketing campaign, "Whatever It Takes," invites people to join a growing movement of those willing to "swing for the fences" in seeking new advancements in cancer research that can have a life-changing impact. Implicit in the campaign are two classes of people: one small and one large—those who struggle together to challenge the ravages of cancer and those who stand on the sidelines and watch. It is the difference between those who are organized around a great cause and those who drift through life with no driving passion to participate in anything great.

The apostle Paul makes the same distinction—a division of people into two classes—here in his letter to the church in Rome. The first class of people is one whose minds and opinions and values are shaped by the world. Uniformity to popular culture extends to dress and manners, speech and thought. They conform to the world and its ways without discerning if participating with everyone else is best for them or even wise. They drift through life as leaves drift down a river. Where life takes them, they go without objection, accommodating to the environment and yielding to social pressures.

The second class is not shaped by the larger culture; they actively seek to transform the culture through a radical commitment to something larger, something nobler than simply going along. They say No when everyone else is saying Yes. They put character into their environment rather than take their character from the environment. Norms and conventions are challenged and a clarion call is made to strive for something larger than one's individual life. In these few words of Paul's letter to the Roman Church, Paul asks that the church pay attention to God and organize its life around God's will.

To which class do we belong? Is society molding us more than we are molding society? Are we conforming to what the world wants us to become or are we being transformed by paying attention to God and seeking God's desires for our lives? Paul is seeking nonconformists, people whose lives are organized around a steady conviction that we were created for something more than just going along with the world. Paul invites us to open ourselves to the shaping influence of God and to experience strength in our inner life by God's active work in our bodies. This is the invitation of Paul when he writes, "be transformed by the renewing of your minds so that you can figure out what God's will is—what is good and pleasing and mature."

Implant within me a spirit that is tireless in running toward the goal of a good and pleasing and mature life in Christ. Amen.

35

The God Who Carries Us

"Bel crouches down; Nebo cowers. Their idols sit on animals, on beasts. The objects you once carried about are now borne as burdens by the weary animals."

ISAIAH 46:1

ONE OF THE MOST moving—and inspiring—moments in any athletic completion is that one where an athlete stumbles and another competitor goes back to offer help. The tone of the moment is transformed from a test of strength and speed to one of mutual humanity, sharing in one another's frailties. Such moments remind us of something nobler than defeating another in a game of skill, strength, and speed. Competition may push each of us to realize our best potential—and that is good. But more extraordinary are moments that reveal our common infirmities; moments where we strengthen one another in the storms of life.

This is not so with God; it must not be so. Unfailing strength is the very nature of God. Yet, here Isaiah fashions for us a sharp contrast between gods that are carried and a God that carries us or, as Henry Sloane Coffin once observed, "Between religion as a load and religion as a lift."[1] In another of Isaiah's tirades against idols, against imaginary gods, he provides the reader with graphic clarity of the gods of Babylon bobbing and swaying in an absurdly undignified fashion on the backs of animals. Weary from the weight

---

1. Coffin, *Joy in Believing*, 8.

of these gods, the animals strain to move forward as the frightened devotees lead the animals to a place of safety away from the invading armies. What a picture; ordinary, mortal human beings struggling to secure the safety of gods! Isaiah intends for this to strike us as absurd.

Isaiah then contrasts this ridiculous image with the living God, the God who bore Israel in his arms from its birth and has carried it ever since. The prophet would have us understand that a burdensome religion is a false religion; that a god which must be taken care of is not a faith that can sustain us. Israel needs, as do we, a faith that takes care of us. Communion with the God of Israel is a faith that always shifts the weight of life to God, not the other way around. And Isaiah wants us to know that if we ever feel that we are carrying our religion, that if faith has become burdensome, then our gaze has moved from the one, true living God.

The wonderful teacher of the Christian faith, Paul Tillich, once commented that we are not asked to grasp the faith of the Old and New Testament but, rather, are called to be grasped by it.[2] A Christian's beliefs are not a set of propositions that we are compelled to accept. That would be a burdensome religion. The Christian faith is an invitation from a living God to come and be held in God's grasp, to be lifted and carried along through the difficulties of life we must all face. We may struggle at times to free ourselves from God's embrace, to go through life alone, in our own strength. But sooner or later, we will become as weary as the animals carrying the idols of Bel and Nebo. And when we are depleted, God will be there.

Almighty God, you created me for life with you. Strengthen me when I am weary, lift me when I stumble, and carry me when I lack strength for the journey. In the strong name of Jesus Christ, I pray. Amen.

---

2. Captured from lecture given by Thomas G. Long in summer of 1992, Princeton Theological Seminary.

36

The Promise of Something New (Location: Jerusalem) (Nathanael Hood)

"As Jesus came to the city and observed it, he wept over it."

Luke 19:41

Pause a moment, and consider the city of Jerusalem as Jesus once saw it. Jesus the man—the Nazarene rabbi—looked upon an already ancient city straining under the yoke of Roman imperialism. Centurions elbowed through marketplaces crowded with Samaritans and Sadducees; self-righteous Israelites prayed in the squares as scabrous lepers scurried through the outskirts. In a few hours, he would be welcomed as a savior by the oppressed masses who would lay their coats and palm branches before him, singing the Psalms of David in joyous delirium. In a few days, those same crowds would scream for his death, demanding his execution at the hands of Pontius Pilate.

There is a small Roman Catholic church on the spot believed to be where Jesus wept in the nineteenth chapter of Luke—shaped like a tear drop, it sits on the Mount of Olives east of the city. Not too far from it is the Church of the Holy Sepulchre, believed to be situated on Golgotha, where Jesus was crucified. Did he know, when he looked upon that city, that in a week's time he would be seeing a nearly identical view, this time tortured, beaten, and nailed to a cross? Yes, Jesus looked upon the city that would be his doom and wept.

Now consider Jesus the Divine, the physical incarnation of the holy Godhead, the living Word that is and was and will be. See the city he saw, the city first inhabited 6000 to 7000 years ago by shepherds thirsty for freshwater springs. See the city ruled in turn by Canaanites, Egyptians, Babylonians, and Romans, dashed by waves of invaders and dynastic restorers. See the city whose legacy is warfare and carnage, as even God's chosen king David took it by force from its Jebusite inhabitants. See the city that would be ravaged by emperor Vespasian less than a century after his death, the second temple reduced to ashes and a single wall while over a million civilians lay dead with another 97,000 enslaved. See the city conquered by Muslims in the seventh century, contested by crusaders in the eleventh, twelfth, and thirteenth, controlled by Ottoman Turks until the nineteenth, and torn between Israelis and Palestinians to this very day. See the city originally named the "dwelling of peace" which would know none for countless generations.

How can we see this city and not weep? Earlier in the Gospel of Luke, Jesus had mourned the sacred city upon learning of Herod's plot to murder him:

> "Jerusalem, Jerusalem, you who kill the prophets and stone those who were sent to you! How often I have wanted to gather your people just as a hen gathers her chicks under her wings. But you didn't want that." (Luke 13:34)

Two thousand years later and the chicks have still not come home. We look out and see a world more bitterly divided than ever, edged on the brink of cataclysm. How similar it must have felt for first-century Jews living under the thumb of Rome where a single order from the emperor could ravage their holiest of holies as was done in the time of Jeremiah. Yet let us not forget that it was out of this swirling void of chaos that God chose to unmake the world itself with a new covenant, one that transcended all the sorrow and brokenness of this life with the promise of a new one. These times are not the end, merely a transition from which to emerge like a certain lowly carpenter all those years ago towards a great glory.

Lord Jesus, help me to be ever attentive to your work of restoration in the world. Use me, and the talents you have given me, in your service. Amen.

37

Holy Moments

"So then let's also run the race that is laid out in front of us, since we have such a great cloud of witnesses surrounding us. Let's throw off any extra baggage, get rid of the sin that trips us up, and fix our eyes on Jesus, faith's pioneer and perfecter."

HEBREWS 12:1, 2

EMERSON WROTE, "OUR FAITH comes in moments; our vice is habitual. Yet there is depth in those brief moments which constrains us to ascribe more reality to them than to all other experiences."[1] Moments that are holy, moments filled with richness, depth, and mystery are rare for many of us. Yet, they do come, however fleeting they may be. They strike us as a welcomed breeze that brushes our face on an otherwise hot and still day. At one moment, it is felt and appreciated. The next, it is gone. The difficulty that often challenges any of us is that we live largely in the ordinary. The exceptional holy moment is dismissed for practical matters of meeting the present struggle of simply getting through the day.

The author of Hebrews urges a redirection of our natural impulse to be carried by whatever distracts us from completing the race that Christ has set before us—the race to know God and live richly that life God desires for us. Here in the twelfth chapter of Hebrews, we are reminded of, "a great

---

1. Emerson, *Emerson: Essays and Lectures*, 385.

cloud of witness surrounding us." That is our encouragement when the race becomes difficult. If we are honest, all races become difficult. Any athlete will acknowledge the multiple forces that pull against a resolve to train—to remain with any athletic endeavor that, in one moment, inspires our best effort. When that resolve becomes weak, nothing holds our eyes on the goal quite as well as family and friends who cheer us forward.

I am a runner. The boldness to declare that comes from multiple books and magazines on running. When I look in the mirror, I see considerably more trunk fat than others who run. I see in others lean bodies covering vast distances. I still have weight to lose and I only run two miles, five mornings a week. Yet, the literature I read each evening declares that I am a runner. A runner is not determined by a measure of fitness or the speed of the run or the distance that is covered. A runner is simply someone who runs regularly. So, I am a runner. But I am a distracted runner. Each morning I walk out the door I am creatively engaged with reasons not to run. That is why I subscribe to *Runner's World* magazine and read books on running. They are my "great cloud of witnesses" that keeps me in the race.

Hebrews encourages that we remain in the race that has been laid out in front of us—the race to know and live for God. And Hebrews urges that we reorganize our life, to throw off any "extra baggage" and "sin that trips us up" that hinders our run. Like an athlete, Hebrews ask that we get rid of all the extra weight of anything that creatively engages us not to spend time regularly with God—time alone in a quiet moment reading God's word and listening. We begin by remembering—remembering a grandmother, or a father, or someone we deeply admire who ran the Christian race before us. They will be our cloud of witnesses that pushes us forward. Emerson said: "When a man lives with God, his voice shall be as sweet as the murmur of the brook and the rustle of the corn."[2]

I ask, O Lord, for a holy moment to brush my face today and the wisdom to pause and reflect deeply upon it. Amen.

---

2. Emerson, *Emerson: Essays and Lectures*, 309.

38

What We Might Be

"But in the days to come..."
MICAH 4:1A

SOME YEARS AGO, I was sharing lunch with my mother in Irving, Texas. A woman seated at a nearby table looked at me, grabbed a notepad from her purse, and approached me, "May I have your autograph?" I inquired of her who she thought I was. She named a football player with the New York Giants and, apparently, she was a huge fan. Naturally, I politely told her my name and that I was a Presbyterian pastor serving a congregation right there in Irving. She refused to believe me. With anger and frustration all mingled together in one burst of emotion, she answered, "If you don't want to give autographs, say so!" and returned to her meal. She saw something in me that I was not—and never will be. And, I fear, I have cost a Giants player one of his fans.

God does something similar. God doesn't mistake our identity, as the woman in Irving, but God does see in us something so much more than is presently true. With a forward-looking eye, God sees what we might become. Think of a teacher that goes into a classroom, a class of girls and boys. The teacher lifts his or her eyes away from the present to see women and men. The best teachers understand that, in a sense, they are architects and builders of the people those children will become. It is the teacher's vision of "what might be" that directs every moment spent with the children. The vision is active in the present, shaping, molding, and encouraging children to do something more. Yet, for the future to be claimed, each child must be a willing participant in the process of learning. In Jesus Christ, God shares God's vision for what we might become. It is a work completed by the Holy Spirit as we willingly participate by paying attention to God.

Our encouragement comes from the rich examples in the Old and New Testament—examples of God's uncommon work in common people. Moses had a speech impediment but would stand before a king and demand that the people of Israel be set free from their bondage in Egypt. David, a shepherd boy tending sheep, would defeat a Philistine giant, Goliath, rescuing Israel from an enemy. Simon, a name that means hearer, or one who simply hears, would have his name changed by Jesus to Peter, a rock, upon which Jesus would build his church. And a woman of sin—an outcast child of the city—would be addressed by Jesus as "daughter" and spoken to as if she had already entered the future as an heir to God's promises. Each story nudges us to come to our present, filled with difficulties and struggle, with a vision of the future, a glimpse of what might be.

Here, in this brief passage, the prophet Micah lifts his eyes away from the present to the days that are to come. By holding clearly before him God's promise of more, Micah finds refreshment in the present difficulty. Without the joyful anticipation of something more to come, without the conviction that the God who worked uncommonly in common people in the past continues the same today, Micah would lose his capacity to hold on, and the spirit of striving would go out of his work. Our vision of the future always determines the behavior and attitudes that we bring to the present. Our dominant thought and hope regulate how we go about our responsibilities today. It is wise to ask what vision pulls us forward? What future do we have in mind? What do we see as the possible consummation of our present work? It is not enough to know what we are doing today. We must draw so close to God that we capture a glimpse of what we are working for—for a glimpse of what we might be.

Forgive me, Lord, for visions that are too small, for little expectations for the future, and for not paying sufficient attention to your work in my life. Amen.

39

The Two Popes (Nathanael Hood)

"Brothers and sisters, I myself don't think I've reached it, but I do this one thing: I forget about the things behind me and reach out for the things ahead of me."

Philippians 3:13

There are not two, but three main presences within Fernando Meirelles' extraordinary film *The Two Popes* about the tumultuous friendship between Pope Benedict XVI and Cardinal Jorge Mario Bergoglio. The first two are the Holy Sees themselves. There's Benedict XVI (Anthony Hopkins), the German successor of the much-beloved Pope John Paul II chosen in large part for his grave, combative conservatism in the face of increasing global secularism. Then there's Bergoglio (Jonathan Pryce), the avuncular Argentinian Jesuit whose liberal theology forged in the furnace of Third World poverty sent shockwaves throughout a church entrenched in tradition and First World luxury. The film sees them butt heads in the wake of a disillusioned Bergoglio's attempted resignation as Archbishop of Buenos Aires. Believing said resignation would be interpreted as a vote of no confidence against his papacy, Benedict refuses. When Bergoglio flies to Rome to confront Benedict personally, the two debate and argue until they slowly become friends.

The third presence only makes itself known gradually, first appearing almost thirty minutes into the film in the midst of their first meeting and, subsequently, their first major argument where they bicker about homosexuality, priestly celibacy, and the provision of sacraments for those out of communion. It's a small, imperious voice from Benedict's Fitbit demanding he remains active to reach his prescribed ten thousand steps a day: "Don't stop now. Keep moving." This voice becomes almost a commentator on the action as the film continues, punctuating arguments and announcing Benedict's unseen presence. It's a marvelous narrative device that keeps the film from getting mired in endless debates about theology, ensuring a sense of forward momentum for both the story and its characters. Indeed, the voice gets the last line of the movie proper before the credits begin as Benedict sits alone in the Vatican after his resignation and Bergoglio's election as pope: "Don't stop now. Keep moving. Keep moving."

As the film continues, it becomes impossible to ignore the Fitbit as an embodiment of the Holy Spirit, gently nudging both Benedict and Bergoglio towards not just reconciliation but friendship. It underscores the film's central thesis that faith and its practice cannot remain frozen in the past. "Time demands movement," Bergoglio challenges during their first meeting. Benedict snaps back with accusations of hypocrisy concerning Bergoglio's former conservative attitudes, particularly concerning homosexuality.

"I changed," he admits.

"No, you compromised," Benedict challenges.

"No. No compromise. No, I changed. It's a different thing."

Such change seems almost blasphemous in an organization like the Catholic Church that lives and dies by its traditions and moves with the speed of centuries, not minutes. But change it must—and not through the rejection of holy doctrine but by faithful, reverent reinterpretation. To paraphrase a great theologian, it's the difference between drinking from a stagnant pond and a flowing river.

There are few places in the Scriptures where this need for faithful, reverent change are better emphasized than in the third chapter of the Epistle to the Philippians where Paul challenges his audience to avoid those who say that believers and converts must strictly adhere to outdated Jewish law and ritual to be saved. Referring to his own upbringing as a Jewish Pharisee as so much sewer trash—sewer trash!—he boasts that he rejected everything for the sake of Christ. It's through living faithfully in God through the Gospel of Jesus Christ that salvation comes, not through outdated ritual and calcified theology. To tear down walls, to shatter the barriers between mankind, this is what living in Christ means. And if any of our practices or beliefs hobble us in this journey, then we must listen for the Holy Spirit which whispers now more than ever to not stop now, to keep moving, to keep moving.

My God, encourage me when I am discouraged. Cast light upon my feet when the way seems dark. Strengthen me when I grow weary. Always help me to look up to the hills and see your glory. Amen.

40

Ministry of Imagination

"There was a Pharisee named Nicodemus, a Jewish leader. He came to Jesus at night and said to him, 'Rabbi, we know that you are a teacher who has come from God, for no one could do these miraculous signs that you do unless God is with him.'"

JOHN 3:1, 2

NICODEMUS CALLS THE CHURCH to a ministry of imagination. A Pharisee, Nicodemus departs from the narrow, walled-in sectarian views of his colleagues and comes to Jesus in sympathetic inquiry. Perhaps Nicodemus is weary of the wooden, cramping, and belittling understanding of the Bible that limits fellowship with others of another point of view. Perhaps Nicodemus fears that barriers of thought and divisions in the fellowship of faith can produce nothing higher than spiritual dwarfs. Perhaps Nicodemus simply wishes for a more expansive and imaginative faith and believes that Jesus can offer the necessary nutriment. For whatever reason, Nicodemus comes to Jesus.

A large faith, a full-grown faith must borrow from others. The genius of maturity is the recognition that a wider vision of this life demands the stimulus of thought found in another's wealth. No one discovers adequate nourishment for their own development within the poverty of self-centeredness and narrow-mindedness. If we are to exercise ourselves in the wider vision of imagination—as does Nicodemus—we must listen sympathetically to understandings not our own. Otherwise, we exist only in an echo chamber, our thought never growing, never expanding. It is well documented that even Shakespeare fetched his water of inspiration from the wells of other great thinkers and writers.

J. H. Jowett reflects that one's life, thinking, and theology will remain comparatively dormant unless it is breathed upon by the bracing influence of fellowship of thought that is beyond our own.[1] Communion with viewpoints on every side, viewpoints to both the left and right of our own grasp of the Bible and the world of thought, lifts our powers for imagination. It is in a grand and inquisitive imagination that our faith discovers strength and grand proportions. It is where we acknowledge that Jesus is more than anyone can ever fully grasp.

It would be well if persons of faith were to exercise the same imaginative curiosity as Nicodemus. Sincere recognition of another's position, appreciation for another's point of view, and discovery of another's purpose and aim in faith strengthen the fellowship of the church. Rather than "leaving the table" when disagreements of faith arise, perhaps it would be a richer and more spacious church if we recall the largest common denominator that has always held the people of faith together, the Lordship of Jesus Christ.

Teach me humility and increase within me the exercise of civility in all my discourse with others. Open my ears, and heart, to hear viewpoints not my own and to value them out of an abundance of love for all people. This I ask, Heavenly Father, in Jesus' name. Amen.

---

1. Jowett, *Thirsting for the Springs*, 193.

41

A Call to Prayer

"Early in the morning, well before sunrise, Jesus rose and went to a deserted place where he could be alone in prayer."

MARK 1:35

MY GRANDMOTHER KEPT A large, white, faux leather cover Bible prominently in her home—usually on a coffee table, though she would occasionally move it about her home as though it was a traveling exhibit. Embossed into the cover was a full-color picture of Jesus kneeling by a great rock in the wilderness. Each time my eyes fell upon that Bible I felt as though it was a call to prayer. The face of Jesus was not anxious, not desperate as my own on those occasions I did pray. His face portrayed confidence, a radiance one has in the company of loved ones who care deeply about us. Absent was worry, doubt, or any trace of anxiety that threaten to consume. Yes, a call to prayer was evident in this picture of Jesus. However, that call made me uncomfortable—uncomfortable because I would experience a lack of spiritual power. With the disciples, I heard my own heart say, "Lord, teach us to pray like that."

In this Scripture, Jesus had just finished a hard, demanding day. Another day of similar demands stretched before him. How could Jesus be ready for it? Mark's Gospel gives us the answer and with it an important insight into Jesus' power, "Early in the morning, well before sunrise, Jesus rose and went to a deserted place where he could be alone in prayer." Jesus was intentional with prayer. Jesus wove into the fabric of each day a time to be alone with God. Jesus regarded this time as a vital part of the human experience, however, one may attempt to define or understand prayer. Prayer was an opportunity to link his life with the purposes of God and cultivate a friendship with God. This friendship produced the confidence that Jesus would not face any of life's demands alone. That would be the source of Jesus' spiritual power.

My lack of spiritual power as a child was from an inadequate view of prayer. I had reduced prayer to those occasions when I would ask God for a favor or for help with a difficulty. Consequently, days without prayer would pass—I simply did not have any request to make of God. Yet, as I matured, I continued to pay attention to that picture on my grandmother's Bible, that picture of Jesus at prayer. It grew upon my consciousness that prayer is the same as time spent with a friend or loved one. I may not have anything to ask of my friend but I did enjoy their company. I felt valued by them, loved by them, and strengthened because of their friendship. The same happens with prayer. A strong hand on the shoulder, and the confidence to face each day swelling within. Power comes as we find ourselves surrounded by God's love, guidance, and strength.

With this refreshing surge of power that flows from regular time in prayer, it is very strange then that we should be content with so little prayer. The weakest, most fearful individual can experience greater strength through the regular rhythm of prayer each day. As this passage of Scripture demonstrates, prayer each day for Jesus was as ordinary as enjoying a meal. Jesus prayed often. Jesus prayed for himself and for others. Jesus prayed when he faced a crisis and Jesus prayed simply to be alone with God. Jesus urged his disciples to pray and Jesus taught prayer by example. What the disciples discovered is that regular prayer did not only sustain Jesus' ministry, it gave direction. Immediately after Jesus rose from prayer this particular morning, Jesus knew what he must do that day. He was not to return to the previous day's work. Jesus was to head in the other direction. God had new work for him there.

Heavenly Father, teach me to pray as Jesus prayed—prayers that seek a vital relationship with you. Amen.

42

Tears in a Bottle

"You yourself have kept track of my misery. Put my tears into your bottle—aren't they on your scroll already?"

PSALM 56:8

MANY OF US HAVE a bucket list—a list of experiences we would cherish before death. They require no explanation to others, no defense. They are deeply personal. Further, an explanation may reduce the depth, color, and richness of personal meaning. Most people recognize that what is experienced deeply can rarely be expressed with words. Words are useful for the communication of thought. They are less useful for conveying deeply held emotions, feelings, and convictions. A strong writer can approach this depth of meaning better than most. But always, words have a reducing effect. Permit me to simply state that high on my bucket list are three experiences I would value: a cameo appearance in a stage production of the musical RENT, a balloon handler in the Macy's Thanksgiving Day Parade, and sharing a cappuccino with David Hyde Pierce.

Some will remember that David Hyde Pierce played the character of Niles Crane on the popular television series, *Frasier*. On three occasions I have enjoyed David Hyde Pierce on a Broadway stage: *Spamalot*, *Curtains*, and *Vanya and Sonia and Masha and Spike*. If I were to have an occasion to have a private conversation with Pierce over coffee my first question to him would be, "What makes you cry?" An answer to that question often points to deeply held convictions; points to those values, struggles, and principles that grip our hearts. Again, words are limiting. But they can point another in the right direction. An answer to the question, "What makes you cry?" provides a window into the depths of another's soul.

Naturally, tears come in a rich variety. A powerful conviction of truth draws tears to my eyes every time. I simply cannot read in Luke's Gospel the story of Simeon taking the infant Jesus in his arms without my chest becoming heavy and tears forming in my eyes. Here, Simeon recognizes this child as God's salvation. This is a story that reaches beyond the descriptive; it is evocative. In faith, Simeon sees God's decisive hand in the unfolding drama of human history. Grief is another variety of tears. Old Testament teacher, Walter Brueggemann helps us with understanding this passage from the Psalms. Here is a confidence that God has kept, treasured, and preserved "my tears"; that is, all the pain and suffering that the psalmist has experienced. "God is the great rememberer who treasures pain so that the psalmist is free to move beyond that pain."[1]

There is an ancient Jewish practice that provides care in times of misery and grief. A small bottle is provided to collect the tears of anguish and loss. The top of the bottle has a small hole in it that would allow those tears to evaporate over time. When the bottle is completely dry, the time for grieving is over. The Psalmist wants us to know that God has a bottle with our name on it. When tears of grief flow, God collects them in that bottle. This is how seriously God takes our grief; how God honors and shares in our loss. But there is a small hole in the top of that bottle. Over time the tears will evaporate. When the bottle is dry, and our eyes are clear, we see that God remains. And God redirects our eyes to tomorrow.

God, thank you for honoring and sharing in our grief. Hold our tears until we can again see your promised tomorrow. Amen.

---

1. Brueggemann and Bellinger, Jr., *Psalms*, 254.

43

When Faith Is Not Enough

"My brothers and sisters, what good is it if people say that they have faith but do nothing to show it? Claiming to have faith can't save anyone, can it?"

JAMES 2:14

SOMEONE ONCE DECLARED THAT promised prayer has no power, only practiced prayer. That same observation can be applied to faith; the profession of faith has no power, only practiced faith. Evidence of this unfolded one Sunday morning during my graduate studies. Sitting in a Sunday school class for young adults at the North Avenue Presbyterian Church in Atlanta, Georgia, a young man asked permission to address the class. His intention was to make a simple observation and ask the class for help. Then the instructor would proceed to teach the lesson he had prepared for the morning. Yet, the young man's comment became the lesson for that day.

This man began his comments by sharing that some years earlier he made a profession of faith in Jesus as his personal Lord and was baptized in that church. He was a graduate student, busy with not only the demanding rigor of his studies and also working a part-time job to help sustain him as a student. Then, there was also this girl. He was "madly in love with her" as he put it and that, naturally, required some of his attention and time. In the economy of a twenty-four-hour day, there simply was no time remaining for the regular reading of the Bible and prayer.

Now, this man has found himself in the middle of a weighty life crisis, one that was causing him to unravel. He turned to his faith. It was then he made a comment that has shaped my own understanding of faith, something that has given more texture, depth, and color to my own relationship with Jesus than anything I found in the classroom. "I turned to my faith and found that I had done nothing with my faith and now my faith could do nothing for me." Then, a long lingering silence draped the room. Wisdom of such depth rarely can be met with words. The instructor then, with a deliberate and careful movement, placed his lesson upon an empty chair and asked, "What can we do for you?"

The only help the student asked for was accountability. "Beginning today, I am no longer neglecting my faith. Hold me accountable. Call me each day and ask what I have read in the Bible and how I am responding. What I need more than anything at this moment is a faith that will sustain me. Hold me accountable. I cannot move forward without God." Here was a young man who discovered the profound truth that merely professing faith in Jesus lacked power. Vital, life-giving faith that sustains us requires practice. This is precisely what James would have us hear, "What good is it, my brothers and sisters, if you say you have faith but do not have works? Can faith save you?"

God, keep me alert to your power, presence, and care in my daily reading of the Bible. Most importantly, direct my thoughts and behavior today by your word. Amen.

44

When We Get God Wrong (Location: Capernaum) (Nathanael Hood)

> *"Now when Jesus heard that John was arrested, he went to Galilee. He left Nazareth and settled in Capernaum, which lies alongside the sea in the area of Zebulun and Naphtali."*
>
> MATTHEW 4:12, 13

SHORT OF THE RESURRECTION, think of Jesus' greatest, most well-known miracles and there's a good chance they happened in Capernaum, a tiny fishing village of about fifteen-hundred people on the north shore of the Sea of Galilee. It was so small and insignificant that its inhabitants never even bothered building a wall—invading armies would pass it by, deeming it too unimportant to occupy; even the Romans ignored it during their ruthless suppression of the Jewish people during the First Jewish-Roman War (AD 66 to 73). Archaeologists speculate that it was cramped and dirty, with several families living together in the same one-story building with no plumbing or drainage. Yet it was this nowhere village, only about forty miles away from his traditional home in Nazareth, that became Jesus' de facto base of operations during his three-year ministry. The Gospel of Matthew even refers to it in its ninth chapter as "his own city."

It was in Capernaum that Jesus found his first four disciples: the fishermen Peter and Andrew and Zebedee's two sons, James and John. (Later, Jesus would recruit Matthew, one of the local tax collectors, as another member of the Twelve.) It was in its little synagogue that Jesus astonished the people with the authority of his teaching and cast out an impure spirit possessing one of the worshippers (Mark 1: 21–27). It was along these dusty streets that Jesus healed the centurion's paralyzed servant (Matthew 8:5–13), an astonishing act of compassion for a gentile living in his country as part of an occupying colonial force. It was in one of these packed, smelly houses that four friends lifted up a mud and thatch roof to lower their lame companion for Jesus' healing (Mark 2: 1–5). It was on these nearby shores of Galilee that Jesus broke five barley loaves and two fish and fed the five thousand, leaving behind twelve baskets of leftovers (John 6:13). And it was on a nearby hillside where Jesus preached the greatest sermon ever known, the Sermon on the Mount (Matthew 5–7).

And yet, it was also the place that Jesus cursed and condemned for its unbelief. "And you, Capernaum," Jesus raged, "will you be honored by being raised up to heaven? No, you will be thrown down to the place of the dead. After all, if the miracles that were done among you had been done in Sodom, it would still be here today." (Matthew 11:23) One of the only recorded times in any of the Scriptures of Jesus getting angry, and it was towards the city he called home for years. It wasn't that the villagers denied the miraculous things Jesus did—their community was too full of those he'd healed for them to claim that kind of ignorance. Instead, they refused to see these signs and wonders as evidence of Jesus' identity as the Messiah, the Son of God. "Their vision of the kingdom," Tom Wright writes, "was all about revolution . . . violence to defeat violence. A holy war against unholy warriors. Love your neighbor, hate your enemy."[1] He was simply the wrong kind of redeemer.

We as believers, much like the people of ancient Capernaum, have our own ideas concerning God into which we cram all our expectations and prejudices. We use Jesus as a crutch for our own political and moral agendas, wielding him more like a weapon than surrendering before him as the Christ. In doing so, we delude ourselves as powerfully as Capernaum did. We appreciate the miracles but ignore the miracle-worker; we eat the barley loaves and fish but blow off the provider; we appreciate the healing but stiff the doctor. As Christians, we must shield ourselves from such arrogance or risk the same condemnation that once echoed down to this little seaside village.

Lord Jesus, help me today to gaze upon you, to understand you with greater clarity, and to welcome my expectations of you to be rearranged. Amen.

---

1. Wright, *Matthew for Everyone*, 133.

45

Paying Attention to God

"When Jacob woke from his sleep, he thought to himself, The Lord is definitely in this place, but I didn't know it. He was terrified and thought, This sacred place is awesome. It's none other than God's house and the entrance to heaven."

GENESIS 28:16, 17

EARLY IN MY RELATIONSHIP with my wife, I learned she liked yellow roses more than any other color. I also learned that she doesn't much care for red roses. Whenever I am shopping at Publix I pass the floral department to see if they have yellow roses. If they do, and they are particularly beautiful, I purchase a dozen for my wife. I have done this now for thirty-three years. It isn't a burden. I delight in making this thoughtful purchase because it brings delight to my wife. It would be a burden if I found that I couldn't afford to purchase roses for her. And I would stop making this purchase if she ever tired of receiving them.

Worship is paying attention to God. Naturally, as a pastor, many Sundays I am in the pulpit—I am at work. But, when I have a Sunday off, I am in worship somewhere. I go to worship not because I feel some professional obligation. Nor do I worship hoping to enjoy some inspirational music or hear a helpful sermon, though both are welcomed. I go to worship to pay attention to God. Paying attention to God causes me delight because I know it delights God. God created man and woman for a relationship with one another and with God and all of Scripture is one long narrative of God pursuing that relationship. As the purchase of yellow roses brings mutual delight for my wife and me, worship brings the same mutual delight for God and me.

During this pandemic, in-person worship is suspended to protect the health and well-being of the congregation. This is no different than persons in the Bible who suffer from a skin disease being required to self-isolate themselves from the faith community until a priest declares them healed. Yet, people miss in-person worship. I get that. So do I. I miss the community, the personal engagement, and the sharing deeply in people's lives before and after the worship service. Yet, the First Presbyterian Church of Delray Beach never suspended worship. Through live stream technology, worship remains available each week. What remains is the opportunity to pay attention to God—to cause God delight and to experience delight as a result.

Here in Genesis, Jacob wakes from his sleep and realizes that God is present. His experience is that he was "terrified" which must not be confused with how that word is often used today. Jacob's experience might better be described as one of astonishment and awe. Simply, Jacob experienced delight in the presence of God and details the experience as "awesome." There may be times when worship becomes routine and rituals are simply repeated week after week. But we continue the routine because, in paying attention to God, we do not want to miss those occasions when, like Jacob, a most adventurous encounter occurs that results in mutual delight.

Come, Holy God, and dwell with me at this moment. Delight and strengthen me today with the certain presence of the risen Christ. Amen.

46

Unbeatable

"I was beaten with rods three times. I was stoned once. I was shipwrecked three times. I spent a day and a night on the open sea. I've been on many journeys. I faced dangers from rivers, robbers, my people, and Gentiles. I faced dangers in the city, in the desert, on the sea, and from false brothers and sisters. I faced these dangers with hard work and heavy labor, many sleepless nights, hunger and thirst, often without food, and in the cold without enough clothes."

2 Corinthians 11:25–27

Sometimes it appears that the apostle Paul had a hidden charm that both protected him from discouragement and defeat while providing navigation for his ministry. With every possible force at work against him—every possible obstacle to moving forward—Paul was simply unbeatable. His journey seemed impossibly long, and there were lengthy stretches that he had to endure much hardship and loneliness. What's more, Paul kept a careful journal of each difficulty encountered, every challenge he faced, and the deprivation he endured. His purpose for recording each was simply to force the question—can anyone survive experiences such as these, one upon another, by their own strength, their own resources?

Paul's answer is, "no." Every difficulty, challenge, and deprivation presented an opportunity for Paul to proclaim available strength that was not

Paul's—the strength of the risen and active work of Jesus Christ. Storms are part of the normal climate and adversity is part of normal life. Paul utterly rejects the false notion that a formula is at work that shields us from the strong winds and turbulence of day-to-day life. Rather, Paul's desire is to point to his own life and demonstrate a steadying hand that holds us and strengthens us in the storms. Life is full of annoying and costly interruptions and opposing forces that are bent on defeating us. Paul urges that we make the winds of opposition occasions for relying upon God.

That legendary football coach of Notre Dame, Knute Rockne once summoned his players before a game and said, "The team that won't be beat, can't be beat."[1] Rockne was not here proclaiming the strength of Jesus for his players. He was appealing to the uncommon courage and strength and persistence that lies within each of us. Many of us engage in the game of life without our best effort, settling for something just below our actual capacity. Tremendous effort to overcome life's difficulties is rare, people often accept defeat easily, naming what is possible as impossible. These are not the challenges Paul speaks of. Paul lifts his eyes to something higher still, to what is impossible were it not for God's strength.

Paul continues this discussion beyond the words printed above. He asks, "Does it sound as though I am bragging about all the challenges I have faced?" "I am!" Yet, Paul quickly states that he brags not to showcase his ability. Paul brags to demonstrate the wondrous work of Jesus through him. There are doors that we cannot walk through and storms we cannot endure on our own. That is when we make every difficulty an opportunity to lean into Christ and draw from Christ's strength. The strength that sustained Paul through every force that sought to stop his ministry is available to every one of us. In our hearts, we may ask, "Can I endure?" Paul gives the answer, "In Jesus, we are unbeatable."

Lord, meet me at every difficulty I face today, strengthen me and show me the way to go. Amen.

---

1. Frank, *"Persistence Is the Key,"* para. 16.

47

The Fear of Insignificance

"Jesus told them, 'When you pray, say: "Father, uphold the holiness of your name. Bring in your kingdom."'"

LUKE 11:2

WHETHER ANYTHING HAPPENS IN prayer largely depends upon what kind of person we are. Many of us want to live a life of significance—a life that impacts our world in a large or small way. Such a life is rarely achieved without preparation, hard work, and the perseverance to move forward in the midst of challenges and difficulties. The road to significance is often hard. Yet, to recall a well-spoken line of wisdom from a movie some years ago, *A League of Their Own*, "It's the hard that makes it great!" The question is one of orientation. Some seek to define for themselves what significance looks like and then move toward that vision. Others seek to know God's will and then move toward that.

Regardless of our beginning place—fashioning our own desired future or seeking God's future for us—we want to take full advantage of the years we are given on this earth. Robert Cohn, a character in Ernest Hemingway's novel, *The Sun Also Rises*, comments to his friend, "'Listen Jake,' he leaned forward on the bar. 'Don't you ever get the feeling that all your life is going by and you're not taking advantage of it? Do you realize you've lived nearly half the time you have to live already?'"[1] Urgency has grasped Robert Cohn.

1. Hemingway, *The Sun Also Rises*, 18.

Urgency grasps us. Looking back we make a judgment, an evaluation of where we have come. Life is going by and the question presses, "Are we taking full advantage of it? Are we making a difference?"

If we are the kind of person that lives as we please, as we have fashioned our future, our aspirations, our will; the prayers we make will lack power. Prayers are rarely made unless our plans get into a snarl. That is the occasion we pray. We ask God to get us out of it, God is reduced to our celestial office assistant. Then we move forward with our own small plans. We remain unchanged. Ignoring God for a long time until our plans become jammed-up is little different from a grasping child. The child asks the parent for unreasonable and selfish things. The parent may give what the child asks on occasion when it seems there is no other way to communicate love. But, as the child matures, parents help the child to think reasonably.

Those who seek to find God's mind and will, experience greater power in prayer. Principally, such persons pray because they love God and God's will. Prayer is a communion between two who seek increasingly to know the other, to please the other. We pay close attention to a spouse or a dear friend to learn about them, to know what they like and dislike. Then we turn the orientation of our life over to causing the other joy. Loving and caring for the other is not separated from life. It becomes our way of life. In the final analysis, prayer implies a conversion, a new orientation to live not solely for oneself but for the other. It is a decision to turn our wills over to the will of God. There, our lives find their significance.

Decrease within me my own selfish desires. Make them unattractive in the beauty of knowing and loving you. Amen.

48

The Sound of God

"After the earthquake, there was a fire. But the Lord wasn't in the fire. After the fire, there was a sound. Thin. Quiet."

1 KINGS 19:12

MY FIRST TRIP TO Washington D.C. was in 1988, attending the College of Preachers located in the National Cathedral. Driving into the city my eyes fell upon the Pentagon—something I had previously seen only in pictures. Looming large out the right side of my windshield, the impressive structure accomplished the intention of the architect—to communicate the presence of the most powerful military force in the world. Though I am proud to be a U.S. citizen, I am a Christian first. And this military center of our nation represented values contrary to the purposes of Christ. A chill gripped me and I was momentarily shaken. Not because our nation had a military force. Even Israel has such a force to protect its freedoms. I was shaken by the enormity of its power.

I prayed—eyes wide open, watching the highway that stretched out in front of me. My prayer wasn't clear. My head wasn't clear. I simply didn't know how to process the unsettledness tumbling within. My father served proudly in the U.S. Navy, as did my father-in-law. Regularly I thank women and men who are in the military or who have served. I thank them for their sacrifice and their service. My prayers for our troops mark my daily prayers. Yet, I was shaken, uncomfortable with the large footprint of our nation's military might. My prayer was not uncommon. Many times I have inquired of God about how to pray. I am troubled by this and that and simply do not know how to pray. "Lord, what do I do with this fear, this uneasiness within?"

I turned off of the highway and onto a surface street, navigating my way to the National Cathedral. My speed reduced along a beautifully landscaped avenue, I noticed a public park, also out the right side of my windshield. This pleasant, bucolic escape from my anxiety was welcomed. This park now occupied the space that was once filled with the enormity of the Pentagon building. The churning, troubled spirit within remained but no longer at the same intensity, no longer causing a death grip on the innocent steering wheel of my car. My prayer continued, thanking God for the change of view from the driver's seat, thanking God that my unsettledness was easing, though only a little.

Traffic dropped my speed to a crawl. More time could safely be given to gazing at the park. Suddenly, God's hand was on my shoulder. Located in the same trajectory as the Pentagon from my driver's seat was a park bench. Seated on the bench was a young woman—approximately my age—in prayer. In her hand was a rosary—a helpful prayer tool used by Roman Catholics. At that moment I was calm, all unsettledness now dissipated. Of the two images—the Pentagon and the exercise of prayer—I was quite certain in which of the two real power dwelt. Each day you and I must choose between the clamor of human strength and power and the silent consecration to God in prayer, between the world's display of self-assurance and the thin, quiet presence of God.

In those unsettled moments when I don't know how to pray, help me to experience your hand upon my shoulder so that I may simply trust in your power, presence, and love. Amen.

49

A Cry of Desperation

"He lifted me out of the pit of death, out of the mud and filth, and set my feet on solid rock. He steadied my legs."

Psalm 40:2

Here is a life that many of us understand. Life is characterized as being a "pit of death—a life of mud and filth." This poignant description betrays that present circumstances did not simply fall upon the one who speaks. "Mud and filth" are not the consequence of disadvantage, not the result of some disaster or illness that comes without personal consent. Rather, this decay of a personal experience of life has been fashioned by intentional choices, one bad choice following another. Perhaps the choices made were hesitant at first, slow, and then questioned. But once a descent into careless living began, movement became more swift and confident. Delight in drinking, or gambling, or immoral behavior brought increasing pleasure.

Then comes the collapse of all self-worth, a reckoning of the internal depravity that begins to reveal itself in physical appearance and behavior. The face can no longer hide the ruin of the interior life. Others clearly see the writing of the unfortunate choices written upon the man or woman. The signs of rot and disorder grow stronger and clearer. Any good or decency that remains continues to diminish until it is nearly smothered as the tyranny of the immoral life assumes command. The individual—both body and soul—once a sweet habitation of all that is good, decent, and holy now entertains what is corrupt and evil. Choices, once deliberate, now are in control. The man or woman is now held hostage in a "pit of death."

Then comes a cry for help. What once was pleasurable has become agony—what once was pursued has become a master. The cry of desperation is made to Almighty God. Some years ago when my daughter, Rachael, was quite young I overheard her telling other little girls her faith story. With four other sets of eyes mesmerized by the narrative that flowed from her libs I heard, "I was a slave girl in Egypt and Pharaoh was so mean to me. But my God is bigger than Pharaoh and God came one day, beat Pharaoh up, and brought me home." For a four-year-old girl, this was her understanding of the Exodus story she had heard from her father so many times. The message was clear and certain. She could count on God.

The one who shares this faith story in Psalm 40 knows they can count on God. A cry of desperation is made to Almighty God to come, overwhelm the master that holds them captive in "a pit of death" and bring them home. The cry may be made at the eleventh hour but God comes. God comes without ridicule, and without mockery, or taunts of "I told you so." God simply comes. From the place of captivity of whatever enslavement, whatever addiction that holds a grip upon the man or woman, the hand of God appears. That hand is stronger. Once more, the enslaved is brought home. His or her feet are set on solid ground, strength is returned to the legs, and life is steadied. A nightmare of horrible dreams ends.

Come, Lord Jesus. Come into all of my dark places that I cannot escape and bring me home once again—a home where my feet are placed on solid ground and my legs are steadied. Amen.

50

Miracle in Bethany (Nathanael Hood)

> *"Having said this, Jesus shouted with a loud voice, 'Lazarus, come out!' The dead man came out, his feet bound and his hands tied, and his face covered with a cloth. Jesus said to them, 'Untie him and let him go.'"*
>
> JOHN 11: 43, 44

IT WAS SPRING THEN, and little pink blossoms peppered the almond trees while the olive groves slept and dreamed of warmer summer winds. Passover was approaching, a time when the crowds of Jerusalem would heave their way towards the Second Temple to slaughter the sacrificial lambs demanded of each family. From their tombs, on the eastern mountain ridge, the old kings and prophets stood a silent guard as the great masses churned their way through the roadside veins of the countryside and the alleyway capillaries of the city. Beneath their lookout lay the tiny hamlet of Bethany, as inauspicious a community as could be imagined in the shadow of God's chosen city. In this place was a quiet and stillness unknown to the commoners, soldiers, and merchants living and working nearby. To the east lay the salty Dead Sea, to the west the fiery Jordan Valley, trapping the village in these brief months in a constant crossfire of desert heatwaves and Mediterranean rains. Imagine for a moment the tranquility of such a place: the steam of rainwater baking on the rocks in the heat; the smell of roasted meat and fresh bread mixed with the scent of new flowers; the comforting silence born of the absence of human hubbub and busyness.

Bethany was a paradise in the shadow of Jerusalem's splendor, one that served as a figurative and literal retreat for Jesus and his ragtag group of Jews in his final days. It's mentioned no less than five times in the Gospels, most often for lodging and eating with friends and family, particularly the beloved sisters Martha and Mary. But we also see it as a place of comings and goings: it was where Jesus prepared for his entry into Jerusalem on Palm Sunday and where he blessed the disciples before the Ascension. Bethany was a place between places, a sanctuary for preparations for bigger and better things.

How odd, then, that Jesus would choose Bethany as the site for one of his most amazing feats, the resurrection of his friend Lazarus. The Gospel of John lists it as the last of Jesus' seven signs or miracles, and none could have been more climactic or astounding. The defeat of death! The pronouncement of a new life after life! The conquest of cosmic entropy and emotional antipathy! Yet notice how Jesus took his time to arrive in Bethany after learning about Lazarus' fatal illness—the ease and casualness with which he delays his departure for two days, with which he teases his disciples with riddles about Lazarus falling asleep. When he finally arrives in Bethany, it's four days too late: Lazarus is dead. The detail of four days is an important one—in that time Jews believed that a person's soul remained with their body for three days. If Jesus had come too early, his raising Lazarus could have been brushed off as an improbable but not impossible phenomenon.

And yet the four days proved nothing before the hand of God as Jesus cried for his friend to come out of his tomb still wrapped in his bandages. Imagine the fear and terror felt by the disciples at such a sight! Imagine the joy and rhapsody! And most importantly, imagine the surreality! Perhaps the most awe-inspiring feat of God's power since the sundering of the Red Sea for Moses or the consumption of Elijah's altar on Mount Carmel . . . and in such a podunk nowhere as Bethany! Jerusalem lay less than an hour's walk away and *here* was where Jesus broke the bonds of death. It's an important reminder of one of the great Christian truths—size and worldly importance matter not to a God who can breathe life upon a mountainside of graves. It is God who makes all things great and mighty, not the designations of man. If a million angels can dance on the point of a pin, then surely God can work wonders in a place overlooked and abandoned by most, even the most insignificant little hamlet as Bethany.

Surprise me, O God, when I no longer expect the unexpected. Startle me again with your surprising grace and power in the ordinary places of my life. Amen.

51

Our Failure With Prayer

"Early in the morning, well before sunrise, Jesus rose and went to a deserted place where he could be alone in prayer."

MARK 1:35

A LITTLE BOY ONCE explained to his minister that he didn't say his prayers every night because "some nights I don't want anything." Many of us are like that little boy. Our view of prayer is a limited one, reduced to asking God for something. Certainly, Jesus invited us to take our request to God in prayer. But that is not all Jesus taught—or demonstrated in his own life—about the subject of prayer. The consequence of an inadequate understanding of prayer is felt in our own lack of spiritual power. We are troubled by doubt, and by fear, and by a sense of weakness to make any real difference in a world of brokenness and need. We miss much of the strength God would provide us through a more expansive understanding—and practice—of prayer.

In this teaching from Mark's Gospel, Jesus had just finished a hard, demanding day meeting the needs of numerous people. Another awaited him. How could Jesus be ready for it? The answer is right here in this one sentence of Scripture; "Jesus rose and went to a deserted place where he could be alone in prayer." Conspicuously absent is any record of the content of Jesus' prayer. In other prayers that Jesus offered, we are told the substance of the prayer. Perhaps the most familiar prayer is the one Jesus offered the night he was betrayed by Judas, arrested, and placed on trial during the night. It is a prayer that is familiar because we have offered it so often ourselves: "Take this suffering from me." But here, in this account of Jesus at prayer, we are not allowed in on the conversation. All we know is that Jesus got up early in the morning to be alone with God.

This little verse teaches more about prayer than most realize. Rather than distract us with the actual dialog between Jesus and God, we are left only with the fact that it was important to Jesus to be alone with God. Before another day of ministry, before another day of addressing the great need of the world, Jesus addressed his own need to be alone with God. Regular time alone with God was the source of Jesus' incredible spiritual power. Here, Jesus teaches us that prayer is more than our formal presentation to God of our various needs. Prayer is a demonstration of a life that is lived with God. Our failure with prayer is that we have reduced prayer to asking rather than understanding that prayer is a real and vital relationship with the divine.

Mark has one additional insight on the wisdom of prayer before we leave this story. Moving the narrative quickly along, we are told that Simon and the other disciples tracked Jesus down, told Jesus that other people, with their various needs, have gathered looking for Jesus, and that Jesus surprises the disciples by announcing that he is going in the other direction. What is apparent is that time alone with God in prayer supplied Jesus with more than spiritual power. Prayer infused Jesus with fresh clarity and focus upon God's intention for Jesus. Jesus was now to go to the nearby villages so that he may preach there also. "That's why I've come," Jesus declared. It is easy to respond to the "asks" of those around us, people asking us to meet their needs. It is the greater wisdom to discern God's intention for us, in prayer, and to respond faithfully.

Grant me today, O Lord, the understanding that regular prayer is the weaving of my life with you and your purposes for me. Amen.

52

Ending Well

"Demas has fallen in love with the present world and has deserted me and has gone to Thessalonica."

2 Timothy 4:10

Harry Emerson Fosdick provides uncommon insight upon this singular verse of Scripture written by the Apostle Paul: "One of the most familiar tragedies in human life (is) a fine beginning and a poor ending."[1] Demas, a colleague with Paul in ministry, lacked the power to see it through. First, Paul writes in his letter to Philemon, that Demas and Luke are coworkers in the cause of Christ Jesus. Paul wrote that letter from a Roman prison. Therefore, Demas, along with Luke, was standing by Paul in his imprisonment—a devoted and promising disciple. Second, Paul mentions Demas in his letter to the Colossians in a rather unusual fashion: *"Luke, the dearly loved physician, and Demas say hello."* (verse 4:14). It doesn't escape the careful reader of this letter that affection is attributed to Luke but not Demas. Luke is "dearly loved." Demas has become merely "Demas." Now, in Paul's second letter to Timothy, we understand what is going on: Demas has abandoned Paul and the Christian ministry. Demas began well enough. But he didn't follow through.

Fosdick reminds us that when Luke wrote his account of the ministry of Jesus Christ, Luke alone among the four gospels shares the teaching about

1. Fosdick, *The Power to See*, 1.

considering the cost before beginning anything: *"If one of you wanted to build a tower, wouldn't you first sit down and calculate the cost, to determine whether you have enough money to complete it?"* (verse 14:28). The one who laid the foundation of the tower was unable to finish it. Luke now warns that people will notice that the builder didn't finish what was started and will receive the ridicule of others. Fosdick imagines that Luke is here pleading with his friend, Demas; pleading with Demas not to leave unfinished the work of ministry he had started so well. Essentially, Luke is saying to his friend, "Don't let it be said by Paul that you abandoned him in the work of Jesus Christ."

Has this become our story? Perhaps we have not abandoned faith in Jesus Christ. But how strongly do we feel about a daily investment in building a relationship with Jesus? Recently a member of this congregation spoke to me following worship and remarked that my suggestion that members spend five minutes each day with a daily devotional was a "big ask." I do hope he was kidding, and perhaps he was. Yet, I wonder how many people actually believe that—that five minutes a day is a "big ask?" It is no secret that all of us find the time for what really matters. The question for each Christian to answer at the beginning of a new year is, "Does my relationship with Jesus really matter?"

However beautiful the beginning of our Christian journey may have been, none of it really matters much without a good end. This is not to suggest that we must demand outwardly successful—and measurable—goals or achievements. Building a deeply meaningful relationship with Jesus is not a contest. It is about minding the heart and seeking positive spiritual change or transformation that is accomplished by God as we intentionally nurture our faith. That is done as we spend time with God reading the Bible, delving into good devotional material, and prayer. At the conclusion of this New Year, it is my hope that it will not be uttered by the angels of us, "Demas, my Demas. Demas has abandoned me."

Forgive me, O Lord, when I permit the busyness of life to take from me what is most important—time each day with you. Amen.

53

When Anger is a Virtue

"He (Moses) looked around to make sure no one else was there. Then he killed the Egyptian and hid him in the sand."

Exodus 2:12

"Looking around at them with anger, deeply grieved at their unyielding hearts, he said to the man, 'Stretch out your hand.'"

Mark 3:5

Moses was born during a time of great darkness. A new king was seated in Egypt and he feared the growing strength of the Jewish people. They were a minority people in Egypt and their growing number unsettled the king. So the king resolved to "deal with them." As a result, the Egyptians organized their military to harass the Jewish people and force them into slave labor. But the more they were oppressed, the more they grew and spread. Pharaoh's contempt for the Jewish people grew until he looked upon them with disgust and dread. More had to be done to hold this growing, minority population in check. The first chapter of Exodus details the evil that was unleashed by the king: young children would be separated from their parents and the male children would be thrown into the Nile River and drowned.

Born to Jewish parents, Moses was numbered among those who would suffer the cruelty of Pharaoh's unsteady and fearful leadership. When his mother saw that Moses was "healthy and beautiful" she hid him from the

Egyptian authorities for three months. When she could no longer hide him, she placed her son in a reed basket, sealed it, and placed the child among the reeds at the riverbank. Pharaoh's daughter came to bathe in the river, found the child, and, moved with compassion, resolved to raise the child as her own. Raised as the son of Pharaoh's daughter, Moses lived a life of ease and privilege in the royal court. Yet, as maturity came on, Moses began to be angry. Perhaps he fought against the anger, this disturbing indignation at the intolerable injustice he saw day after day propagated against the Jewish people—his people! Nonetheless, anger took possession of Moses.

Pay close attention to the developing narrative here in Exodus: it is when Moses found something to be angry at that he found God. Perhaps Moses' anger was foolish. It did explode in such grand fashion that he killed the soldier that was beating a Hebrew slave. Yet, Moses could no longer watch something so unbearably wrong and not take action. We might imagine the consequences to a pastor today for speaking the truth to power. Moses knew immediately that his response might not have been wise. He sought to cover it up. But intrinsic to this story is that Moses' anger unleashed the beginning of the real Moses—the Moses portrayed on the silver screen and proclaimed from the pulpit. A quiet Moses would have made little difference, and would not have been remembered. Soon, following this explosion of anger, Moses came down from Sinai with the Ten Commandments that have shaken generations. As Henry Emerson Fosdick writes, "His indignation against evil got him somewhere."[1]

Each generation presents some incarnation of injustice and evil. Occasionally it is hard to see God when the suffering of the present age presses so profoundly upon our consciousness. Well, perhaps if we permit the present injustice to arouse our indignation we will see God. We will experience God's nudge to quit our moral apathy, untether our passion for fairness and justice, and in our own response experience something of the holy ground that Moses stood on. When our Lord, Jesus Christ saw a deed of mercy being withheld by some misplaced ceremonial allegiance, he looked around with anger and took action to correct an injustice. Jesus teaches us by his response that, in the face of evil or injustice, we are not Christian if we are not angry. Martin Luther once wrote that it is when he is angry that he preaches well and prays better.

Forgive me my inaction in the face of evil and injustice. Direct my steps that I may be useful to you in ushering in your justice for all people. Amen.

---

1. Fosdick, *What Is Vital*, 4.

54

A New Outlook

"Therefore, you are no longer a slave but a son or daughter, and if you are his child, then you are also an heir through God."

GALATIANS 4:7

WHEN SARA ROOSEVELT WAS asked if she ever imagined that her son, Franklin Roosevelt, might become president, she replied: "Never, no never! That was the last thing I should ever have imagined for him, or that he should be in public life of any sort." Both she and her son, she insisted, shared a far simpler ambition—"The highest ideal—to grow to be like his father, straight and honorable, just and kind, an upstanding American."[1] An only child, and with few playmates his own age, Franklin viewed his attentive and protective father as a companion and friend. Presidential biographer, Doris Kearns Goodwin observes that Franklin's optimistic spirit and the general expectation that things would turn out happily is a testament to the self-confidence developed within the atmosphere of love and affection that enveloped him as a child.[2]

The prevailing wisdom today—and imbedded in many approaches to psychological counseling—is that all of life consists of two elements: first, the facts, and second, our way of looking at them. Few of us escape some disappointment, some physical or mental limitation, or some distressing

1. Goodwin, *Leadership In Turbulent Times*, 50.
2. Goodwin, *Leadership In Turbulent Times*, 43.

circumstance. It is a fact of life. We have very little control over these facts. Yet, what is largely within our power is how we look at these facts. We may permit these facts to debilitate us, ruin our temper, spoil our work, and hurt our relationships with others, or we can become a master over their influence. Any cursory examination of Franklin Roosevelt's life reveals a good measure of challenges, disappointments, and loss. But Roosevelt remained a master over everyone, convinced that there was a larger purpose for his life and nothing would stop his pursuit of that purpose. A positive home environment and the knowledge that he bore a strong and respected family name directed Roosevelt's outlook.

The Christian faith is a call to a new outlook—a call to a changed point of view on the facts of life. In this teaching from Paul's letter to the church in Galatia, Paul reminds us that we were once slaves and, consequently, of diminished value. And those who perceive to have a diminished value as a person have a dim view of life. But now, in the person of Jesus Christ, we are no longer slaves but children of God. If children of God, then an heir. Our name has been connected, as was Roosevelt's, to a strong and respected name. For Paul, this makes a profound difference in how we are to live. We live as members of a royal household.

The deep divergence that commonly separates those who move positively through life from those who don't lies in their outlook. Jesus' word for "repent" meant to "change your mind" or "look at things differently." When Jesus called those who would become his disciples he didn't ask them to join a church or subscribe to some creed. He asked them to look at the facts differently. The laws concerning the Sabbath were reconsidered. The place of children was elevated. For those caught in the very act of sin, grace prevailed over punishment. Jesus called for a radical shift in how life would be lived—a shift that now recognized that with God on our side any handicap could be overcome and every challenge met positively. When we get a new way of seeing things it is then that we find a new life.

Remind me of your love and concern for me that I may radically change how I see disappointments, failures, and loss. I am a child of a living God. Amen.

55

The Remarkable Power of Story

"In the future, your children will ask you, 'What is the meaning of the laws, the regulations, and the case laws that the Lord our God commanded you?' tell them: We were Pharaoh's slaves in Egypt. But the Lord brought us out of Egypt with a mighty hand."

DEUTERONOMY 6:20, 21

MY DAUGHTER, RACHAEL, WAS five years old at our move into a new home in Coppell, Texas. Shortly after settling into our new home, Rachael and I went exploring our new community. Near our home was a large, beautiful park and, within the park, a smaller, enclosed playground for children. Naturally, she wanted to meet the other children there in the playground, all engaged in their own play. I saw it as an opportunity to read while Rachael did what she does best—meeting strangers and forging deep and abiding friendships in little time. The playground was enclosed with a gate that had a safety design that only adults could open. Rachael would be safe as I turned my attention to my *The New Yorker* magazine.

After completing a short article, I thought it wise to have "eyes on" my daughter. I did not see her. I wasn't concerned because of the safety design of the gate. But I did think it prudent to place my magazine down and find her. What I found was Rachael being Rachael. Seated on the ground in a semi-circle were four other little girls, approximately Rachael's age, with their focus fixed upon Rachael, who was also seated. Not wanting to disrupt whatever Rachael was saying that held the attention of four strangers, I drew near quietly. What I heard from the heart of a five-year-old was, "I was a slave girl in Egypt and Pharaoh was so mean to me. But my God is bigger than Pharaoh and God came for me one day, beat Pharaoh up, and took me home. I don't exactly remember it because I think I was asleep in my daddy's arms."

Where did Rachael get that story? From her father, who had received the story from his father who received the story from the Bible. It is a story that is captured here in Deuteronomy that occurs at a crucial juncture of Israel's journey from slavery in Egypt. Just before the people leave their forty-year journey in the wilderness, cross the Jordan River, and take possession of the land promised to them, Moses instructs them how to shape and mold their children into one powerful, corporate story. It is a story that will give meaning, purpose, and understanding of who they are as a people of God. The story will be a response to the children's inquiry, an inquiry that asks, what is the meaning of the laws God has "*commanded you*." In a subtle shift, the children express a certain distance from their parent's faith—"*commanded you*."

Just as subtly, the parent's answer is to break down the separation suggested by the children and includes them in the remarkable story of God's deliverance, "*We were* Pharaoh's slaves in Egypt," and "But the Lord *brought us* out of Egypt." Questions about rules and laws in the faith community are answered in stories. Stories are imaginative and embody fascination and richness that simple, direct explanations fail to provide. Stories invite the listener to enter, poke around a little, and locate a comfortable place to settle and claim a unique place in the larger narrative. The remarkable power of stories was realized one bright, sunny day in a children's playground area in Coppell, Texas: "I was a slave girl in Egypt," spoke my daughter to four strangers. In those few words, Rachael entered the story, poked around here and there, and found herself belonging to something so much greater than one small girl. Rachael belonged to a people who have captured the heart of God.

God, open my heart to understand where I fit within your one, great story of redemption and love. Amen.

56

The Dust of Qumran
(Location: Qumran)

"Every Scripture is inspired by God and is useful for teaching, for showing mistakes, for correcting, and for training character, so that the person who belongs to God can be equipped to do everything that is good."

2 TIMOTHY 3:16, 17

OVERLOOKING THE DEAD SEA at a site not far from Jerusalem is a place that is widely considered one of the most important archaeological finds of modern times. It is called Khirbet Qumran. Here in 1947, an Arab shepherd boy entered one of the numerous caves that dot the landscape looking for a lost sheep. Throwing a stone into a dark portion of the cave, hoping to frighten the sheep back out, he heard breaking pottery. Closer examination would reward the shepherd with the discovery of ancient scrolls that were over two thousand years old. After his discovery, archeologists conducted a search in other caves in the region. More than eight hundred ancient manuscripts were found, known today as the Dead Sea Scrolls.

What is significant about this discovery is that included among the scrolls were the oldest copies of every Old Testament book, except the Book of Esther. Each manuscript was approximately a thousand years older than those used to translate the Bible from Hebrew into modern languages.

Perhaps even more remarkable was the discovery that, upon close examination of each book of the Old Testament, there was very little that had been altered during the thousand-year interval between these scrolls and those used to make the translations of the Bible we have now. This provides strong evidence that the manuscripts available today are extremely close to the original writing of these books.

Interestingly, it is precisely these Old Testament books to which Paul refers here, in his second letter to Timothy, since the New Testament had not yet been written when Timothy was a child (verse 15). Paul reminds Timothy that the chief aim of Scripture is for both information and transformation. It is not enough to learn more about God. Through Scripture, each person of faith experiences an encounter with God that tears out what is old and corrupt and refurbishes their life with what is new, holy, and necessary for doing what is pleasing to God. Becoming well-formed spiritually is the essential function of God's Word.

My first visit to Qumran was the most meaningful portion of my trip to the Holy Land. It is here that an ancient faith community, the Essenes, labored carefully to preserve Holy Scripture for future generations. These Scriptures, the Dead Sea Scrolls, are gone now, placed in a museum in Jerusalem for optimal preservation and enjoyment by the thousands who visit the museum each year. What remains in Qumran are empty caves, parched earth, and dust. It is that dust, the dust of Qumran, that remains to remind the spiritual pilgrim of what life would be without the living waters of God's Word.

Father, give me ears to hear your truth, and a heart to respond obediently, so that I may glorify you without ceasing. Amen.

57

God's Purpose. God's Call. God's Power

". . . so is my word that comes from my mouth; it does not return to me empty. Instead, it does what I want, and accomplishes what I intend."

Isaiah 55:11

Reading the Bible, with a fresh and alert mind, impacts and stirs the reader in extraordinary and often unanticipated ways. Because the printed words belong to a real, present, and active God, the words are used imaginatively and purposefully, in a tailored fashion, for each individual reader. Reading the Bible is never a solo activity. God, in the Holy Spirit, is always present, accomplishing a purposeful work in the mind and heart of the individual who comes expectantly to experience something new. When the mind is dull and expects little from reading the Bible, this dynamic and amazing power is absent. In my own engagement with the Bible each morning, I experience three reoccurring themes.

First, the Bible reveals the purposefulness of God. Perhaps in no other place in Scripture is this more clearly and directly presented than in the twelfth chapter of Genesis, verses 1–3: God promises to bless Abraham. But, with penetrating clarity, this blessing is ultimately for the purpose of blessing all of humanity. A blessing to all people, of all nations, is the bottom line of God's promise to Abraham. God's unfolding purpose may be too vast and, at times, imperceptible, to be grasped this side of the grave, but, at least, we are assured by the Bible that the world has been delivered from meaninglessness. With this knowledge, we can live quietly and confidently, trusting the care of the future to God.

Second, the Bible reveals God's call upon each person. Assuming a robust theological posture, the Apostle Paul declares in Ephesians 2:10 that we were, " . . . created in Christ Jesus to do good things. God planned for these good things to be the way that we live our lives." Candidly, Paul corrects the notion that followers of Jesus Christ are to participate, here and there, in good work. No; good work, or doing good things, is to be our way of life. It is all part of God's divine activity that our own lives be caught up in the one grand purpose that God is continually unfolding in the world. Each person's life is made integral to God's resolve to gather the nations under the Lordship of his Son, Jesus Christ.

Third, the Bible reveals God's power. God is not defeated. With panoramic vision, Paul captures the human condition in Romans 8: "Who will separate us from Christ's love? Will we be separated by trouble, distress, harassment, famine, nakedness, danger, or sword? As it is written, we are being put to death all day long for your sake. We are treated like sheep for slaughter. But in all these things we win a sweeping victory through the one who loved us." (verses 35–37) Contrary to appearances, difficulties, hardships, and death will not defeat God and those who belong to God. The struggle will certainly manifest itself in every life. But in the end, we will discover that our life has been guided and loved, and that disaster is overruled. More, we will find that nothing of value is lost.

God, make me alert to your purpose, you call upon me that I may be useful to you, and grant me a fresh encounter of your power at work in the world. Amen.

58

Conch Shell

> *"The kingdom of heaven is like a man who was leaving on a trip. He called his servants and handed his possessions over to them."*
>
> MATTHEW 25:14

SINCE I WAS A child I have collected—and adored—conch shells, more specifically, the queen conch variety. I grew up in Atlanta, Georgia. But once every two years my family vacationed in the Florida Keys. A family tradition that developed was a stop at Shell World located in the first key, Key Largo. It is a tradition I have now resumed with my wife each time we travel to the Keys. Whether for the day or a weekend, each trip to the Florida Keys includes a stop at Shell World. And, on most of those stops, I select and purchase a queen conch. It is a meaningful tradition and I now own dozens of these beautiful shells—six of them in my office! Each purchase connects me to a cherished childhood memory.

The queen conch is found off the coast of Florida and throughout the Caribbean. The shell is valued as a decorative souvenir and—historically—by Native Americans and indigenous Caribbean peoples to create various tools. The animal that lives within the shell, a marine mollusk, is enjoyed in a variety of seafood preparations. Though not an endangered species as a whole, the queen conch is now protected in Florida waters due to extreme overfishing. The queen conch shell sold by Shell World is responsibly sourced from various Caribbean islands where the conch populations are healthy.

As a child, I chose to collect the queen conch over other varieties of beautiful shells because of their affordability. There are other varieties of shells that many would consider more striking in their complexity and beauty than the queen conch. And they are much more expensive to purchase. But today, as an adult, I have found a deeper and richer appreciation for surrounding myself with this beautiful shell, in both my home and office. In some South Pacific cultures, a speaker holds a conch shell as a symbol of a *temporary* position of authority. "Leaders must understand who holds the conch—that is, who should be listened to and when," writes Max De Pree.[1] As a follower of Jesus Christ, I also have been given temporary authority to declare God's love for a hurting world.

In this rich passage from Matthew's Gospel, Jesus teaches this spiritual principle in a parable, commonly called the Parable of the Talents. In the story—or parable—a man is leaving on a trip. He calls his servants and distributes his possessions to them. What becomes clear in the larger story is that these possessions are not transferred property. The man who is leaving retains ownership. The possessions are simply entrusted for a period of time to the management of the servants. And upon the man's return, the servants will be held accountable for their temporary responsibility with his possessions. The queen conch shells in my home and office remind me each day of the tremendous privilege—and responsibly—that has been entrusted to me to declare the depth of God's love until the day Jesus returns.

Lord, we are not here on our own behalf but on behalf of those you have called us to love. Purify my lips and reshape my heart so that I may declare your love this day. Amen.

---

1. De Pree, *Leadership Is an Art*, 20.

59

When We Struggle
(Location: Mount of Olives)

"Jesus left and made his way to the Mount of Olives, as was his custom, and the disciples followed him. He withdrew from them about a stone's throw, knelt down, and prayed. He said, 'Father, if it's your will, take this cup of suffering away from me. However, not my will but your will must be done.' Then a heavenly angel appeared to him and strengthened him."

LUKE 22: 39, 41–43

RECENTLY, THIS HAS BECOME one of my favorite passages in the entire Bible. After thirty years of doing ministry, I expected that desiring and living by the will of God would come naturally. It has not. In fact, as I approach fifty-four years of age, the struggle between my will and God's will has become more intense. It is some consolation that Jesus experiences the same struggle here on the Mount of Olives. Such was Jesus' struggle that he asked that the suffering he faced be taken away. I need no further proof than this request that Jesus was, in fact, fully human as we are.

We all face individual moments of struggle. Some struggle with seeking a new way forward after a major life change such as the death of a loved one or divorce. Others struggle with inadequate financial resources. Still, others struggle with poor health, estranged relationships with loved ones, or any number of new disappointments that come all too regularly. To all of us, in these moments of struggle, the message of these few sentences is loud and clear: do not imagine that because life has suddenly become difficult that you have made a wrong decision, followed a poor pathway in life, or arrived at the wrong place. The idea that faithful Christians always have days without struggle is simply a romantic misunderstanding of what it means to follow Jesus; following Jesus always leads to the Mount of Olives.

It is particularly comforting to know that it isn't unusual to experience the struggle of our will and God's will. The Apostle Paul once cried in utter despair, *"I don't do what I want to do. Instead, I do the thing that I hate."* (Romans 7:15) Paul knows well the common struggle of self-will and God's will. We are routinely betrayed by forces—within and without—that cause us to make decisions contrary to our desire to follow Jesus. In these moments, we may be tempted to abandon hope; to throw in the towel and give up the struggle.

In those moments, Jesus demonstrates an alternative to abandoning the struggle; Jesus invites us to pray on the Mount of Olives. Jesus' own prayer is a powerful witness to the difficulty of the struggle. Such struggle is too great to face alone. Our strength is not sufficient. In prayer, Jesus not only demonstrates his inadequacy to meet the challenge, Jesus' prayer results in receiving uncommon strength from above. And Jesus wants us to know that if we share his struggle, we will also share in the power of God that gave him strength. In those moments when we face difficulty, when we struggle with what we want and what God wants for us, the Mount of Olives reminds us that the battle must be won on our knees.

Heavenly Father, as you met your Son on the Mount of Olives and gave him strength, I ask that you meet me now in my struggle. By the same power that Jesus received, help me to stand in the midst of difficulty and not be defeated. Amen.

60

Vintage Sand Pails

"They call all sorts of people to the mountain, where they offer right sacrifices. It's true: They're nourished on the sea's abundance; they are nourished on buried treasures in the sand."

Deuteronomy 33:19

A THROWBACK BEACH TOY, vintage sand pails "carry summertime nostalgia in spades," writes Betsy Cribb in a recent issue of *Coastal Living* magazine.[1] Cribb laments the loss of the old metal beach pails that have now been given away to their plastic counterparts. The first of these colorful metal sand pails popped up on American beaches in the mid-1800s. But it would be another thirty years when trains made travel to the beach available to a wider population that the little pails skyrocketed in popularity. Cribb writes that early versions were hand-painted in just one or two colors and lacquered for a glossy finish. But chromolithography (a multicolor printing process) enabled toy-makers to crank out pails with detailed illustrations in bright, saturated hues. Original metal sand pails are now in demand by a new generation as great decorative and collectible pieces as plant holders or vintage décor pieces for beach homes and cottages.

Often, children used sand pails for building sandcastles—some pails included a shovel and a variety of molds with which one could make interesting sand sculptures. Also popular with children was the use of the pails,

---

1. Cribb, "Vintage Sand Pails," 24.

with contrasting handles, to gather collectibles from the sea and the beach such as seashells, sea glass, buttons, and pebbles. The ocean and the shore presented gifts in abundance for the curious seeker with the determination and energy to scan the water and sand for them. With lighthearted and cheerful illustrations, these metal sand pails offered families colorful, and inexpensive, mini-beach playsets that provided hours of enjoyment for their children.

Here, in this rich passage from Deuteronomy, God speaks of extracting from the sea's abundance the nourishment the people required and gathering multiple treasures from the sand. As children on our beaches, running cheerfully with a sand pail in hand, collecting from the abundance of God's varied gifts, God invites us to notice and collect the gifts God has given us. The days of limited resources for God's people are over. God has a new lifestyle in mind for us. The time of struggle has passed and now, as the people settled in God's promised territory, they would be nourished on, "the sea's abundance; they are nourished on buried treasures in the sand." The function of these few verses is to shift the focus from Israel's behavior to God's ultimate purpose to bless God's people.

And here is the good news! The law of God, with all its demands upon the people, is thus subordinated to the overriding purpose—and desire—of God for his people. God's love and concern for the welfare of the people are declared in spite of the people failing God and one another. In the end, our disobedience to God will not stop God from blessing us. God simply cannot help but shower blessings upon those God loves. This becomes an occasion for joy in every aspect of our lives—an occasion for us to respond by coming before God, on God's mountain, where we present "right sacrifices" that we might share God's blessings with others.

Lord, open the eyes of my understanding, so that I may see the abundance of your blessings and be filled again with vigor, energy, and enthusiasm. Amen.

61

How Shall We Rebuild?
(Nathanael Hood)

"Isn't this the fast I choose—releasing wicked restraints, untying the ropes of a yoke, setting free the mistreated, and breaking every yoke? Isn't it sharing your bread with the hungry and bringing the homeless poor into your house, covering the naked when you see them, and not hiding from your own family?"

ISAIAH 58:6, 7

THEIR BONDS BROKEN AND shackles shattered, the ancient Judeans returned from their Babylonian captivity to find Jerusalem a wasted ruin. In the city of the Davidic kings, Solomon's Temple, and the Ark of the Covenant, the refugees found this former center of Jewish religious, political, and social life a shell of its former self, destroyed, depopulated, profaned. The Holiest of the Holies was violated, the treasuries looted, the buildings smashed, and life could never go back to normal for the Jewish people. And indeed the exile permanently changed the face of their religion. Once a faith that acknowledged the existence of other gods, this new Judaism was doggedly monotheistic. Once a people ruled by kings, now they were led by scribes, sages, and priests. And where once the thought of a religion without a central temple was unthinkable, now they praised a God who faithfully followed his children throughout the world. As prominent Israeli scholar,

Yehezkel Kaufmann once wrote: "With the exile, the religion of Israel comes to an end and Judaism begins."[1]

The fifty-eighth chapter of Isaiah offers us a glimpse into the metamorphosis of post-exilic Judaism. While the entire book is traditionally attributed to the eighth century BCE prophet, the last ten chapters are now believed by scholars to be a collection of anonymous oracles recorded three hundred years later during the reconstruction of Jerusalem. The portrait they paint is not always comforting. Much like the Pharisees of Jesus' time who competed to see who could pray the loudest in public, this chapter depicts the wealthy ostentatiously mourning and praying for restoration while ignoring the poor and needy among them. Specifically, the wealthy are shown to brag about their extravagant ritualistic fasting where they starve themselves in sackcloth and ashes. To which the oracles respond with a simple and direct how dare you? Isn't the fast that God demands, the salvation of the helpless among them? The literal feeding of the hungry, the literal housing of the homeless, the literal clothing of the naked? The God of this new Judaism cared not for their theatrics. Instead, this new god who was God demanded concrete, literal solutions to economic and social injustice among his children. Only then could Jerusalem truly be rebuilt.

Almost two and half thousand years have passed since the time of Isaiah, and the world finds itself again in a time of devastating crisis. As the Coronavirus pandemic forces the international community into a global quarantine, it feels like things will never be the same again. The wealth and prosperity we assumed would protect us have proved worthless as even the richest countries with the best medical resources have been devastated. The stories we hear in the news are horrific: farmers forced to let food rot in their fields; doctors and nurses forced to care for the diseased without Personal Protective Equipment (PPE); millions—including this writer—being forced into unemployment with no lasting economic safety net. We hear of the homeless in Las Vegas being made to sleep in parking spaces in parking lots so they won't infect each other. We hear of the government wasting millions on Blue Angels flyovers to honor the very healthcare workers they refuse to properly fund. And we hear of people like Leilani Jordan, a twenty-seven-year-old grocery store clerk in Maryland who died after being forced to work without gloves or hand sanitizer. When her family received their daughter's last paycheck—literal blood money—they found that they'd lost their little girl for only $20.64.

Much like the post-exile Judeans, we find ourselves on the threshold of total societal transformation. Things won't go back to normal because

---

1. Young, "Secrets of Noah's Ark," October 7, 2015.

things can't go back to normal. Too many systems have been proven ineffective, too many laws have been proven useless, and too many people have been proven expendable. Not only can't things go back to normal, but things also shouldn't go back to normal. Not, at least, if we want to honor God, the God who demanded the end of useless fasting and the implementation of social and economic reforms in the fifty-eighth chapter of Isaiah. How do we rebuild after the quarantine ends? By working to ensure there are no homeless to stuff into parking lots, by fighting to properly equip healthcare professionals and first responders, by tearing down the systems of old to make sure nobody dies for a $20.64 paycheck ever again.

Lord, we live in a time of great fear and anxiety. Calm our nerves and give us the peace we need to survive, the peace we need to recover, the peace we need to rebuild. Remind us of your instructions in Isaiah that we work to make a world of economic and social justice for all your children, now and forevermore. In the name of Christ Jesus, we pray. Amen.

62

Prescription for Unhealthy Anger

"Instead, dress yourself with the Lord Jesus Christ, and don't plan to indulge your selfish desires."

ROMANS 13:14

"Be angry without sinning. Don't let the sun set on your anger."

EPHESIANS 4:26

IF YOU ARE LIKE most people, you were raised with the old maxim, "feed a cold, starve a fever." Writing for ScientificAmerican.com, Mark Fischetti has traced this maxim to a 1574 dictionary by John Withals, which noted that "fasting is a great remedy of fever. The belief is that eating food may help the body generate warmth during a 'cold' and that avoiding food may help it cool down when overheated."[1] But recent medical science says that that old wisdom is wrong. It should be "feed a cold, feed a fever." Naturally, doctors advise meals that are balanced and nutritious for optimal support of the body's struggle to overcome the illness. Apparently, what still holds true is the value of a simmering bowl of chicken soup.

That old maxim has been disproved by modern medicine but a portion of it—"starve a fever"—is precisely the spiritual prescription the Apostle Paul advises for unhealthy anger: "don't plan to indulge your selfish desires."

---

1. Fischetti, "Fact or Fiction," January 3. 2014.

Anger is one of the most common sins when it stirs within us a passion of fury that can result in threats and violence. The world has witnessed this anger in the increased level of violence often done in the name of religion. Fear occupies the thoughts of many simply because they may be found to have a different religion or point of view. Broken relationships and estrangement from loved ones due to anger also rips at the fabric of God's good intention for all of humanity. Paul offers counsel: let the selfishness of anger be destroyed by the withholding of appropriate support—"don't plan to indulge."

There is no method more efficient and assured of victory over the sin of anger than destruction by neglect. As another maxim goes, "deny the fuel, you exhaust the flame." In practice, what Paul urges in all of his letters is that we redirect our thoughts from those things we disagree with to the one conviction that holds each of us together, the Lordship of Jesus Christ. Dwelling on the things that divide us results in aroused feelings. Unchecked, those feelings boil over and scalds and destroy the more gentle places of our spirit. We can control our passion by wisely directing our thought to our unity in Jesus and a common striving to love our neighbor as ourselves.

Paul is clear that anger itself isn't a sin. Anger often signals that something is wrong, requires attention, and calls for a measured response. At the deepest level, anger demonstrates that we are awake, aware, and care deeply about the world we live in. "Be angry," writes Paul to the church in Ephesus, "without sinning." Those last two words must not be glossed over. We are not to sin whenever anger is present. There is no consideration given to whether the anger is justified or not. And when we do experience anger, resolve it quickly before it arouses those passions that lead to destruction. We have been baptized into the life of Jesus Christ. At its most basic meaning, that means that Christ is placed first in our lives, not our ideology, our prejudices, and our convictions. If we keep our eyes on what our baptism means, we will make no provision for the care of selfish desires. And, an unhealthy anger withers.

Cool my temper, O Lord, even when my cause is just. Teach me to speak words of gentleness so that Christ may be honored by my behavior. Amen.

63

The God We Don't Expect (Nathanael Hood)

"Then Jesus said to his disciples, 'All who want to come after me must say no to themselves, take up their cross, and follow me. All who want to save their lives will lose them. But all who lose their lives because of me will find them.'"

MATTHEW 16:24, 25

OF ALL JESUS' DISCIPLES—SAVE perhaps Judas Iscariot—it is Peter Simon, that lowly fisherman, who comes across to us from the pages of history as the most fully realized and most fully human. The Gospels paint him as a man of great, seismic contradictions: confident enough in his faith to leap upon the waters of Galilee yet doubtful enough to sink below them; brave enough to attack the Sanhedrin in Gethsemane, yet frightened enough to deny Christ three times in the high priest's courtyard. In the sixteenth chapter of Matthew, we see yet another demonstration of Peter's conflicted faithfulness. Upon reaching Caesarea Philippi, Jesus asks his disciples "Who do people say the Human One is?" Eleven of them mutter noncommittally, but Peter leaps in: "You are the Christ, the Son of the living God." Many forget that when Jesus first began his ministry, he hid his lineage as the Son of God from his followers, instead of presenting himself as a rabbi preaching radical reform of Jewish tradition in the face of Roman imperialism. It was here, at this moment, that a fisherman's faith revealed Jesus' true identity to the world.

In response, Jesus praises Peter and declares him the rock upon which he will build his church. But pay very close attention to what happens next, particularly to the language used in the Common English Bible translation. After Jesus explains his mission to suffer and die at the hand of their Roman oppressors, Peter "took hold" of him, "scolds" him, and "began to correct him." Certainly, Jesus, the promised Messiah, would tear down the Romans, reunite the Twelve Tribes, and restore the Davidic monarchy to power once and for all. Yet Jesus savagely scolds him with one of the most cutting rebukes in Scripture: "Get behind me, Satan."

But just as Jesus condemns he comforts, immediately informing Peter and the rest of the disciples that his is not the way of meek surrender, but the path to everlasting life. Again, pay close attention to the language: "All who want to come after me must *say no to themselves, take up their cross*, and *follow me*." [Emphasis mine] We find three demands—one of self-denial, one of self-sacrifice, and one of self-submission. First, we must reject all our preconceptions about who God is or what God wants. Second, we must humble ourselves before him in front of the whole world. And third, we must follow in his footsteps, not in the footsteps we proscribe for him.

Peter's mistake wasn't his lack of faith, but rather its willfully misguided application. Unable to envision a Messiah who didn't avenge and conquer, he literally tried to seize and bully God incarnated in flesh. And how often have we seen the same thing happen today? It seems we can't turn on a TV or open a newspaper without hearing or reading somebody screeching about what God wants or what God needs. God has become a cudgel with which to assault political adversaries, a club to self-righteously attack those who don't fall into the proper ideological or moral line. In these troubling, divisive times, we must look to the words of the Gospel of Matthew: to find one's life, one must lose it. Just as Peter was rebuked, so we must rebuke ourselves and humbly follow.

Grant me the wisdom and courage to follow you, O God, and not the god or gods I fashion in my mind. Amen.

64

Thanksgiving Day in Bonaire

"After giving thanks, he broke it and said, 'This is my body, which is for you; do this to remember me.'"

1 Corinthians 11:24

This year my wife, Grace, and I will celebrate Thanksgiving Day on the Caribbean Island of Bonaire. Our thirty-fourth Thanksgiving together, this one will be different. Most of our celebrations of this holiday have been with family—our children, our parents, or our siblings. Some years ago, our children and Grace's mother celebrated Thanksgiving with us in New York City, kicking the day off with the Macy's Thanksgiving Day Parade. During our twelve years in Bucks County, we shared a number of celebrations with another family in that church, each year alternating homes for the meal. Since moving to Florida, several celebrations were with a family of this congregation, breaking from meal preparation in the home to celebrate over a sumptuous buffet provided by the former Marriot of Delray Beach. Guests around the table may have varied through the years. However, there were always guests.

This year, neither of our children is able to make the trip to Florida. Our daughter, Rachael, has now made her home in Seattle, Washington, and our son, Nathanael, will be preparing final papers for the fall semester at Princeton Theological Seminary. My brother, Wayne, and his wife, Nancy, have now retired from their ministry in Florida and have moved to Tennessee, and Grace's siblings will be out of the country. The church family we shared several meals with at Marriott has moved on and Grace and I have buried both of our parents. This year Grace and I will be alone for Thanksgiving Day. It is a familiar story. Each year brings change to every one of us—and our families. Since the beginning of this pandemic, it seems the speed of change has only accelerated. Disorientation is the result, often accompanied by some level of grief.

This year's celebration will be a significant departure from our first thirty-three together—a holiday that always included either family or friends at the table. Therefore, Grace and I will celebrate Thanksgiving Day in Bonaire. It is a decision to embrace what is inevitable in all of our lives—change, and to make imaginative use of that change. Most of us have little control over our future. Change is a reliable companion that shares life with all of us. What we do have is the ability to take charge of that change, to make creative use of it in a manner that creates blessings. Without purposely choosing how we will adapt to change, the consequence that results may produce sadness and grief that is difficult to navigate. The inevitable change in the seasons of life may produce a deeper, richer experience than we ever thought possible or it can diminish life. The choice belongs to every one of us.

Therefore, this year, Grace and I are going to Bonaire. Moreover, I have purchased a fruitcake. Not any fruitcake. Like many people, I usually do not care for fruitcakes. However, for decades I have delighted in the fruitcake from Collin Street Bakery in Corsicana, Texas. It has become a Thanksgiving Day tradition and it is hard to imagine Thanksgiving without it. I will take this fruitcake to Bonaire and, only there, remove it from its packaging and enjoy it. This year, Thanksgiving Day will be a significant departure from previous celebrations. That is why this fruitcake is so important. In the midst of inevitable change, I need to remember—to remember the journey that now takes me to Bonaire. This fruitcake will connect me meaningfully to the richness of the past as I experience the present moment and anticipate the Thanksgivings that lie in the future. "After giving thanks, he broke it and said, 'This is my body, which is for you; do this to remember me.'"

Jesus, bless this day that I share with you. Help me to look upon yesterday with gratitude as I anticipate your goodness today and tomorrow. Amen.

65

The Disciple's Rest

> *"'Come to me, all you who are struggling hard and carrying heavy loads, and I will give you rest. Put on my yoke, and learn from me. I'm gentle and humble. And you will find rest for yourselves.'"*
>
> MATTHEW 11:28, 29

THERE IS A SAYING among pastors that in every congregation a third of the people are in a crisis, a third of the people are coming out of a crisis, and a third of the people are about to go into a crisis. If you are not in a crisis, chances are, there is something out in front of you heading your way. Anxiety and uncertainty seem to mark the countenance of many people today. Everywhere there is evidence of a certain strain—exhaustion from struggling to carry more than one person can reasonably bear. Attempting to face challenges that are beyond our strength, people move with fear, the wrinkle of worry etched deeply in their faces. Absent are the rest, the assurance, and the strength available in the person of Jesus Christ.

We require the stimulus of companionship with Jesus—the restful realization of God's presence and care for us. Such rest is offered here by Jesus, "Come to me . . . I will give you rest." This rest is always a gift. It is not earned. This rest comes as the fruit of a relationship. It is not from our labor. It is an immediate gift but its value is continuously experienced as we probe deeply into the riches of the relationship with Jesus. Much as falling in love, there are continually rich discoveries that are uncovered and realized as the relationship grows deeper, is explored, and cherished. The invitation to, "Come to me" prepares for, and actually leads to, the second part of the invitation, "Learn from me."

Author, and teacher, Richard Foster once declared that if you are too busy to read, you are *too* busy.[1] Similarly, if we are too busy to spend time each day with God, to read the Bible and devotional literature, to "learn of Jesus," then we are too busy. Each day is then powered by our own strength, which, eventually, becomes exhausted. Writers cannot write from exhaustion. Musicians perform poorly without adequate rest. Those who fight experience defeat without the replenishment received from time off on the battlefield. Woven into the fabric of God's good creation is the "seventh day" that is for rest and simply knowing God. Jesus asks that we learn from him that the gift of rest might be fully experienced.

Instead of living with aimlessness and exhaustion as though we were on our own, Jesus invites us to a sure and restful intimacy with him. A person who comes to Jesus and spends time in that relationship—learning from Jesus—discovers someone whose strength and force are tremendous! Such people move through the darkest storms of life with apparent ease. But it is the ease that is linked with the infinite—the very God who created all there is. Such people possess spiritual energy rather than manifest symptoms of panic. They recognize the wealth and power of allies in God and face the difficulties of life with restful assurance. "Come to me" invites Jesus, and we will be distinguished from the world. We will have rest.

Forgive my busyness that makes little time for you. I accept your invitation to "Come" and "Learn" that I might find rest this day and in all of my tomorrows. Amen.

---

1. Foster, *Freedom of Simplicity*, 160.

66

Fast Food Religion (Nathanael Hood)

> *"Look! I'm standing at the door and knocking. If any hear my voice and open the door, I will come in to be with them, and will have dinner with them, and they will have dinner with me."*
>
> REVELATION 3:20

WE LIVE IN A world of fast food religion. In the breathless hustle and bustle of modern life, we all too often find ourselves without the time, without the means, or without the energy to devote ourselves fully to belief, so we settle for bite-sized servings of faith, prepackaged, precooked, pre-delivered. Difficult concepts and truths get chopped, frozen, and flash-fried into simple aphorisms and decontextualized verses to give ourselves a warm, fuzzy feeling of comfort. Consider Revelation 3:20, a favorite of fast food religion, one that promises that Jesus is at the door to our lives knocking, waiting for us to let him in. Go to any store that sells religious tchotchkes and you'll inevitably find a refrigerator magnet or painting referencing this verse, usually featuring a barefoot, white-robed Jesus expectantly knocking on a literal door, eager to be let inside. The message is simple: Jesus is always there, waiting to be let into our lives if only we'd listen. And yes, Jesus *is* always at the door of our lives, knocking to be let inside. But much like a fast food cheeseburger, slightly cold and greasy, it only provides so much nutrition, and one certainly can't sustain a healthy diet eating it every day. The truth, the deeper meaning, is much more complicated and difficult. But much like a proper home-cooked meal, prepared with love and careful attention, the results are worth the effort.

The key to understanding this verse is its larger context within the book of Revelation. To most, the last book of the Bible is a wellspring of apocalyptic visions and awe-full imagery—multi-headed dragons and multi-colored horsemen wreaking havoc on a doomed world of unrepentant sinners. But the book itself was actually a letter written to the "Seven Churches of Asia" located in modern-day Turkey that made up much of early Christendom. As such, the first several chapters of Revelation are highly specific messages admonishing and encouraging them. Revelation 3:20 is part of the larger message to the church in Laodicea, the easternmost of the seven and also one of the wealthiest, an ancient banking hub and manufacturer of medicinal eye salve and luxurious black wool used for expensive black clothing. Such was their wealth that within the span of a few decades they managed to completely rebuild their city not once but twice following a series of deadly earthquakes—and all without imperial aid. And what does John of Patmos, the author of Revelation, say to this city of wealth and luxury? "You don't realize that you are miserable, pathetic, poor, blind, and naked." (Revelation 3:17)

Take a closer look at 3:20, specifically what John writes after the over-digested bit about God knocking at their door. I will come in and have dinner with them, he writes, and they will have dinner with me. Biblical scholars believe that John wasn't being metaphorical here but literal—the meal is the sacrament of communion, and Christ is asking to be let in to share it. All this begs the question: how were the Laodiceans eating? The answer, again according to biblical scholars, was probably at the tables of their Roman neighbors, feasting on the sacred meat sacrificed to pagan gods, the consumption of which ensured upward financial mobility and consolidated class status. The Laodiceans church may have been Christians, but they were lukewarm ones who compromised their faith with foreign rituals to increase and protect their wealth.

Suddenly Revelation 3:20 doesn't fit the mold of fast food religion anymore. It's no pithy reminder of God's omnipotence, but a call to reject the world of its sinful trappings and to embrace the true community of Christ. Turn away from the meat of the Romans and partake of the bread of Christ, it commands; drink from the living water promised to the Samaritan woman at the well in the Gospel of John from which none ever thirst again. To sit at this table, to eat this meal is to set oneself apart from the world and all its alluring trappings. It's a difficult order, particularly for those accustomed to luxury and easy living. But it's a necessary one. Only then can the banquet—home-cooked and piping hot—truly begin.

Teach me the meaning of discipleship. Lift my thoughts above my personal wants and comforts that I might be useful to your continuing work today. Amen.

67

Breakfast with Harry Emerson Fosdick

"I tell you that you are Peter. And I will build my church on this rock. The gates of the underworld won't be able to stand against it."

MATTHEW 16:18

IN A RECENT EPISODE of the television show, *Young Sheldon*, we see hanging on a bedroom wall a poster of Albert Einstein. This particular episode develops as its primary storyline Sheldon's desire to become the next Einstein. Those familiar with the character of Sheldon from the television show, *The Big Bang Theory*, or this show, *Young Sheldon*, are quite acquainted with the breath of Sheldon's intelligence. It often eclipses everyone in Sheldon's orbit. What is often irritating about Sheldon's character is his inability to be gracious about his intellectual capacity. Here, in this particular episode, young Sheldon has determined to learn all he can about the one he idolizes. Learning that Einstein was Jewish, it seems reasonable to Sheldon that his journey to becoming like Einstein must include conversion to the Jewish faith. In one poignant moment, Sheldon is counseled by a Jewish Rabbi that when Sheldon came to the end of his life, God would not ask him why he didn't become like Albert Einstein. Rather, God would ask Sheldon why wasn't he Sheldon.

I am as guilty as young Sheldon. Near my desk is a framed picture of Harry Emerson Fosdick, a great preacher of another generation. I have read Fosdick's autobiography and a biography of this man who was once called, "the least hated and best-loved heretic that ever lived."[1] Many mornings I enjoy breakfast with one of Fosdick's forty-seven books of sermons, biblical studies, and Christian apologetics. His life had sharp parallels to my own; his thinking stretched my thinking, and his writing informed my own reading—and understanding—of the Bible. Often, I place Fosdick quotes in the Sunday morning worship bulletin, and my preaching sparkles with Fosdick insights. A liberal Christian and preacher in those decades of our nation's history when that was much more dangerous (Ordained in November of 1903, retired in May of 1946), Fosdick has shaped my own theological convictions and reading of the Bible to be more gracious and generous, less narrow and restrictive. Perhaps the critical difference between young Sheldon and me is that I harbor no illusion of becoming another Fosdick.

Young Sheldon desires to be the next Albert Einstein and I deeply value the ministry of Harry Emerson Fosdick. The danger for both Sheldon and me is that we pay little attention to who God has uniquely created each of us to be. We are not alone. Many people today habitually wish they were someone else, or at the minimum, they wish they could be more like someone else. They wish they could possess qualities that they lack, to be more attractive, more intelligent, or have a more outgoing personality. Perhaps their longing is simply to claim more courage, more patience, or more talent. The result is always a disappointment. As Fosdick once shared from the pulpit, "Nobody can put qualities into us from the outside."[2] This lesson from Matthew's Gospel suggests coming at this dilemma from another angle: claim who God has made us to be, "I tell you that you are Peter!" Jesus tells Peter that there is something already in Peter that is sufficient for planting and building the church.

This presents both an encouragement and a challenge. It is an encouragement to accept that God has already made us sufficient for the work God has for us. It isn't necessary to be someone else or to import into our lives qualities we don't possess. "I tell you that you are Peter." Jesus is asking Peter to claim that; to claim that God has uniquely and purposefully made Peter to be the man he is. The same is spoken to us through this text. We already possess all God needs for us to be useful. This also presents a challenge. Jesus saw something deep inside Peter that Peter didn't see. Peter would be a rock, a strong foundation for the church of Jesus Christ. When Peter saw a reflection of himself in the waters of a lake, he saw a man that was temperamental, emotional, and lacking courage. Peter's challenge was to see what Jesus saw, to reach down deep into himself, claim what Jesus saw, nurture

---

1. Durant, "Fosdick Calls Wise," header.
2. Fosdick, *The Hope*, 186.

it and make that quality the driving force of his life. It is our business in life to get out of ourselves what is already there; to lay hold of those virtues, qualities, and passions that lay dormant within. It is then that we realize we don't need to be anyone else. God's grand purpose requires exactly who we were created to be.

Jesus, you have claimed me to be useful to you. Even now you are changing me, transforming me, pulling me toward yourself. Remake me that I may be a faithful disciple as you would have me be. Amen.

68

Weekend Tomb
(Location: The Garden Tomb)

"There was a garden in the place where Jesus was crucified, and in the garden was a new tomb in which no one had ever been laid."

JOHN 19:41

OUTSIDE THE CITY WALLS of Old Jerusalem, near the Damascus Gate, is The Garden Tomb, one of two tombs that are believed to be the burial place of Jesus. The Garden Tomb challenges a sixteen-hundred-year-old tradition that the site of Jesus' burial is marked by an ancient church located within the walls of the Old City—the Church of the Holy Sepulchre. Those who argue in favor of The Garden Tomb as the burial place of Jesus point to its close proximity to a hill with a rocky face that bears a resemblance to a skull, a probable place of the crucifixion. This is a highly visible location to people traveling the main road north from the city, a place that was intentionally chosen for crucifixions to discourage challenges, or disobedience, to the religious or civil law of the day.

The strongest argument against The Garden Tomb as the burial place of Jesus is archeological evidence that suggests that the tomb was used as a burial site in the period of the Old Testament. The witness of John's Gospel is that Jesus was placed in "a new tomb in which no one had ever been laid." If The Garden Tomb is not actually the burial place of Jesus, it is most certainly what the tomb would have looked like—located in a lovely garden that dates back to Jesus' day, a place of considerable calm and beauty. Jesus' tomb was in a garden and this garden now provides spiritual pilgrims a meaningful center of quiet meditation, worship, and devotion.

There are still others who suggest that neither of these two tombs was the actual place of Jesus' burial; that in all probability, the actual spot of Jesus' crucifixion and burial is located several feet beneath the accumulated ruins of the city of Jerusalem. It is a fact of history that since the death and resurrection of Jesus, the city of Jerusalem was destroyed and rebuilt multiple times. What all of this suggests to me is that, perhaps, we are struggling with matters that are unimportant. What is important to the Christian witness is that the tomb, regardless of its precise location, was in fact, simply a weekend tomb. It was only used for three days.

The power of the Christian faith is not located in a specific place. The power of the Christian faith is located in a person, the person of Jesus Christ. Pinpointing the actual place of Jesus' death and burial is less important than what followed those events—Jesus' resurrection from the tomb, from death, and his continuing life today among those he loves. To stand in Jerusalem, that place where Jesus taught and worshiped, that place where Jesus was betrayed and crucified, that place where Jesus was buried and defeated death, is perhaps one of the most meaningful experiences available to a person of faith. But what is absolutely critical to the existence of a vital faith is the conviction that the tomb of Jesus, wherever it may be, is empty; that Jesus walks this day and each day with those who seek him.

Creator of all things, you bring life from death and give birth to hope where there is discouragement. Cause miracles to happen in my life so that I may be a living witness to your power and love. Amen.

69

Throwing Away Self-Pity

"Awake, awake, put on your strength, Zion!"

Isaiah 52:1a

Captivity for Israel has ended. God has defeated the powers of Babylon and has authorized Israel to depart and head for home to Jerusalem. A new day, with a strong future, now rises for God's people. "Awake, awake!" is God's double imperative to Israel. "Put on your strength, Zion!" The call sounds strangely familiar. "Up and Adam! Let's get going!" is the more common usage today. These, or similar, words have been uttered by most parents summoning their children awake from their sleep. The image of sleepy children, resisting the call to leave the comfort of a warm bed, is sharp and crisp. The parent can wake the child with a shout and can summon the child from the bed, but it must be the child's own strength that moves them from slumber to a fresh engagement with a new day.

God's present difficulty is that Israel doesn't want to get out of bed. During their captivity in Babylon, Israel has become dulled, inattentive, hopeless, and grief-stricken.[1] Israel has been humiliated by Babylon and has spiraled into such despair and self-pity that they no longer want to live. No longer did life offer a driving purpose, only a memory of brighter days. Absent was a radiant hope, only a fading dream. A captivating vision has fled from their sight. What remained was a history. "Awake, awake!"

---

1. Brueggemann, *Isaiah*, 136.

is God's response to Israel's self-pity. "Put on your strength, Zion!" God is reminding Israel that there is still strength in the people and is here urging them to summon that strength and toss off that negative attitude that has consumed them.

Psychotherapist and author, Amy Morin writes that feeling sorry for yourself is self-destructive.[2] Though we all experience pain and sorrow in life, dwelling on your sorrow and misfortune can consume you until it eventually changes your thoughts and behaviors. Morin contends that any of us can choose to take control. "Even when you can't alter your circumstances, you can alter your attitude."[3] This is the clear declaration of God to Israel; the clear call to shake off their indulgence in self-pity, claim the strength that remains in them, and move positively forward toward the future God has prepared for them. God's strength comes alongside our own. It does not do for us what we can do for ourselves.

After Victor Hugo was exiled from his beloved France, he spent eighteen years in the Channel Islands. Hugo once described this exile from the nation he loved as worse than death. Each afternoon, at sunset, Victor Hugo would climb to a cliff overlooking a small harbor and look longingly out over the water toward France. Legend tells us that each day, following his meditations, Hugo would pick up a pebble and throw it into the sea. One day the children who developed an affection for him asked why he threw a stone in the sea each day. "Not stones, children, not stones. I am throwing my self-pity into the sea." Little wonder that during those eighteen years of struggle, Victor Hugo gave the world his best and most profound work of literature.

Give me a fresh perspective of the challenges I face today and a new conviction of the uncommon strength I have because of your love. Amen.

---

2. Morin, *13 Things*, 20.
3. Morin, *13 Things*, 18.

70

Prayer and Responsibility

"Hezekiah turned his face to the wall and prayed to the Lord. Then Isaiah said, 'Prepare a bandage made of figs.' They did so and put it on the swelling, at which point Hezekiah started getting better."

2 KINGS 20:2, 7

THEODORE ROOSEVELT, OUR NATION'S twenty-sixth president, was born a frail, sickly child with debilitating asthma. At seventeen, Roosevelt was as tall as he would grow, five feet eight inches, and was just shy of 125 pounds. His health, a continual concern of his parents, prompted Theodore Senior to decide that the time had come to "present a major challenge to his son."[1] At the age of twelve, Theodore—nicknamed, Teedie—was told by his father that he had a great mind, but not the body. Without the help of the body, the mind could not go as far as it should. "You must make your body. It is hard drudgery to make one's body, but I know you will do it."[2] Teedie made the commitment to his father that he would do so. The promise was adhered to with bulldog tenacity. The young Theodore Roosevelt took personal responsibility for his physical health and development.

Hezekiah, king of Judah, became a very sick man during his leadership. He had a wound that had become so serious that his spiritual counselor, a prophet named Isaiah, informed him that he should put his affairs in

1. Morris, *The Rise*, 32.
2. Morris, *The Rise*, 32.

order because he was dying. That diagnosis came like a bolt of lightning to Hezekiah. In desperation, Hezekiah "turned his face to the wall and prayed to the Lord." He pled with the Lord to reward his faithfulness as a man of God and to spare his life. Then, the Scriptures tell us, that Hezekiah cried and cried. Before Isaiah had left the courtyard of the king's residence, God sent him back to Hezekiah with another and more hopeful message: "I have heard your prayers and have seen your tears. So now I'm going to heal you. I will add fifteen years to your life."[3] Then follows something that is most curious: Isaiah orders a bandage made of figs to be placed on the swelling. Hezekiah prayed and Isaiah prepared a bandage: prayer and responsibility.

With powerful clarity, this passage of Scripture teaches us that two things were responsible for Hezekiah's rapid recovery: prayer and a bandage, faith and personal responsibility. If the king was to recover his health, both were required. The Bible refuses to indicate which of the two was the more important. We cannot know which was the most effective. The message is that without either of them Hezekiah would have died in the prime of his life and at a time when his country most needed his leadership. The power of the Assyrian king, and his armies, threaten the peace of Judah. The death of Hezekiah would have made Judah most vulnerable to their enemies. With his health restored, Hezekiah was able to defend his nation from the Assyrian threat. This story provides an important lesson for God's people: While prayer is essential it must never be made a substitute for personal responsibility.

There are people who make the mistake of choosing between the two, prayer and responsibility. We have seen in the news recently where parents of a particular Christian sect refused medical treatment for their young son because they chose the avenue of prayer alone. A choice between faith and medicine is simply not supported by this Bible lesson. Each is a gift of God and each has its own power. Faith and medicine are both means of healing. They belong together. Both are agents of a compassionate God. Prayer and personal responsibility cooperate closely in effecting the highest well-being of those who struggle with illness. This story from 2 Kings reminds us not to neglect either. The second-century French physician, Paré, reminds us of this truth when he wrote, "I dressed the wound and God healed it."

Merciful God, your goodness and mercy surround my life. Grant me the wisdom to do what I can and a heart that trusts in you. Amen.

---

3. Portions of 2 Kings 20:5, 6

71

Christmas Begins with Wonder

"She gave birth to her firstborn child, a son, wrapped him snugly, and laid him in a manger, because there was no place for them in the guestroom."

Luke 2:7

My wife, Grace, and I collect nativity sets. Over the course of our marriage, we have collected over thirty, each beautiful and unique in their own way. Several have come from Congo, Africa, where my wife was born and raised by missionary parents. Others are from Guatemala, Argentina, Peru, Mexico, and Israel. There are also beautiful sets from Alaska and from Native American reservations in the west. Two are whimsical sets from North Carolina—one that depicts every character of the nativity as black bears and another as red cardinals. They have been fashioned from metal, stone, clay, wax, and wood. Each represents a cherished memory and all stir the wonder of that first Christmas.

Christmas begins with wonder. It is a story whereby we are reminded that God has come into the world for every generation and for every person. It is a story that defies reasonableness. God, the creator of the heavens and the earth and all that is them, comes to earth as a vulnerable baby, to parents of little material possessions, in the nondescript town of Bethlehem. The parents have no stature, no power, and no capacity to provide anything more than a manger to place their first child. Absent is any hint of privilege, any suggestion that this family will ever attract the notice of others. Yet, shepherds are drawn to the nativity, leaders of great nations travel considerable distances to bring gifts of substantial value and angels sing from the heavens of the birth of Jesus. The story is astounding, incredible, and outside the parameters of credible story-telling. Serious engagement with the Christmas story begins with wonder.

Wonder is not doubt. For those who doubt, they are unable to see. Their eyes are clouded by a determined focus on what they understand. Wonder exists where there is hope in inexplicable love, and uncommon generosity. Wonder springs from believing that there is more in life than can ever be explained and the deep desire to be surprised. Christian wonder arises from the ancient promise of a God who cares deeply for us, clinging to that promise tenaciously, particularly at those times when there seems to be so little evidence for it, and paying attention, recognizing that God may surprise us at any moment. The shepherds and the magi arrived at the nativity, not because of incontrovertible proof that the Holy Son of God was born but because they were paying attention to a God that surprises.

For Christmas to be more today than a nostalgic glance backward there must be a recovery of wonder. We cannot rejoice at Christmas unless we rejoice that this is a season where images of the nativity—in our homes and churches, on Christmas cards and wrapping paper—remind us that God comes to us in unexpected moments, in a surprising fashion, and always in a manner that is beyond our ability to understand. We live in a world that doesn't know what to make of the love of God; a love that is free of ulterior motives. God baffles us and mystery and wonder permeate God's presence and activity in the world, including the Christmas story. The Christian faith has never asked that we dismiss our questions. But its promises are realized only when we permit ourselves to experience expectant wonder once again.

O gracious and surprising God, thank you for moments of wonder. This Christmas, surprise me again with your power and activity in my life. Amen.

72

Rethinking Sabbath (Nathanael Hood)

"The synagogue leader, incensed that Jesus had healed on the Sabbath, responded, "There are six days during which work is permitted. Come and be healed on those days, not on the Sabbath day." The Lord replied, "Hypocrites! Don't each of you on the Sabbath untie your ox or donkey from its stall and lead it out to get a drink? Then isn't it necessary that this woman, a daughter of Abraham, bound by Satan for eighteen long years, be set free from her bondage on the Sabbath day?"

Luke 13:14–16

THE JANUARY 12, 2010 Haiti earthquake was one of the greatest humanitarian crises of the last decade. The 7.0 magnitude quake demolished huge swathes of the countryside and multiple cities, destroying or damaging a quarter-million homes and with them upwards of 316,000 lives. Millions of survivors suddenly found themselves homeless and forced to sleep out in the street or makeshift shanty towns with little access to drinkable water. The lack of proper sanitation and hygiene led to the first major cholera outbreak of the modern era, eventually infecting over eight hundred thousand with a disease that hadn't been seen on the island in over a century. Corpses literally festered in the street as the government scrambled to dig mass graves. Though the international community quickly rallied to provide relief, delays in distribution led to widespread looting and violence among the survivors. But into this hell rescue workers continued to flood, despite the terror, despite the carnage, despite the destruction.

Among these was a six-man delegation from Israel's ZAKA International Rescue Unit that performed crucial rescue operations in the capital Port-au-Prince. The team was comprised of Orthodox Jews who insisted on being flown out to rescue sites despite it being the Sabbath, the day when traditionally no work is allowed. According to Talmudic sources, there are thirty-nine categories of work prohibited on the Sabbath, many of them necessitated by emergency rescue work like sifting ("merakaid"), demolition ("soter"), and extinguishing fires ("mehabeh"). And yet these six Orthodox Jews sifted, demolished, and extinguished, taking time off from their work only to wrap themselves in prayer shawls and recite Shabbat prayers. When asked about violating the Sabbath, ZAKA commander Mati Goldstein explained that they did it with pride: "We did everything to save lives [despite Sabbath] . . . we are here because the Torah orders us to save lives."

Those familiar with Judaism might recognize this as the fulfillment of "pikuach nefesh"—Hebrew for "saving a life"—a deeply held principle derived from both the Torah and Talmud which argues that the preservation of human life overrides almost every religious rule. For Jews, when human life is on the line it's blasphemous *not* to violate God's commands. Christianity also has the principle of "pikuach nefesh" hard-wired into its DNA, demonstrated by Jesus' deliberate defying of the religious authorities of his day in the Gospel of Luke by healing a woman crippled for eighteen years on the Sabbath. When challenged by the Pharisees, Jesus publicly humiliated them, pointing out their hypocrisy for taking more care of their animals than their fellow human beings. As Jesus echoed elsewhere in the Gospel of Mark with his declaration that the Sabbath was made for man not man for the Sabbath, religious laws exist to help mankind. Mindless zealotry at the expense of people is itself blasphemous.

During this time of crisis, communities of faith from all the world's major religions are struggling to cope with maintaining their traditions in the face of social distancing orders and quarantines. Christianity in particular is feeling the sting of isolation: Sunday services are being live-streamed, baptisms delayed, funerals performed without the deceased's loved ones. We can't even observe Communion, one of our most important sacraments. Ask any pastor, deacon, or elder and they'll tell you that the emotional and psychological toll of these restrictions on their congregations is devastating. But perhaps we as Christians can recontextualize these absences as a sacrament in itself. By not gathering in person to worship, we're slowing the spread of the disease. By staying apart, we're keeping our communities safe.

By not keeping the Sabbath together, we respect the "pikauch nefesh" and the true Sabbath taught by Jesus, the one based on human life and dignity.

Lord, in these difficult times, help us remember that even separated we are one body of believers in your Son Christ Jesus. Help us feel whole in this time of separation as we all work to protect the sick, elderly, and most vulnerable around us. Amen.

73

Living Positively with Our Handicaps

"So I'll gladly spend my time bragging about my weaknesses so that Christ's power can rest on me."

2 Corinthians 12:9b

Bragging about our weaknesses is uncommon. What is customary—even encouraged—is that we "hide" our weaknesses and present the illusion of a life that is lived in a tranquil manner that is deep and even and unhindered by frailties. One unfortunate result is the deep disillusionment that is experienced when we find our heroes far too human, with frailties and weaknesses like our own. We look for people who seem to have no limitations, no handicaps, and no imperfections and we aspire to be like them. In no small manner, people with weaknesses are not considered worthy of our admiration and praise.

Naturally, the danger of finding such a person, a person who is unencumbered by difficulties and imperfections, is to know someone who also possesses considerable conceit. They need no one; they require nothing for their journey through life, not even God. Worse, when understood correctly, their perfection fails to inspire those of us who struggle with handicaps. Another's perfection can only result in our despair. This is why Paul "brags" about his weaknesses—Paul's interest is that we praise only God and that we find in his broken, imperfect life reason for encouragement as we struggle with our own handicaps.

Paul did pray multiple times that his handicap might be removed. That is a demonstration of his humanity. It is an honest prayer that we have no doubt prayed ourselves. Yet, our spiritual condition is developed, positively or negatively, from the place of our weaknesses. For many, the first and instinctive reaction toward our limitations is a negative attitude—a rebellion or self-pity. We revolt against our limitations. Such a negative struggle often advances to cursing God. What we fail to see is that disappointment with our imperfection arises from conceit—we expect to be perfect. That is a poor spiritual condition indeed!

Paul's positive and hopeful response to his weaknesses demonstrates that anyone, regardless of his limitations, can make a spiritual contribution to the world. History is replete with stories of people who rise up and make great contributions in spite of handicaps. These are the stories that inspire each of us to push through whatever difficulties hinder us and advance our lives and the lives of others. Anyone fortunate enough to have the charm and looks of a prince, excellent physical and mental health, and is untroubled by limitations, fails to inspire those who struggle daily under limitations. It is not easy to estimate the spiritual stimulus that comes into human life from handicapped people who have found that Christ's power is sufficient for them.

Remove from me my shame and embarrassment for where I am weak, grant me the humility to accept help from others, and teach me to live each day in gratitude for the gifts and strengths I have. In Christ's name, I pray. Amen.

74

The Plain and Simple Gospel

"'Come, follow me,' he said, 'and I'll show you how to fish for people.'"
MATTHEW 4:19

WE ARE ALL LIVING a deeply entangled, complex life. As complexity increases, so does our exhaustion. We run faster, master complex planning calendars that were designed to make life less cumbersome, and come to the end of many days feeling that we have been defeated. Present is a growing nostalgia for a simpler world—a desire for a plainer, clearer path forward. This general desire includes the spiritual realm. The hope is that the church would provide a rediscovery of God, a reclaiming of God's strength for daily living, and direction for a larger purpose to which we may attach our lives. Unfortunately, what many find are cumbersome requirements for membership and multiple invitations to serve on committees that multiply our exhaustion. With church participation, we discover that there are now more oars in the water that requires our attention.

How can we return to a simpler time? Jesus is instructive. Notice that Jesus does not invite people to register for a six-week new member class. Jesus does not make committee assignments. Jesus does not examine doctrinal purity or demand conformity to creedal statements. Jesus quite simply asks that we follow him. To follow Jesus is to share life with Jesus in the fullest sense: to go where he goes, to listen to what he taught, and to participate in practices and disciplines that were important to him. An invitation to follow is the suggestion that there is something of value to be found. Naturally, to accept such an invitation begins with an acknowledgment that the present life isn't working anymore. Unless we really believe that another approach to life is required, we will continue trying to make the present one work.

The one other thing that Jesus asks for is a posture of humility, a desire to learn, and a willingness to participate in Jesus' work: "and I'll show you how to fish for people." All the work of Jesus is about one thing—looking for those who have wandered far from God and bringing them back home to the Father. As with any great work, there are multiple functions that must be accomplished. None of us are asked—or equipped—to do them all. Some of us are to be teachers, some will show hospitality, and others will be administrators, caregivers, and evangelists. Others will provide care and comfort to the broken. The various jobs to be done are many. But one goal remains: "to fish for people" so that they may return to God. Jesus will show us the way.

None of this suggests that boards and committees are without value to Jesus. Leadership boards must be populated with those who have demonstrated the capacity to respond to the promptings of God, to show people where Jesus is moving and call them to follow. Committees provide a responsible means for organizing a great workforce for accomplishing all that Jesus seeks to do in a particular community. But, in this over-complicated world, the church must not add unnecessary complexity to the simple call of Jesus to follow him and to participate with him in his grand redemptive purposes: a cup of cold water to the thirsty, a helping hand on the roadside, an encouraging word softly spoken. These are all within our reach. Nor are we called to carry the whole world on our backs. Our chief function is to point to the one who does, Jesus Christ. That is the Gospel, plain and simple.

Heavenly Father, make me more aware of your leading and grant me the courage to follow unreservedly. Amen.

75

Surrender (Nathanael Hood)

"That's enough! Now know that I am God!"

PSALM 46:10

MARTIN LUTHER WAS, TO put it mildly, a busy man. Born of respectable middle-class means, his parents instilled in him a dogged Teutonic work ethic that saw him beginning his college education at the University of Erfurt at only seventeen years old. Once there, he blitzed through a wearying curriculum of law (which dissatisfied him), philosophy (which frustrated him), and theology (which electrified him). After a near-death experience during a lightning storm in 1505 where he promised Saint Anna he'd become a monk in exchange for his life, he abandoned his secular studies to enter an Augustinian monastery. Within two years he was ordained. In three, he was teaching theology in Wittenberg. In four, he'd earned two more bachelor's degrees with a Doctor of Theology following in seven. In just a decade, this tireless young man became a provincial vicar charged with overseeing eleven monasteries in eastern Germany.

The rest of his story is one many of us are more familiar with. The Ninety-five Theses are nailed to the church door. Justification by faith alone. Excommunication by Pope Leo X. Cross-examination at Worms. Flight to Wartburg Castle. Translation of the New Testament into German vernacular. Peasant revolts and uprisings. The break with Catholicism, the founding of Lutherism, and the birth of Protestantism. And through it all

Luther maintained a steady, prolific output of catechisms, commentaries, pamphlets, treatises, masses, hymns, books, and sermons. By the end of his life, he'd accumulated over one hundred folio volumes of original writings. And all this while fleeing various authorities, both papal and secular, as the Turks ravaged Hungary and Austria, waves of plague swept England, and the Holy Roman Emperor's own troops sacked Rome. The world was turning itself to ashes.

During his whirlwind life, Luther found himself time and again facing the darkest corners of doubt, sorrow, and exhaustion. According to various sources, Luther repeatedly turned toward the forty-sixth Psalm for comfort and respite. Stories go that he would ask his close friend and fellow reformer Philip Melanchthon to sing it with him: "Come, Philip, let us sing the forty-sixth Psalm." Such was his love for the Psalm that opened with the triumphant declaration "God is our refuge and strength, a help always near in times of great trouble" that he officially set it to music to write one of the greatest hymns in Christendom: "A Mighty Fortress Is Our God."

But it's in the tenth verse that the psalmist's triumphant bombast gets tempered by a proclamation from God, telling them to be quiet, be still, and know that God is God. This is a psalm for boasting in the strength of the Almighty, but it's also a command for one of the hardest things that man can do: surrender oneself. There comes a moment in the depths of adversity where one must remove oneself from trying to control the forces of fate and simply trust in our creator. To do otherwise would be to lose ourselves to our own neuroses and anxieties. It's only in this quiet and stillness that we find our center, and it's there—much like Moses in the desert, Elijah in the cave, or Paul on the road to Damascus—that we can finally find and know God. And it was in this emptiness inspired by reading the forty-sixth Psalm the night before his incendiary refusal to recant his beliefs at the Diet of Worms that Martin Luther found the courage to face his accusers and make one of the bravest stands in the history of Christendom: "I cannot and will not recant anything, since it is neither safe nor right to go against conscience. May God help me. Amen."

Surrender is so difficult, O Lord. It is comfortable to be in control. Grant me courage today to surrender my life and future to your care. Amen.

76

Speaking Wisely

"Do you love life; do you relish the chance to enjoy good things? Then you must keep your tongue from evil and keep your lips from speaking lies!"

PSALM 34:12, 13

IT IS A RHETORICAL question, of course. Who doesn't want to be thoroughly alive, enjoying all the good things that life has to offer, to be lifted above the plane of mere existence? To live a large life, a life of spacious activities and with a grand purpose captures our imaginations. This is a life of abounding energy and possesses a deep awareness of the things that bless—both personally and those around us.

The Psalms offer treasured insight for such a life, insight for embracing a spacious life of blessedness, of extracting the secret flavors and essences of things as we live into each day. Very specifically, we are instructed in the wisdom of many who have traveled before us; we are told to exercise wise government over our tongues. Relationships with one another rise to unimaginable heights as the tongue is disciplined and directed to build, edify and, exalt those who hear us. It is as though life receives its nutriments from careful and blessed speech.

Our speech is too often destructive. Poison-soaked speech first poisons the speaker. "Every word we speak recoils upon the speaker's heart, leaves its influence, either in grace or disfigurement," writes that wonderful preacher,

J.H. Jowett.[1] Where the tongue is untrue the heart is afraid of exposure. Life is diminished. One may also argue that such speech is lazy speech. Where there is no exercise of restraint or government of the tongue; it is free to roam at will. Therefore, urges the Psalms, to keep your tongue from evil and speaking lies. The tongue that is held in severe restriction, the tongue that only shapes words that are good and encouraging to others results in quiet and fruitful happiness.

Undisciplined tongues seem to flourish today. And the world is the poorer for it. Yet, our own lives may move to a higher plane simply by a personal revolt from the disorderly conduct of tongues. The best way to affect a departure from the guile and venom that flows freely around us is to exercise one's self in active good, of words spoken kindly, with pleasantness and grace. The fragrance of our speech will tickle the hearts of others. It may invite them to share in the same wisdom of the Psalms, an invitation to experience a blessed life, full, safe, and abounding in good things.

Grant me the wisdom and strength to govern my tongue, O Lord. Help me to use my speech only to encourage, build and edify all who hear me, so that my life and theirs will be blessed. Amen.

---

1. Jowett, *Thirsting for the Springs*, 188.

77

The Great Wisdom of Prayer

"Early in the morning, well before sunrise, Jesus rose and went to a deserted place where he could be alone in prayer."

MARK 1:35

IT WAS SAID OF the disciples long ago that people held them in wonder and awe that they had been with Jesus. To be with one of the disciples was to experience one degree of separation from our Lord. That close proximity to Christ resulted in an experience of spiritual vitality and power. God's love, wisdom, and strength were no longer limited to one's imagination as stories of Jesus' life and ministry were shared. In the company of a disciple—or disciples—God's presence seemed to come near. The vision of God's glory grew more expansive in the heart as a result of being in the presence of one of the disciples. Perhaps that same fascination is what drives each of us to be photographed with those we admire. There is an unmistakable attraction and thrill to standing in the presence of those who have acquired a larger-than-life persona.

In this passage from Mark's Gospel, Jesus had just finished a hard, grueling day. A similar day would follow. How could he be ready for it? What would be the spring of fresh physical, emotional, and spiritual strength from which he would drink? Mark gives us the answer and with it the key to Jesus' vitality and stamina, "Early in the morning, well before sunrise, Jesus rose and went to a deserted place where he could be alone in prayer." This one verse suggests the great wisdom of prayer: Every morning, draw from the inexhaustible power of God by drawing near to God's presence. That is done in prayer. Once when a man was asked what he was doing each day sitting alone in a church, gazing upon a picture of Jesus, he answered, "I am simply looking at him and he is looking at me." Prayer is time with God.

The weakest, humblest life can be made stronger when placed before God. As we pray, the Bible promises that God will be there. There will be days when God seems absent. The Psalms tell us this. Pray anyway. Know that God is present. Day after day the eyes of the soul become more sensitive to God, the heart more aware of God's still small voice speaking. Eventually, prayer becomes that daily practice by which the individual soul becomes intertwined with the presence and strength of God. The fact of intimate communion with God is the great reality of true, regular prayer. In prayer, we come to see ourselves surrounded by God's love and concern for us as we begin each new day.

How strange, how foolish it must seem to God that we should be content with so little prayer. This particular occasion, mentioned in this one verse of Scripture from Mark's Gospel, was no unusual occurrence for Jesus. Jesus prayed often; Jesus prayed for himself and for others. Jesus took time for prayer before each day and before every difficult challenge that drew near to him. Jesus teaches prayer to us by example, for he knew from his own experience that prayer was a vital part of navigating the inevitable difficulties that each one of us must face. Today, many Christians are troubled by weakness, doubt, and fear, largely because they miss the help that prayer might provide. The greater wisdom of prayer is simply discovering—and experiencing—that we never have to face a day alone.

As I move into the joys, opportunities, and challenges that this day holds, strengthen me by the certainty of your presence. Amen.

78

Praying As Jesus Prayed

"Jesus was praying in a certain place. When he finished, one of his disciples said, 'Lord, teach us to pray, just as John taught his disciples.'"

LUKE 11:1

SOME YEARS AGO I returned home from a business meeting in South Carolina. After claiming my baggage at the Tampa International Airport I proceeded to my car which was parked in the short-term parking garage. I found a flat tire. Only once in my life had I ever changed a flat tire. That was before I was married. That one time it took me nearly forty minutes. I remember my father once telling me that I wasn't worth much with my hands. I never disappointed. Exhausted from my trip and staring down at a flat tire I made the decision to call my father-in-law who lived near the airport. He giggled—he giggled at me often, wondering what kind of man his daughter married—and said he would be there in ten minutes. In about the same amount of time it took him to arrive, my tire was changed and I was ready to go. I thanked him, we hugged and each of us said "I love you" to the other. On my drive home I realized that it had been nearly a month since the last time I spoke with my father-in-law.

Often, this is what our prayer life looks like. Life is moving forward in a pleasant manner, we are happy, and our needs are few. Conversation with God—in prayer—is virtually non-existent. Suddenly we look down at a flat tire and a phone call is made to God. For many, it completely escapes them that there is anything deficient in their practice of prayer. All that has been understood about prayer is that God is the great giver who shows up when we make the call. Some of you reading this will recall the major home appliance manufacturer, Maytag, and their television commercials of the Maytag repairman sitting by the phone waiting for a call. When our flat tire is not resolved quickly we question, "Where is God?" Our confidence in the power of prayer wanes. Perhaps even more tragic is that some may begin to question the very existence of God.

Jesus' practice of prayer astonished the disciples. Such was their amazement at Jesus' prayers that they asked him to teach them to pray. As far as we know from the Gospels, this is the only thing the disciples explicitly asked Jesus to teach them. Notice that this fresh interest in prayer does not arise from the study of an apprentice manual for discipleship or from a conversation with Jesus on the topic. It followed immediately after observing Jesus at prayer. There was something about Jesus' prayer life that was different from their own practice of prayer; something that evidenced a greater sense of intimacy with God, and something that gave release to more power. As Harry Emerson Fosdick so clearly expressed it, Jesus went into prayer in one mood and came out in another. Praying was not a form but a force.[1]

Fortunately for the church today, the Gospels have captured many of Jesus' prayers. A close examination of those prayers reveals a surprise for many: absent is any hint of begging. Jesus does not approach his heavenly father with pleas for his personal welfare, as though a disinterested God must be cajoled or convinced to offer a blessing. What becomes startlingly clear is an affirmative tone to Jesus' prayers. Jesus turns his back on any doubt of God's goodness and stretches out his hand to appropriate the inexhaustible resources available to any one of us. Such prayer retires for a moment from the swirling darkness that may surround us from time to time and affirms that God is present and active in our life. Such prayer, Fosdick affirms, "does not so much ask as take; it does not so much beg for living water as sink shafts into it and draw from it."[2] That is praying as Jesus prayed.

Lord, by your grace, help me this day to lay hold of the inexhaustible power available to me in prayer. Amen.

---

1. Fosdick, *Riverside Sermons*, 112.
2. Fosdick, *Riverside Sermons*, 116

79

Where God Is Found (Nathanael Hood)

"The Lord said, 'Go out and stand at the mountain before the Lord. The Lord is passing by.' A very strong wind tore through the mountains and broke apart the stones before the Lord. But the Lord wasn't in the wind. After the wind, there was an earthquake. But the Lord wasn't in the earthquake. After the earthquake, there was a fire. But the Lord wasn't in the fire. After the fire, there was a sound. Thin. Quiet. When Elijah heard it, he wrapped his face in his coat. He went out and stood at the cave's entrance. A voice came to him and said, 'Why are you here, Elijah?'"

1 Kings 19: 11–13

God had won. His fire had come down from the heavens and devoured the sacrifices of grain and meat, scorching the very alter to ashes. The 450 prophets of Baal who had desecrated his temple with pagan worship and idols had failed to summon their god, and in the face of the God of Israel's majesty were seized and slaughtered on the spot. We don't know how many witnessed this miracle orchestrated by the prophet Elijah on Mount Carmel, but all who did were amazed. All fell on their faces and worshipped the God of Abraham and Isaac. Among them was the wicked king Ahab, the very king who had welcomed the prophets of Baal. For a moment sanctity seemed to be restored to the throne of David, and Elijah rushed to the then-capital city of Jezreel in triumph.

But it was in this greatest moment of victory that Elijah experienced one of his greatest moments of defeat. Unmoved by her husband's recounting of the miracle, queen Jezebel threatened to have Elijah executed, forcing him into exile in the wilderness. And if we pay close attention to the text, we see that nobody tried to stop or help him, not even those who had seen the Lord's fire with their own eyes.

After fleeing over 250 miles south of Jezreel, an exhausted Elijah hides in a cave on Mount Horeb—the same mountain upon which Moses received the Ten Commandments. After spending the night, the Lord arrives and asks what he was doing there. Elijah explodes in panicked fury: he's hiding for his life! Despite all his work, despite the prophecies and warnings, despite the miracles and wonders, the Israelites haven't repented of their wickedness and now seek *his* life! He has, in short, done everything right. How can he be repaid like this?

What follows is one of the most famous theophanies—or physical appearances of God—in the Old Testament. God calls Elijah to come outside the cave and stand before him. But before Elijah can, three calamities wrack Mount Horeb: a calamitous wind, an earthquake, and a fire. And yet, the Lord was not in them. Pay very close attention to the language being used here. Before Elijah's eyes three earth-shattering, world-ending cataclysms erupted. And yet the Lord was *not in them*. As Terence E. Fretheim points out in his commentary on First and Second Kings, the pagans believed that Baal manifested in such disasters; he was "in" them. But these pass "before" the God of Elijah's fathers. He is absent from their ravages and destructions, absent from the despair they cast and the ruination they bring.[1] Only then does a soft, quiet sound come. Only then does Elijah wrap his face in acknowledgment of being in the presence of the one true God. Only then does God speak to him again, asking him the same simple question. Why are you here, Elijah? You still have so much work to do.

One of the most common misconceptions Christians share is that faith in God is some kind of shield that protects one from tragedies and disasters. But they happen every day, even to the most sincere and devout followers. Jobs and opportunities are lost. Friends and family succumb to disease and accidents. Storms rage and devastate entire seaboards. What we must *not* do is mistake these things as righteous retribution from a vengeful God. A God concerned with heavy-handed retribution for even the most minor of mistakes would not send his only Son to die for us. Ours is not a God who

---

1. Frerthem, *First and Second Kings*, 111–12.

speaks with fire and fury. Ours is one who seeks a relationship with us, one who sees and knows all and loves us in spite of it. What we must do is seek it. And we can start by listening for his gentle voice of reassurance and comfort in our most trying times. Only then can we start to rebuild.

Heavenly Father, may my spirit and heart be willingly grounded in which you can cultivate the relationship you desire, that I may know you more fully and trust you more deeply. Amen.

80

Hungry for God

"Just like a deer that craves streams of water, my whole being craves you, God."

PSALM 42:1

ON A RECENT VACATION, my wife, daughter, and I climbed the Dunn's River Falls in Jamaica. This world-famous waterfall cascades six hundred feet down a giant rock staircase to the Caribbean Sea. Visitors to the falls are divided into teams of eight, join hands, and follow a guide up the natural stepping platforms as they are showered with cool, clear water all the way up. There are various places on the way up where we stop, let go of one another's hands and rest, splash each other, and take photos. But movement toward the top always requires holding onto one another to assist a secure footing on slippery stones. Naturally, each person experiences moments of awe at the tropical beauty around us and laughter as we struggle together toward the top, firmly holding onto each other. Yet, at a deeper level, I experienced something of God's Kingdom surrounding the whole experience. We were joined together—by hands—in a common quest to reach the top without any consideration of the other's political, educational, or ethnic identity.

Similarly, all people are possessed by a common quest that has taken hold of the human heart. It is a quest that leaps across the borders of religious affiliations, races, and nations. It cuts across generations and continually challenges women and men. What I speak of is a deep and increasing desire to know God. Every person, atheist or religious, experiences a desire to connect with someone or power greater than their individual self. We may disagree on much and desire different things in life. But, in the last analysis, behind every search in life, there is one, eternal, common quest. It is a quest driven by questions such as, "What are we here for?," "What is it all about?," and "Is there one, singular purpose in life." Those who are honest admit to an inescapable yearning for fellowship with the one who is above and beyond this life.

This quest is driven by disillusionment—disillusionment with striving for more stuff, disillusionment with political activism to correct social ills, and disillusionment with charitable organizations' ability to meet increasing human needs. At one time believing that human power, intellect, and resourcefulness were sufficient for every need, all things spiritual were neglected. That abandonment of the spiritual has shown up in the Christian pulpit. The pulpit is asked to support ministries that address homelessness, hunger, addiction, and broken relationships rather than proclaim the presence and power of God. What has been experienced is little contentment and even less peace of heart. What eventually dawns upon the church is that all alone, we are not sufficient. The revolt against God has not turned out very well. We need God

Episcopal pastor and author, Barbara Brown Taylor once heard from church members that they were hungry to know the Bible. She hired professors from a nearby seminary and offered regular courses on the Old and New Testaments. The classes were small and sporadically attended. After multiple starts and failures with various Bible studies, Taylor finally realized that "Bible" was a code word for "God." People were not hungry for information about the Bible; they were hungry for an experience of God.[1] Naturally, Bible study is important. Also important is housing the homeless, feeding the hungry, caring for the addicted, and helping people mend broken relationships. But these are on the circumference rather than the center. It's like tinkering with a sprinkler system without watering the grass. Without water, the grass dies. Without God, our faith withers.

God, you are the beginning and the end. Help me to remember that my deepest hunger in life is a hunger for you. Amen.

---

1. Taylor, *The Preaching of Life*, 49.

81

Waiting to Understand

"Jesus replied, 'You don't understand what I'm doing now, but you will understand later.'"

JOHN 13:7

RECENTLY MY WIFE, DAUGHTER, and I enjoyed a late breakfast at Benny's On the Beach in Lake Worth. After we parked, Grace and Rachael walked directly to the restaurant while I moved toward the parking kiosk to pay. As I waited behind two women, who were together, I overheard a most absurd conversation between them. After one had completed the payment transaction and received her receipt, the other woman remarked, "We need to place the receipt on our car's dash before going to the beach." She was answered by her friend, "The receipt says that there is no need to place it on the dash." That was followed by the other, "That has to be wrong! There is no way for the police to know that we have paid." Undeterred, the other woman began reading the receipt once again, "There is no need . . . " She was interrupted, "That is simply ridiculous! We are placing the receipt on the dash!" I watched as the two women returned to their car and placed the receipt on the dash.

I confess to not understanding how the police will know. The spaces are no longer numbered. The parking kiosk simply asks for the license plate number for the payment transaction. But I trusted what I did not understand. I took my receipt, placed it in my wallet, and moved toward the restaurant to join my wife and daughter. Perhaps I will understand later. Nonetheless, I did not demand to understand before following the instructions provided. This is precisely what Jesus is asking the disciples to accept: "You don't understand what I'm doing now, but you will understand later." These words were probably spoken on the night that Jesus was betrayed and arrested. As apparent from Jesus's remark, the disciples are puzzled. They have tried to follow Jesus—and left a great deal behind to do so—and now Jesus is speaking to them about going away. They may have had questions during Jesus' ministry. But now they are thoroughly unsettled.

Often we are unsettled. There is much in life that we don't understand. Present in life are inequalities that are terribly unfair, injustice that appears insurmountable, and cruelty that is incomprehensible. This past week many returned to the safety of their homes from work to learn from the evening news that fifty people are dead in a New Zealand mosque shooting. It is a violence that simply doesn't make sense. What are we to do in the face of such challenging problems? Jesus acknowledges that we don't understand. Then, Jesus gives to us a divine promise: "But you will understand later." Until then, Jesus asks us to trust and wait. The difficulty for many of us is that we don't like to wait. Telling us that we will understand later seems a feeble thing to say to people who want to understand immediately and have a thoughtful grasp of how this world works. Yet, that is precisely the problem—we are a tiny power trying to comprehend what God is doing.

In a previous meditation, I wrote of a Broadway musical my son, Nathanael, and I enjoyed this past December, *The Band's Visit*. In that meditation, I shared that for the first thirty minutes of the musical I came to the conclusion that I had wasted a rather large sum of money on two expensive tickets. The narrative was slow to develop, held little interest for me, and lacked the sparkle and energy I have come to expect from big-budget Broadway musicals. If I were to invite someone to see the musical with me today I would ask of them to give the musical a chance—to wait patiently through the first thirty minutes until the inevitable grasp it will have on their heart. Something happens in the story that unfolds that results in identification with the brokenness of the characters, a longing for good on their behalf, and even prayers sent upward to heaven that they each find some measure of joy. Then the musical concludes. An actress steps to center stage and speaks the final words of the production to each of us, the audience: "Once a band came to town. You probably didn't hear about it. It wasn't very important." It is then your heart shouts, "That's not true! It is important. It mattered. It mattered very much!" That is because, after a period of time when we didn't understand, it suddenly was clear. And Jesus said to the disciples, "You don't understand what I'm doing now, but you will understand later."

Compassionate God, never let me forget that you love me. In those moments when the world doesn't make sense help me find comfort in the knowledge that you remain Lord of the heavens and earth. Amen.

82

From Why to Where (Nathanael Hood)

> *"As Jesus walked along, he saw a man who was blind from birth. Jesus' disciples asked, 'Rabbi, who sinned so that he was born blind, this man or his parents?' Jesus answered, 'Neither he nor his parents. This happened so that God's mighty works might be displayed in him.'"*
>
> JOHN 9:1–3

ON DECEMBER 26, 2004, the third-largest earthquake ever recorded struck the west coast of northern Sumatra, rocking the fault-lines with the power of over fifteen hundred atomic bombs, vibrating the entire planet by one centimeter. The cataclysmic shockwaves birthed a series of apocalyptic tsunamis that reached upwards of one hundred feet high. Due to the relative historical scarcity of tsunamis in the Indian Ocean, the surrounding coastal communities had no practical tsunami warning systems, guaranteeing local populations were unaware of their impending doom while the waters rushed their way. Almost a quarter million in fourteen different countries were killed, making it one of the deadliest natural disasters in human history. A global humanitarian relief effort was swiftly organized, with food, medicine, and over $14 billion in international aid distributed to survivors and first responders. When the waters finally receded and the destruction cleared away, millions were left with a simple question: why? How, in a just, sane universe, could this happen?

In the January 8, 2005 issue of *The Los Angeles Times*, reporters Teresa Watanabe and Larry B. Stammer published an article that examined the different theological responses to the 2004 tsunamis from the major world religions. Their findings revealed stark differences in how mankind's great faith traditions grappled not just with tragedy, but with the theodical implications of disaster. Buddhists, according to a former Sri Lankan ambassador, believe in the doctrine of karmic law, not random chance, implying that the casualties received their just reward for the sins of their past or current lives while the survivors benefitted from their past or current goodnesses. According to a prominent Hindu faith leader in southern California, Hindus also believe in karma, but their belief in god(s) implies the intercession of a divine will: the god(s) sent the tsunamis to punish the afflicted communities' bad karma. Meanwhile, a Wiccan high priestess in Wisconsin explained that earthquakes and tsunamis were the result of "Mother Nature stretching—she had a kink in her back and stretched."

The responses from the Abrahamic faiths were different. When asked, a prominent rabbi teaching at the University of Judaism in Los Angeles responded that such disasters were a "natural consequence of God's decision to make a finite world." But this begs the question of why, if God deliberately created a finite world, he couldn't design one without physical and natural laws that periodically drown a quarter million innocent people. Meanwhile, according to the leader of the Islamic Shura Council of Southern California, mankind is called not to ask "why" but "what now": "We should take it as a test from God to see how human beings respond." It's this last interpretation that perhaps comes closest to the Christian theological outlook, finding the idea of God's causing the tsunamis a non-issue. As Baptist minister Douglas McConnell explained to Watanabe and Stammer, "believing that God deliberately caused the [tsunamis] is a difficult leap for those who believe God was revealed in the compassionate Jesus."

We see this belief here in the ninth chapter of the Gospel of John where Jesus' disciples ask him if the suffering of a man blind since birth was karmic punishment for his family's sins. Notice how Jesus responds. He doesn't just reply in the negative, he rejects their premise that mankind's suffering is ordained. Jesus changes the question, instead of saying that what matters now is that in his presence, the mighty works of God might be displayed. Just as Jesus rejected their premise, this text invites us to change our question from why there is suffering to the location of Christ in the midst of said suffering. The answer can always be found in the midst of the church's response to devastation: the donating of money, the sharing of shelter, and the giving of food and medicine. It's in the healing of the world that we come closer to Christ. We have no time for wondering why.

Lord Jesus, draw me from a preoccupation with searching questions that cannot be answered to experiencing your presence and love more deeply. Amen.

83

Brush Strokes

> *"Don't be conformed to the patterns of this world, but be transformed by the renewing of your minds so that you can figure out what God's will is—what is good and pleasing and mature."*
>
> Romans 12:2

Gilbert "Dibo" Doran holds the Curacao's 2019 title as the King of Tumba, Curacao's Carnival anthem. A music genre indigenous to this area of the Caribbean, Tumba has its roots in the history of slavery and remains popular for ending parties on a high note. "Nowadays, the Tumba Festival is the biggest music festival on the island. Local composers and musicians compete for living their culture to the max."[1] Doran self-identifies as a "patriot to the bone" asserting that one's culture and tradition are part of your identity. It's your roots. Through his original music compositions, Doran desires to leave his mark on the music genre, to be an example, and contribute to the longevity of the cultural imprint of the Tumba Festival. Perseverance is key, adds Doran.

Gilbert Doran is a man whose life is organized around a central purpose. Raised in a single-parent home, Doran neither ran away from life nor ran along with life. He set himself apart from other children by intentionally directing his life around a core passion—a passion for the culture, folklore, and tradition of Curacao, particularly as expressed in music. "Instead of a

---

1. Rosa, "I Want My Legacy," 85.

bike or a Nintendo, I would ask for drums, a piano, or cymbals as a gift."[2] Doran stands proudly among women and men who have done the most for the world precisely because they are nonconformists. He has elevated the level of life for ages to come for the people of Curacao because of a driving passion to contribute positively to his corner of the world.

This is precisely what the Apostle Paul is asking of those who would follow Jesus Christ. Be a nonconformist! Don't go along with life, drifting wherever the flow of life may take you, becoming shaped by whatever forces surround you. Set your mind on God. Learn of God. Seek to know God's will and discern all that is good, pleasing, and mature. As Doran held, perseverance is key. The distinguished preacher from another generation, Robert J. McCracken once observed, "The reason why so many people are at the mercy of circumstance is that they have neither discovered a faith by which to live nor a cause to serve."[3] The "patterns of this world" exert a powerful shaping influence upon each person. The Apostle Paul provides another way. Draw on spiritual resources greater than your own. Fix your eyes on God.

Many people today take the path of least resistance. Without a driving conviction to mature in the faith through regular time with God by prayer and reading the Bible, they are caught by the flow of life and carried along paths and channels they have not chosen. The usual result is that their life begins to reflect the standards and practices of their environment. The people they meet and the things that happen to them likely shape who they become. It is as though they surrender the brush strokes that paint their life portrait to an unknown hand. Here, in his letter to the church in Rome, the Apostle Paul urges that we submit the brush strokes that will paint our portrait to the hand of the Master, Jesus Christ.

O God, lift me into your light today! May I not follow the path of least resistance. Direct my steps according to your truth that I may become all you intend. Amen.

---

2. Rosa, "I Want My Legacy," 85.
3. McCracken, "The Peril of Conformity," 24.

84

A Life Unnoticed

> *"One poor widow came forward and put in two small copper coins worth a penny. Jesus called his disciples to him and said, 'I assure you that this poor widow has put in more than everyone who's been putting money in the treasury.'"*
>
> MARK 12:42, 43

TOM TEWELL ONCE SHARED with me that the deepest brokenness experienced by the homeless is that they go unnoticed. The desire that others see them and acknowledge them, the longing that others acknowledge them as people who share this earth with them, is deeper than the hunger of an empty stomach or the fear for personal safety. Every person longs for a sense of value, love, and for recognition. The homeless are no different. Nor are the homeless alone in this struggle. People who are older and single, those who struggle with addiction, and the under-resourced all experience the fear of remaining unnoticed. We do not live in the most compassionate of times, and such people join the great shuffle—where our communities move them out of sight and mind. Our full and frantic lives may be partly to blame. We simply do not have the time or emotional energy to acknowledge these people and be available to them.

Here, in Mark's Gospel, there are two stories at play, each unfolding simultaneously. The legal experts comprise the cast for the first narrative and a poor widow in a solo performance for the second narrative. In the first story, the legal experts go to considerable effort that others see them for their devotion and sacrifice. In the second story, a widow has probably abandoned any hope that anyone will ever notice her again. There is no attempt by this woman to ensure that people see her. She simply makes her gift to the temple treasury from an impulse of faith, an impulse that discloses her quiet gratitude and trust in God. Jesus notices both, the legal experts and the woman. Yet, what is remarkable in this text is that those who desired an audience received Jesus' displeasure. The one who did not seek any notice is held-up by Jesus as an honorable example of authentic discipleship.

The poor widow is invisible—that is, invisible to everyone except Jesus. Moreover, what Jesus sees is that the woman is contributing—however small—to a cause that is larger than her own life. There are "invisible" people in our communities who feel unattractive, have little to offer anyone, and are lonely. The despair that they experience makes moving through each day unbearable. Each invisible person in our orbit presents an opportunity to share the companionship and compassion of Christ. An invitation to dinner, to family celebrations, and even acknowledging their birthdays, proclaims that they are people with dignity and worth. We are the children of a God who notices and protects the unnoticed, and therefore, we are to be agents of God's protecting and providing grace. Additionally, we are to recall that the woman's gift reminds us that each person has something to contribute to the work of the church.

Perhaps the deepest impact any church can have on a community is to invest in the lives of persons who may go unnoticed where we live. There is a story in the Jewish tradition of a rabbi who was so holy that the rumor developed that on Sabbath afternoons he ascended into heaven to personally commune with God. The rumor grew from the observation that this rabbi simply seemed to disappear from sight in the local community until the end of the day. Several boys decided to follow, in secret, the rabbi. Throughout the afternoon and into the early evening, they saw the rabbi go into the homes of the elderly, the sick, and the poor. He cooked meals, cleaned homes, and read Scripture to the lonely. The next day the people inquired of the boys; did the rabbi really ascend into heaven? The boys answered, "No. He went much higher."

God of all people, remove from my eyes those things that prevent me from seeing others, especially those who are lonely. Then direct my response to them so that they may experience your grace. Amen.

85

Knowing God's Will

"Don't be conformed to the patterns of this world, but be transformed by the renewing of your minds so that you can figure out what God's will is—what is good and pleasing and mature."

ROMANS 12:2

RECENTLY, MY FRIEND TOM Tewell shared with me a basic and helpful approach to seeking God's will—an approach he had learned years earlier from Lloyd J. Ogilvie. The place to begin is a careful reading of the Bible and prayer. Seeking God's will in a particular circumstance, or more generally for one's life, must always begin with some grasp of who God is. What can we know of God and how God has worked through human history from God's Word in the Holy Scriptures? God's desire for today will not contradict God's character as disclosed in the Bible. If God is opposed to adultery in the Bible, for instance, God remains opposed to adultery. Simply, we will never discern that God may be calling us to violate our marriage vows.

The second movement to discerning God's will is by consulting with a few trusted people who have demonstrated, in some way, that they listen carefully for God's direction. These will be people who have been widely noticed by others as "paying attention to God" as they live each day. Share with them what you think God may be calling you to do. Then invite them to place what you think you hear alongside what they know of God and God's activity. Is there consistency? Does what you believe God is saying match up with the God your friends have come to know from years of following Christ? Some Christian leaders refer to this practice as "discernment in community." Bring what you hear to a faithful community so they can say if it makes sense to them from what they know of God.

Finally, pay attention to the opportunities that present themselves—and those that don't. What some may simply call "circumstances" may be powerful indicators of what God is up to in your life. If you believe God is calling you to missionary work overseas and no doors seem to be opening for that to happen, it is well to rethink if God's will has been properly discerned. On the other hand, if you sense God is calling you to partner with Habitat for Humanity for building homes for the poor, and you have particular skills for building homes, and have discretionary time available in your routine rhythm of life and then hear of a specific need from that organization that you can meet, and feel a burden for those who can't afford a home—well, you see where I am going.

Many ask why finding God's will has to be such a struggle. My own take on that is that God planned it that way. It is in the struggle that we go deeper and deeper in a relationship with God. Think of it this way. A meaningful relationship with a spouse is built by paying close attention to their likes and dislikes over a long period of time. We listen carefully when they speak. We watch what makes them happy and what discourages them. We take notice of their idiosyncrasies. This takes effort, naturally. But it is the effort—over time—that results in a deep and satisfying relationship with another. God wants no less from us.

Father God, today I pray that you will instill in my heart patience to seek your will, clarity of understanding, and a passionate desire to obey everything Jesus commanded. Amen.

86

Success in the Spiritual Life

"Train yourself for a holy life! While physical training has some value, training in holy living is useful for everything. It has promise for this life now and the life to come."

1 TIMOTHY 4:7B, 8

THOREAU SAID, "IF ONE advances confidently in the direction of his dreams . . . he will meet with a success unexpected in common hours."[1] Advancement in a chosen direction is intentional movement, not simply a longing or a dream. One is aspirational; the other is a determined pursuit. One person may aspire to learn the Italian language; another enrolls in a language class. Therefore, we need to ask ourselves, "Have I determined a pathway for realizing my dreams? Am I now pursuing that path?" Success, says Thoreau, belongs to those who begin to move in the direction that is right for them. That is when things start to go our way.

In this letter to Timothy, Paul uses an athletic metaphor to describe, "Advancing confidently in the direction of a holy life." He urges the reader to "Train yourself," that is, to advance intentionally and confidently in the direction of living like Christ. The Greek word Paul uses for "train" is the word from which we get "gymnasium." It would be odd for anyone to go to a gym simply to watch others train. Gyms have value, not as "observation posts" for people who dream of better health, but as an "action center" for

---

1. Thoreau, *Walden*, 326.

advancing toward better health. When Paul speaks about training in holy living, he is talking about activities that engage us—activities that make a demand upon us.

It is good for us to reassess our priorities from time to time. Often we speak of our aspirations: an aspiration to learn a musical instrument, an aspiration to travel, or an aspiration to return to school. Yet, without "advancing confidently in the direction of our dreams," they remain aspirations. Absent is a commitment and plan to advance toward them. Someone once observed that our priorities are transparent for the world to see—they see our priorities in what we do each day. The mature person understands that what is important receives time, energy, and intentionality. If consistently arriving to work on time is important for job security, we arrive to work on time.

Thomas Long writes that if the holy life is our aim, we go to the theological gym to do curls, crunches, and run laps to train, not to run a marathon but in order to be people of love.[2] Naturally, observes Tom Long, it does not take much training to love the lovable. However, when Christ calls us to love those who are difficult to love—or to love our enemies—then, that takes practice. That takes time in the theological gym. "Train yourself for a holy life!" writes Paul. The great Swiss psychiatrist Carl Jung said that the supreme goal of men and women is to fulfill themselves—to honor their unique calling in life. The apostle Paul is asking that we now honor our baptismal vows—to become like Christ.

Creator God, show us real and concrete ways for developing a life that is marked by holiness. Amen.

---

2. Long, *Belief*, 131.

87

Religious Dropouts

"At this, many of his disciples turned away and no longer accompanied him."

JOHN 6:66

IT IS NOW FAIRLY common knowledge that Christian churches across the United States are experiencing decline—a decline in membership, decline in worship attendance, and decline in financial support. Diminishing interest in the church has resulted, in many congregations, a shift from full-time pastoral leadership to part-time, reduced opportunities for spiritual nurture and growth, and a smaller impact on the local community. As congregations grow smaller they are faced with difficult decisions such as merging with other churches or closing their doors permanently. Causes for the decline of the Christian Church across our nation have been studied and solutions have been scarce.

What has received less attention is a phenomenon I will call the "religious dropouts." These are the people who are regularly present in services of worship, engaged in personal spiritual growth, and participate in the church's mission to feed the hungry, house the homeless and care for the broken. Vibrant and robust churches are built upon their dedication to Jesus and Jesus' work through the local congregation. It is not difficult to see that the church is stronger for such people. Then, they simply aren't present anymore. The place they once occupied in worship is empty. It is a phenomenon that dates back to the earthly ministry of Jesus: "many of his disciples turned away and no longer accompanied him."

The primary reason for the "religious dropout" remains the same from Jesus' day until ours: frustration and disappointment. There are present in every faith community people who turn to religion for some things the Christian faith never promised to provide. They expect in religion a kind of magical solution to their problems, anxieties, and illnesses and it hasn't worked out. Some expect that faithfulness to the church will protect them from job loss, marital discord, and safety from the violence in the world. Others look to the church to shelter their children from everything that is unpleasant and distasteful in the dominant culture. When they fail to receive what they were looking for, they are cool to religion and simply drop out.

After many who followed Jesus turned away, Jesus turned to his disciples and asked, "Do you also want to leave?" It is a good question for each one of us to ask. People who come to our churches expecting only to "get something" or find easy solutions will be frustrated and disappointed. Somehow they have missed that Jesus was betrayed, beaten, and crucified. As William Willimon once commented, why do the followers of Jesus expect to get off any better? What is required is a return to the promise that the faith has always made available: In Jesus Christ, God walks with us through the storms, difficulties, and struggles of life, strengthening us along the way. Life will take us to the depths. When we arrive, Jesus will be there. We are not alone.

God of new life, help me recover faith in your presence and love in the midst of life's struggles. Amen.

88

Unfinished Discipleship

"Every Scripture is inspired by God and is useful for teaching, for showing mistakes, for correcting, and for training character, so that the person who belongs to God can be equipped to do everything that is good."

2 Timothy 3:16, 17

There are people in the church who have a favorite hymn but not a favorite Scripture. They have picked out a favorite piece of music to feed their soul, but they do not have a favorite selection from the Bible to feed their mind. The soul is well nourished. The mind is not. Why would this be? I recall a woman telling me that she does not need to study the Bible. She studied the Bible formally in college classes. That was forty years ago! Asked what her favorite Scripture was, she responded, "To thine own self be true." That is not from the Bible. It is from the Shakespearean tragedy, Hamlet. Yet, she sings in the church choir each week. Classic, traditional church music feeds her soul, she told me. Nourishing the soul while neglecting the mind.

Paul writes to Timothy that God inspires Scripture for expanding the mind. The essential value of Scripture is to teach, show mistakes, for correcting, and for training character. Beautiful sacred music inspires and takes a weary soul to a place of rest and nourishment. That is important in the life of a disciple. However, it is not enough. Paul reminds us here, as he does in other places, that God created us for a purpose. God created each person to be useful to God. Scripture makes us useful. Scripture shapes us, forms us, and equips us to be participants in God's work in the world. Inspired by sacred music while lacking usefulness to God is unfinished discipleship.

We belong to God. Paul is clear on that point. Can you imagine staffing your business with people who lack the basic skill set to get the work done? Christian baptism is Kingdom staffing. Baptism is God's claim on us. God chooses us and provides the Bible as a training manual for equipping us to be useful. Baptism is also our promise. We promise to make God's work the very center of our life. That means that we will expand our capacities for accomplishing each task God places in our charge. Done well, God's Kingdom expands continually affecting positively more and more lives. That results in the exponential growth of God's purposes in the world. That is, if each newly baptized disciple is useful.

I am asking that you feed your mind daily on God's word in the Bible. Memorize passages that seem particularly meaningful. Throughout the day, as you go about other tasks, recall to mind those passages you have memorized. Think deeply about why that particular passage is important to you. That simple process accomplishes a big part of God's work in each person— reflecting on what God intends for us to hear from a portion of Scripture that resonates with us. Prayerfully ask two questions: "What would you have me hear, O Lord?" and "What would you have me do, O Lord?" Day after day, you will discover that God's Spirit is upon you, equipping you for God's good purposes in the world. That is what discipleship looks like.

Lord, I am frequently distracted from reading the Bible. Yet, I know that I make time for those things I most want to do. Stir my heart with a deep hunger for your word. Amen.

89

In the Silence We Hear, In the Stillness We See (Nathanael Hood)

"My heart is not proud, Lord, my eyes are not haughty; I do not concern myself with great matters or things too wonderful for me. But I have calmed and quieted myself, I am like a weaned child with its mother; like a weaned child I am content. Israel, put your hope in the Lord both now and forevermore."

PSALM 131

SINCE IT BEGAN EARLIER this year, the global Covid-19 quarantine has had some truly remarkable effects on nature and the environment. Earlier this month an international team of scientists announced that the sudden halting of, among other things, factory production and car usage has resulted in global carbon emissions dropping by 17 percent. All around the world this reduction has revealed itself in shocking, unexpected ways. The perennially smog-drenched skies of Los Angeles are clean and blue for the first time in many people's memories. The sediments traditionally churned up by Venetian boats have settled so completely that animal and plant life has returned to the city's formerly mud-choked waterways. In Delhi—the most polluted city on earth—pollution has dropped so drastically that residents can now see the stars at night. I've personally experienced the effect this quarantine has had on New York City: for the first time since moving to

Brooklyn almost three years ago, I can actually smell the salt water of the Atlantic Ocean.

Writer Julio Vincent Gambuto has described this period as the "Great Pause," and indeed it seems as if the entire world is holding its breath.[1] But it's not just the environment that's paused, it's life itself for billions of people. Jobs have been lost, leaving countless families in financial limbo. Close-knit communities have been disrupted as people have been forced to abandon public gatherings. Parents have been stressed as schools have closed, forcing them to provide 24/7 childcare even while working. Marriages have been strained and tested as some couples have been separated by hospitalizations and others cloistered together in tiny living spaces for months on end. And for those self-isolating in quarantine, the days themselves have become a blur, the days running into weeks, the weeks running into months. Is it Monday, Wednesday, or Saturday? March, April, or May? What does it matter when they all seem the same?

Yet this pause need not be a negative one. In a recent sermon, Rabbi David Edleson of Temple Sinai in South Burlington, Vermont explained thusly: "I think it is very tough for many if not most of us just to sit still, just to be home, to be present and to be content. This is a spiritual opportunity for growth. For stopping the focus on what we can't do, and finding ways to be more content doing nothing, or doing simple things with those with us." Indeed, the need for peace, silence, and nothingness is baked into the very DNA of the Abrahamic faiths whose God rested on the seventh day of creation. Our Scriptures are all filled with visions of quiet and calm, of sabbath rests and high holy days, of fasting and contemplation. When Jesus calmed the storm on the Sea of Galilee, he rebuked the very winds with the word "peace." Perhaps this "Great Pause" isn't a curse but an opportunity to draw closer to God.

Psalm 131, one of the shortest psalms in the Bible, provides one of the most striking visions of finding contentment in times of stillness and quiet. One of the fifteen Songs of Ascent—Psalms believed to be sung by worshippers traveling to Jerusalem during pilgrim festivals—celebrates calming oneself as an act of surrendering one's pride before God, and with it, one's anxieties about the present and future. This ego-destruction frees us from the illusion that we can control our destinies, and that we are therefore responsible for the unexpected catastrophes and uncontrollable setbacks in our lives (a delusion common in America's up-by-the-bootstraps culture). By submitting ourselves to the stillness of God, we release ourselves from

---

1. Gambuto, "Prepare For the Ultimate," April 14, 2020.

psychological self-bondage. In this way, we find contentment in peace that is healing, not distressing as we rest in a pause that is holy, not destructive.

Peace, O Jesus, we pray for peace in these times of stress and anxiety. Help us find solace in our stillness and contentment in our contemplation of your power and majesty. Remind us to put our hope in you just as the psalmist did on the steps leading to Jerusalem so many millennia ago. Amen.

90

Christ's Own Denial

"Jesus replied, 'My kingdom doesn't originate from this world. If it did, my guards would fight so that I wouldn't have been arrested by the Jewish leaders. My kingdom isn't from here.'"

JOHN 18:36

THIS IS A REMARKABLE passage of Scripture! Captured here is Jesus' own denial; Jesus' denial of sovereign territory, "My kingdom isn't from here." From inside the governor's house, a center of power for a defined territory, Jesus disclaims royal territory. Certainly, Jesus' denial is on the geographical level, his royal authority lies elsewhere. This confuses Pilate. For Pilate—and for us—sovereignty implies a specific place, such as the British Empire. That empire has clearly defined borders, though the contours have changed over history. Christ denies any claim to this kind of power or rule. Incredibly, Christ seems to be placing his credibility on the line.

Many are well familiar with Peter's denial. On the night of Jesus' arrest, Peter denies three times ever knowing the man, Jesus. Yet, that same night, Jesus is also making a denial. The difference between Peter's denial and Jesus' own denial is not subtle. Peter's denial is about self-preservation; Peter fears arrest if he is honest about his relationship with Jesus. Jesus' denial is something much deeper than self-preservation. Jesus is pointing from the physical world to the spiritual. The exchange between Pilate and Jesus becomes a struggle between political power and spiritual power. Political power exerts its influence on people's outward behavior. Spiritual power changes people from the inside.

One Easter morning a couple spoke to me following the first service. They said they had lived only a few blocks from the church for years and had never worshipped with us before that morning. They continued by sharing that though they had not worshipped before they were always grateful that the church was here. Politely and carefully, I asked, "Why?" "Why were they grateful that the church was here?" Their answer is, "Each day the church reminds us that there is something more." They promised to return and then proceeded to walk down the street—presumably to their home. Spiritual power is about something more than the eye can see, "My kingdom isn't from here."

Jesus' denial is all about lifting our eyes above political alliances, carefully defined and defended borders, and self-preservation. Jesus wants, "something more" for each of us. Political power bends a people to the will of the state. Spiritual power molds and shapes a people to the wholeness God once fashioned at creation but lost through rebellion and estrangement from God. Jesus' confrontation with our political systems, in the form of Pilate, suggests that his kingship not only challenges the political state, but it also judges and calls into question the ability of the state to provide the life God desires for us. It would appear in the crucifixion of Jesus that Pilate won, that the political systems of the day have the upper hand. Nevertheless, the resurrection remains only a few days away.

Holy God, teach me today how to worship! Grant that I might understand the things of real value and commit my life to them. Amen.

91

Undefeated

"We know that God works all things together for good for the ones who love God, for those who are called according to his purpose."

ROMANS 8:28

RECENTLY, THE CAPTAIN OF the Ruby Princess, of the Princess Cruise Line, made this disembarkation announcement to the crew who were leaving the ship due to the disruption of cruising by the Covid-19 virus: "This invisible virus has incredible power. We can't see it but we see the results of what it is doing. One thing, though, this virus cannot do; one thing in this virus that makes it imperfect. This virus can't break us. This virus actually has one design flaw. It makes us stronger." From our struggle and pain with this pandemic, communities are coming together, a great resilience is emerging, and people are experiencing strength unnoticed before. We are becoming the kind of people and the kind of world that the power and goodness of God have set out to make from the beginning of time.

Disruption is underway—a disruption that is deeper and more profound than the economic and political narratives that receive nearly uninterrupted coverage in the news. The sheer magnitude of this crisis is forcing a personal and cultural "repentance" or reexamination of those things that have ultimate worth and value in our lives. A strong economy failed to protect us from the ravages of this unseen virus. Political ideology is powerless to turn back the pain, suffering, and death left in its path. Misplaced priorities and values are exposed as having insufficient value for adding richness and depth to life. What remains are the questions as old as the Scriptures—questions of purpose and meaning and love.

First responders have brought fresh clarity to the values of compassion, cooperation, and confidence in an unseen power and strength to change lives and communities. New Yorkers, and other municipalities, celebrate these values each day by stepping onto balconies and the street to applaud the new heroes among us as they struggle to save lives impacted by this virus. This crisis presents an opportunity to build a different life moving forward, a life where we immerse ourselves more deeply into the lives of our spouses and children, a life where we seek opportunities to help vulnerable people in need of support and love, a life that is less about placing self first and more about caring for our neighbor.

A pastor of another generation, Phillips Brooks, wrote that we should not pray for easy times. Rather, pray for strength, courage, and grace enough to meet hard times and come off victorious.[1] If we long for a return to the normal that was prior to this virus we are already defeated. The apostle Paul would urge, rather, that we keep our eyes fixed upon the living God who is at work in the midst of this pandemic, working for our good. This pandemic is not a good thing by any measure. Nor is it the work or will of God. But Scripture bears witness that God was always present in the very center of a crisis, working to bring God's people through stronger, more confident, and with a new appreciation for what really matters in life.

Lord, enable me to see that in the midst of the challenges, difficulties, and disappointments I struggle with, you are right there with me, loving me and strengthening me. Amen.

---

1. Brooks, *Twenty Sermons*, 330.

92

When You Don't Know

"Don't be conformed to the patterns of this world, but be transformed by the renewing of your minds so that you can figure out what God's will is—what is good and pleasing and mature."

ROMANS 12:2

My wife, Grace, and I celebrated our twenty-fifth wedding anniversary with an eight-day Caribbean cruise. That was in November of 2012—four months after beginning a new ministry that took me from the Philadelphia area to Delray Beach, Florida. The last day was a sea day, the ship making its way back to Port Everglades, Fort Lauderdale, Florida. Placing an assortment of oatmeal cookies and chocolate chip cookies on a plate someone approached me, thrusting his hand toward me for a handshake, and said, "Hello Dr. Hood." Naturally, I was startled. I am on a cruise ship of nearly three thousand strangers. Who could possibly know me? The stranger continued, "I am a member of the First Presbyterian Church of Delray Beach. I saw you board the ship. I've been watching you during this cruise. I wanted to see what kind of man you were when you didn't know you were being watched."

That is a good question for any of us. What kind of man, what kind of woman are we when we don't know we are being watched? This question reminds me of a presidential race several decades ago. Suspicion whirred around one candidate, suspicion about his private life and fidelity to his marriage vows. The candidate boldly told the press, "Follow me. Watch me!" Apparently, he didn't believe they would. They did. And he was caught being unfaithful to his wife. That was the end of his presidential run. What kind of man, what kind of woman are we when we don't know we are being watched? It is a good question.

The apostle Paul teaches us in his letter to the Roman Church that each of our lives is being molded and shaped by one of two forces, either by the world or by God. The world has its patterns and desires which would shape our lives and God has another pattern and desire for us. Fortunately, says Paul, we have a choice in the matter. It is a matter of where our attention is focused. Attention to the values and priorities of the world will result in feelings of scarcity, a fear that there is simply not enough to go around. Our response becomes one of struggle—wrestling with others to ensure our fair share. Attention to God and God's values and priorities results in concern for others and generosity. The world will create a man or woman that is selfish, self-centered, and fearful. God creates a man or woman that is secure in God's care and embodies hope for the future. Again, teaches Paul, that we have the freedom to choose.

The Christian life is a life lived in, through, and for God. Attention to God through regular prayer, reading the Bible, and intentional practices of obedience to what we hear in Scripture increasingly conforms us to the image of Christ. Neglect of these things thrusts us into a default position of being conformed to the brokenness and disintegration of the world. Over time, we become someone who lives in the dark, fearful that someone will see what we are ashamed of. The apostle Paul is urging the church to recognize the negative and destructive forces of the world that seek to grasp us and shape us. "Don't be conformed to the patterns of this world," writes Paul. Rather, "be transformed by the renewing of your minds." That is accomplished by living into a relationship with God. It is then we are not ashamed of what others see when we don't know we are being watched. My conversation with the man on the ship ended that day with his gentle and gracious comment, "I look forward to you being my pastor, Dr. Hood."

Gracious and loving God, thank you for intertwining my life with the life of Jesus through prayer and the reading of the Bible. Make of my life one that is whole, gracious, and never ashamed. Amen.

93

Breaking and Remaking the Temple—Faith in a Time of Rioting (Nathanael Hood)

"At that moment the curtain of the temple was torn in two from top to bottom. The earth shook, the rocks split ... "

MATTHEW 27:51

ONCE AGAIN, WITHIN OUR lifetimes, our country is torn by civil unrest. Enflamed by widely disseminated smartphone footage of a Minneapolis police officer kneeling on the neck of George Floyd, an unarmed black man, until he suffocated to death, organized protests have popped up in more than two hundred cities demonstrating against police brutality. For many, particularly those in minority communities, the George Floyd killing was the final straw: memories of Rodney King in Los Angeles, Michael Brown in Ferguson, Eric Garner in New York City, Breonna Taylor in Louisville, and untold more have boiled over into an angry wave of civil disobedience. While the vast majority of the protestors have been nonviolent—living less than a mile from Barclays in Brooklyn, one of the national hotspots for the demonstrations, I can personally attest to this—there has still been looting, vandalism, and the wholesale destruction of property on the part of many so-called "activists." And while many police have acted responsibly and even admirably—in several cities officers have actually marched with and demonstrated alongside the protestors—there are still widespread reports of unprovoked police violence such as the use of rubber bullets against non-protesting bystanders and tear gas toward accredited members of the press.

Social media has been awash with images of the unrest, and several are undoubtedly bound for the history books. But one of the most powerful, in my opinion, shows the walls of St. Patrick's Cathedral in New York City on the morning of May 30 after demonstrators desecrated them with antipolice slogans the night before. It's an image to make one pause: here's one of the oldest, grandest, and most sacred cathedrals in America, one which since its initial dedication has seen two World Wars, twenty-seven presidents, and countless worshippers baptized, married, and eulogized. Images like these shatter the aura of timelessness surrounding our holy spaces, reminding us of their presence in the eternal now. The church's eyes might be lifted towards the eternal, but these pictures force us to remember and reexamine God's mission in our everyday lives. So yes, the graffiti is a tragedy. One day the spray paint will be washed away and St. Patrick's Cathedral will seem as timeless as ever. But right now it—and the rest of the Christian community—is on the frontline of these riots.

How then should we react to these demonstrations? First, we must remember that civil disobedience and nonviolent protest are baked into the very DNA of Christianity. Jesus himself preached in the shadow of a violent colonizing force. His teachings flipped the societal status quo on its head, forcing the authorities to acknowledge the humanity of their subjects even as they repressed them. Consider Jesus' command to turn the other cheek: by doing so, victims would force assailants to strike them a second time with the palm of their right hand (the left hand being unclean and unsuitable for striking), which in the customs of ancient Rome signified them as socioeconomic equals. We must also remember that destruction need not be a profane act. In fact, destruction is frequently a prelude to renewal. Remember that upon Jesus' death, the Temple in Jerusalem was struck by an earthquake, the Temple curtain being torn asunder and the very stones smashed apart. The old ways needed to be destroyed before they could be restored with God's new covenant. But—and this is important—nowhere do the Gospels say that anyone in the Temple was harmed or killed. In stark contradiction, the violent upheaval of the Temple led to the breaking of tombs and the resurrection of many "holy people" who returned to Jerusalem and "appeared to many people." (Matthew 27:52, 53) The destruction sanctified and gave life, it did not take it.

Perhaps we would do well to remember the teachings of Martin Luther King Jr., one of the architects of the American Civil Rights Movement. In a speech given at Stanford University in 1967, King famously reflected on the widespread rioting that ravaged the country. "I think America must see that riots do not develop out of thin air. Certain conditions continue to exist in our society which must be condemned as vigorously as we condemn riots," he declared. He then delivered one of his most shocking (and frequently decontextualized) statements: "But in the final analysis, a riot is the language of the unheard. And what is it that America has failed to hear?" When we see the riots in our streets, the protests, the demonstrations—and yes, even the vandalism and destruction—we Christians must ask ourselves what we have failed to hear. What must we do to restore the Temple now that it's being smashed again? How do we preserve and protect life without denying it?

We pray to you, great God, for peace and restoration in these terrible times. Bring your justice and mercy to the protestors and the police. Protect us from ourselves and from each other. Let these be merely growing pains in the continued development of your work here on this earth. Amen.

94

When God Says No

> *"Then he went a short distance farther and fell to the ground. He prayed that, if possible, he might be spared the time of suffering. He said, 'Abba, Father, for you all things are possible. Take this cup of suffering away from me. However—not what I want but what you want.'"*
>
> MARK 14:35, 36

I REMEMBER IT WELL. It was two days before Christmas. All the gifts for our children had been purchased, wrapped, and placed under the family Christmas tree. I had the day off and invited my four-year-old daughter, Rachael, to join me in enjoying the holiday decorations at the local mall and lunch in the food court. In one brief moment, she was no longer by my side—something in the mall bookstore caught her eye and she was gone. As I entered the bookstore, Rachael presented me with a Barbie Doll calendar. She saw it from the mall. "Please, daddy, will you buy this for me?" Two thoughts swiftly took residence in my mind: First, I could hear my wife making fun of me, "Christmas is two days away, and you bought her a gift?" My defense would be simple and honest, "You were not there looking into those four-year-old, imploring eyes." The second thought was more profound. It shook me. And it caused me considerable pain. For the next fourteen years, until she was an adult, I would have to look into those same eyes and, on many occasions, answer, "No." This one moment became an easy "Yes."

Parenting isn't for the faint of heart. Certainly, it is filled with considerable joy, warmth, and love. But there is also pain. Some of that pain is from looking into the eyes of a child, deeply loved, and answering, "No." Children can't see what parents see. They do not have the deeper understanding of life that parents possess. The consequences of a poorly chosen, "Yes" are not understood. Responsible parenting sometimes demands, looking into the eyes of your child, and answering, "No." Children will not always understand. They will be disappointed. Occasionally, they may express both anger and sadness. The flood of emotions experienced and expressed, is unpleasant for both child and parent. But love, on occasion, demands, "No."

Jesus teaches us to pray, in the Lord's Prayer, to pray to our spiritual parent, "Our Father who is in heaven (Matthew 6:9)." Here, on the night that Jesus would be arrested, Jesus prays. In the shadows of the night, alone in a garden, Jesus addresses his father, "Abba, Father," which literally means, "Daddy." Jesus, the Son of God, is frightened, on his knees in a garden, and begins his "ask" of his Father, "Please, Daddy." What is God to do? As Christians, we know well that an answer of "Yes" would prevent Jesus' suffering and death. It would also mean our destruction. For without the cross, each of us would be held accountable for our sins. There would be no forgiveness. Jesus is pleading. What is God to do? God answers his Son, "No."

Someone has taught Christians a lie. Someone taught Christians that fervent, deeply felt and faithful prayers to God would always be answered with a, "Yes." That promise is never made in the Bible. What is promised is that God hears every prayer. What is promised is that God draws near to us in prayer. And, additionally, what is promised is that there is nothing, absolutely nothing, which will ever separate us from God's love. But God sees what we cannot see. God understands more deeply what we cannot understand. And it is precisely because of that love that God has for us that, sometimes, God's answer is "No."

Once more, O God, so embrace me today in your loving arms that your presence, and love, are unmistakable. Particularly, when your answer must be, "No." Amen.

95

Never Alone

"Even when I walk through the darkest valley, I fear no danger because you are with me. Your rod and your staff—they protect me."

Psalm 23:4

Every parent knows what it is like to be awakened in the middle of the night by the cry of a child. "Daddy, there are monsters under my bed," my daughter, Rachael insisted. "No, sweetheart, there are no monsters under your bed." "How do you know?" "I'll turn on the lights and together we will take a look." Not only under the bed, but we also looked in her closet and under the pile of clothes, Rachael promised her mom she would pick up and put away properly. "No monsters." I kissed my daughter goodnight—again—and I turned off her light and returned to bed.

Years later and a little older, Rachael had other fears but was less willing to voice them. Fortunately, parents develop the capacity to notice little nuances here and subtleties there that betray their child's fears. Parents stumble over an appropriate response—a response that protects the child's dignity while comforting the fears. Words are often used. Words of reason, words of encouragement, words of assurance that everything will turn out exactly as it should be. And then, one day Rachael arrived at a place where she was able to tell me exactly what she needed, "Would you stay with me?" "Yes, yes, of course, I will stay with you."

Then the day arrived all too soon, the day I would drop my daughter off for college. After her mother and I helped her move her things into her dormitory room, toured the campus, and said our goodbyes, my wife and I went to dinner without our daughter. I remember that day well. My wife, Grace, and I were seated at a Longhorn Steakhouse restaurant, and menus were placed in our hands. There was an empty chair at the table, one always occupied by Rachael. One glance at the empty chair and the tears flowed. I sobbed.

The tears were less about missing my daughter, though I certainly was missing her. I sobbed because I now understood that I wouldn't be there when Rachael sensed monsters under her bed. I wouldn't be there to take her hand when life became less certain. I wouldn't be there when she simply needed me to "stay with her." Moravian College was only an hour away but it seems so much further when it's your child that is now starting out on their own. I had only one thing I could do now for my daughter. I prayed. "Keep your promise, God. When Rachael steps into that dark place, be with her. Your rod and staff, use them to guide her and protect her. I am calling you out, Oh, God, on your promise."

Father, I am so grateful that there is no road that I can take, no uncertainty I may encounter that I must travel alone. I claim this promise for each member of my family. Amen.

96

The Allure of a Defeated Life

"I was given a thorn in my body."
2 Corinthians 12:7

Few things are as unfortunate as to see a woman or man losing heart and all sense of hope, drifting into apathy, and finally despair. When a sense of defeat is permitted to take residence in life, frustration and inaction are too frequently the results. The face becomes sullen, the head is held low, and the shoulders sag. Bitterness grows, the result of an erroneous belief that life has dealt a raw deal or that others have received better opportunities. Left unchecked, the self-pity sentences them to low levels of achievement. A strange comfort is found in simply giving up—experiencing a certain allure of being defeated.

History is replete with men and women who have experienced hardship, anguished over setbacks, and struggled with handicaps—physical, mental, and emotional. Anyone of them may have been resentful and rebellious—and many have—with bad behavior the consequence. Yet, there are others who rise above the circumstances of their lives, press forward with unbelievable determination and consecrate their lives to the service of others. The apostle Paul stands among them. Paul moved through life hindered by "a thorn in the body" but produced nearly two-thirds of our New Testament.

Rather than giving up and accepting defeat, Paul labored under his handicap. Naturally, Paul—like any of us—preferred that the handicap be corrected, the difficulty removed. On three occasions Paul asked the Lord for this. But the handicap remained; the thorn wasn't removed. But Paul's prayers were answered. "My grace is enough for you," answered God. With God's answer, Paul committed himself to do the very best he could do with what he had. His life and ministry were a vessel of hope for everyone he encountered. To his children, Theodore Roosevelt continually cultivated a hopeful disposition—and in doing so charged the atmosphere of his home with hope.

Paul sought to demonstrate in his life that there is no limitation, no misfortune, no burden of sorrow, suffering, or loss that the human spirit cannot rise above. He endured much of each. But Paul went deeper than self-discipline and self-determination. Paul triumphed over it all because he sought God. Perhaps this was the finest message that Paul left the church—that when the allure of defeat tempts the heart Paul calls us to that deeper place where our life is open to the grace and power of Almighty God.

Heavenly Father, forgive me when I choose hopelessness rather than hope, despair rather than confidence in your love when confronted with difficulty. Amen.

97

Smash Your Statues, Drown Your Idols (Nathanael Hood)

> *"When he got near the camp and saw the bull calf and the dancing, Moses was furious. He hurled the tablets down and shattered them in pieces at the foot of the mountain. He took the calf that they had made and burned it in a fire. Then he ground it down to crushed powder, scattered it on the water, and made the Israelites drink it."*
>
> Exodus 32:19, 20

Every November 13th in Bristol, England, schoolchildren are given large sweet buns mixed with dried fruits and tasty spices. These massive buns come with eight wedge marks, all the better for breaking off and sharing with other children and their families. It's a fine lesson in practical charity, and the buns themselves are named after Edward Colston, one of the most noted philanthropists in Bristol's history. When he died in 1721 he left a legacy of giving that continues to this day—walk the streets of Bristol and you'll see buildings, schools, and churches founded or sponsored by Colston still bearing his name. The one thing you won't see, at least anymore, is the statue of Colston that used to stand in the city's center, as it was toppled, desecrated, and shoved into the nearby harbor on June 7, 2020, by protestors enraged by the police murder of George Floyd in the United States. Edward Colston, benefactor of Bristol, model of Christian charity, and namesake of a delicious children's treat, made his fortune selling kidnapped Africans into slavery.

We live in the midst of a literal historical reckoning. As millions spill into the streets the world over to protest police brutality and anti-black violence, people are taking long, hard looks at their countries' histories and reconsidering who is worth revering. These "reconsiderations" are particularly pronounced here in America, a land still steeped in legacies of racial hatred and mob violence. Statues of colonizers and slaveholders dot our public buildings and national landmarks, and even now there remain an estimated eighteen hundred monuments, statues, and official symbols memorializing the Confederacy (most of which, tellingly, were erected during the Jim Crow era to intimidate newly freed black communities). And now many of these are getting the Colston treatment. In Richmond, Virginia a statue of Robert E. Lee was desecrated with graffiti. In New Orleans, a bust of John McDonogh, public school patron, and slave magnate, was toppled and smashed. And in Boston, a famous statue of Christopher Columbus, one of the greatest butchers in human history, was beheaded.

The point of these protests isn't to erase history, but to tear down the false idols erected to enshrine false legacies. How can any nation that purports to believe in egalitarian equality dedicate public space to men who enslaved their fellow human beings or fought a war to keep them in shackles? In the Book of Exodus, we can find an eerie parallel to our current national crisis of conscience when the Israelites, fresh from a four-hundred-year captivity in Egypt, turned from the God who freed them and erected a golden calf while Moses was on Mount Sinai. This golden calf was more than just an idol, as some scholars believe it was an Apis Bull, an object of cult worship in Egypt. It would seem that just as the Israelites grumbled in the desert for the bread and meat of their captors, they grumbled too for their gods. Just as we in the West cling to the imagined legacy of charitable slaveholders and magnanimous colonizers, the Israelites clung to an imagined history of prosperity in bondage.

Moses' response was swift, brutal, and effective. Not only did he destroy the golden calf, but he also had it crushed, mixed with water, and consumed by its worshippers. They were, quite literally, forced to choke on their blasphemous idolatry. So now must we in the West also choke on our own false worship. In particular, we as a larger Christian community must stand as an example and follow Moses' example and exorcise the false idols of white supremacy and racial violence from our pasts. Though we believe in the sanctity of all God's children and the ultimate salvation of all who truly repent of their sins and follow Jesus—slaveholders and colonizers included—there's no reason to preserve their legacies of bloodshed and terror.

It's not just the moral thing to do, it's the biblical thing to do. It's time we cast our idols into the harbor next to the golden calf and Edward Colston.

O God, lift the fog of idolatry from our eyes and guide us to reconcile with our pasts so we may achieve a better, brighter, and more just future. In Jesus' name, we pray. Amen.

98

A Life Trained By Christ

"Train yourself for a holy life!"

1 TIMOTHY 4:7B

A PHYSICIAN ONCE TAUGHT me an important lesson about spiritual growth—there is simply no substitute for regularly paying attention to God. He shared this story with me. In the midst of a successful practice as a doctor, he had little time for his wife, and for his children. Seventy and eighty-hour workweeks were customary. He loved his patients. He loved his work. Time at home was for rest and renewal for the next day. Dinners with his family were rare. Hard work seemed to pay dividends. His salary rose steadily each year. Admiration for him and his exceptional work held a privileged position in the community. Everything seemed right until it did not. Both his wife and his children had found a way to get on in life without him. "The day I realized that was the most painful day of my life," the doctor said.

The doctor held a stethoscope in his hand. "Perhaps, this is the most important tool for a physician's work," he shared. Doctors study and train to know how to listen to a patient with this tool. What is supremely important is to know what "regular" sounds like when we hold the stethoscope to a patient's chest or back. If the doctor does not know what "regular" sounds like, then the doctor simply does not know what they are listening to with a patient seated in front of them. Doctors must learn well what "regular" sounds like so when using a stethoscope, they can recognize immediately what sounds "irregular." Once an "irregular" comes through the stethoscope, a decision, with the patient, is required. This one part of practicing medicine is all about listening carefully, listening correctly.

"I was failing at listening carefully to my life, to my family," said the doctor. "Then, I almost lost them." "That terrified me." The difficulty was that I did not know what "regular" was, or what "regular" sounded like as a part of a family. Here is a man who is an excellent doctor but is a poor husband and father. Training was required. Good training is about consistent, regular effort over time. Good training demands the proper tools. "I went back to school," said the doctor. The textbook was the Bible. The classroom was a chair in his backyard for one hour at the close of every day. Reading the Bible every evening, the doctor learned what "regular" sounded like. Then he listened carefully to his own life, his daily practices, and his priorities. What the doctor heard was irregular.

It is remarkable what listening to God will do for a life. A "regular" life, a healthy life, is a lived experience of faith in God. Practices change and as practices change, a reshaping occurs. Each life that listens carefully to God, in regular time reading the Bible and prayer, redevelops from the inside out. Such a life embodies more and more the way of Jesus. Trust in God increases, persistent hope in the coming of God's reign expands, and love overcomes hatred and selfishness. Life moves from unhealthy "instinctual reactions" to learned behaviors—behaviors that enter the heart from habitual practice in the way of Christ. This is a trained life. A life trained by Christ.

Holy God, teach me this day to listen deeply to your word in the Bible. Scatter the many distractions that assail me that I may hear clearly your guidance and follow. Amen.

99

The Gift of Encouragement

"So continue encouraging each other and building each other up, just like you are doing already."

1 Thessalonians 5:11

In the January, 2020 issue of *Runner's World* magazine, a woman shares her struggle to complete the New York City Marathon. Halfway through the twenty-six-mile run, personal resources ran out. Physical and emotional resources depleted, she would walk to the sidelines and drop out. Except, there were people on the sidelines. Strangers to her. Moreover, not one of them would let her stand with them on the side of the street. They were not rude. Rather, they shouted, cheered, and pushed her forward with words of encouragement. Strangers would not allow her to quit. She finished the marathon in last place. However, she finished the race!

That is the business of the church! We encourage people not to give up on the race. We shout words of encouragement. We urge them to continue, particularly when it is difficult. We do so in the certain confidence of God's strength that never falters. Showing up for worship is a shout from the sidelines. Serving in some ministry, alongside others, is a shout from the sidelines. Financial giving to ensure that the church continues to move forward is a shout from the sidelines. Paying attention to others, listening deeply, and caring with an expansive heart, is a shout-out from the sidelines.

Each is a real and meaningful means of urging people forward when they face every kind of struggle, difficulty, and challenge.

Some years ago, the distinguished Christian thinker and teacher, Lesslie Newbigin taught that the primary task of the Christian is engagement. Preaching is important. Teaching is important. However, the primary task of the Christian is deep and meaningful engagement in the lives of those we encounter every day. What the church preaches and what the church teaches is not the primary concern of most people. What is most urgent in the lives of the common person is the question "Is there someone who cares?" Authentic engagement in the life of another, championing them through difficulty, create a ripple effect that changes multitudes of lives.

The single greatest mistake that Christians make is the assumption that their faith is a private matter. Such an assumption directs the believer down the path of selfishness. Comments such as, "I can be a good Christian without going to church" reveals that selfishness. As Newbigin argues—and as the apostle Paul asserts here in his letter to the Thessalonian Church—Christians are to gather so that they may mutually encourage one another. Demonstrations of care, support, and encouragement are shouts from the sidelines to those discouraged and defeated by life. These "shoutouts" become enough for those whose own resources have become depleted to finish the race.

Gracious God, grant me the opportunity to elevate and encourage another person. I want to see others as people precious to you. Deliver me from all pettiness and selfish compulsions so that I may love others deeply. Amen.

100

Stuck Like Stockdale (Nathanael Hood)

> "Now, compelled by the Spirit, I'm going to Jerusalem. I don't know what will happen to me there. What I do know is that the Holy Spirit testifies to me from city to city that prisons and troubles await me. But nothing, not even my life, is more important than my completing my mission. This is nothing other than the ministry I received from the Lord Jesus: to testify about the good news of God's grace."
>
> ACTS 20:22–24

ON SEPTEMBER 9, 1965, naval pilot James Bond Stockdale was shot down while flying a mission over North Vietnam. Forced to eject from his disabled plane, Stockdale parachuted down into a village where the inhabitants brutally beat him and turned him over to the North Vietnamese as a prisoner of war. For the next seven-and-a-half years he was held in the Hỏa Lò Prison—the notorious "Hanoi Hilton"—where he held the dubious honor of being the most senior naval officer in captivity. During this time he and his fellow captives (including future senator John McCain) were savagely tortured, starved, and interrogated. Their treatment was so severe that inmates took it for granted that they'd eventually be broken through torture and forced to make anti-American statements. New arrivals were coached by other prisoners to do whatever it took to survive. "But you first must take physical torture," they were solemnly warned.

As an officer, Stockdale's captivity was particularly brutal; when he was repatriated in 1973 as part of Operation Homecoming he couldn't stand upright or walk. But he nevertheless maintained what little composure he could, implementing a code of conduct for his fellow prisoners and routinely disfiguring himself so he couldn't be used for North Vietnamese propaganda. Reflecting on his captivity in later years, Stockdale explained his mindset to business writer James C. Collins for his book *Good to Great*. He said that the prisoners who didn't survive the Hilton were the optimists, the ones who believed that they'd be rescued or freed in no time. He explained that the key to withstanding extreme hardship was brutal realism: "You must never confuse faith that you will prevail in the end—*which you can never afford to lose*—with the discipline to confront the most brutal facts of your current reality, whatever they might be." [Emphasis added] Collins would term this seemingly contradictory duality of hope and realism as the Stockdale Paradox.

Around the world, millions, if not literally billions, of people are finding themselves in another form of captivity while under quarantine for Covid-19. The physical, mental, and psychological effects have been staggering. According to federal studies, binge drinking among those trying to self-medicate has skyrocketed. Many living alone have found themselves trapped in impromptu solitary confinement. Domestic violence has exploded around the world and with it a new wave of divorces and separations. Unemployment rates not seen since the Great Depression have thrown the lives and welfare of tens of millions of Americans into chaos, anxiety, and disarray. And with so many governments, both local and federal, domestic and international, treating the pandemic with a hands-off attitude exacerbated by widespread distrust of the scientific establishment, the global rate of infection doesn't show any signs of slowing down.

To weather this storm, we Christians need to take a good, hard look at the Stockdale Paradox. We will not be able to pray this away, and neither will the virus suddenly vanish overnight. It will take great discipline and fortitude to make it to the other side. For guidance, we can turn to the Apostle Paul, who in the book of Acts racks up one of the most prominent records of suffering in Scripture, being arrested, imprisoned, and shipwrecked numerous times. Paul was never deterred from his calling to spread the Gospel, but neither was he unrealistic about its cost. While preparing to depart for Jerusalem in the twentieth chapter, he explained that he fully expected another round of imprisonment. That was the harsh reality. But the hope that tempered it—the hope Stockdale would insist on almost two millennia later—is the grace and strength of Jesus Christ. May we find the same strength and comfort as we steel ourselves for the worst to come.

Gracious God, grant us the courage and fortitude to weather life's storms of injustice and circumstance. Help us to never forget that you are our savior and protector, even when things seem their worst. Amen.

101

Brokenness at Christmas

"Joseph her husband was a righteous man. Because he didn't want to humiliate her, he decided to call off their engagement quietly."
MATTHEW 1:19

THOMAS LONG TAUGHT A three-week class, *Preaching the Gospel of Matthew*, during the summer of 1992. On the first day, we were assigned homework that seemed daunting—prepare for the next day a mini-biography of each name in Matthew's genealogy, which begins his Gospel. Each student worked late into the night in the Princeton Seminary Library, occasionally looking up at one another to gauge one another's reactions to the surprises we were uncovering. As we proceeded with name after name in the family tree of Jesus Christ, it seemed we were reading the scandal page of one of those sensationalist newspapers found in larger cities. Sprinkled throughout the bloodline of Jesus were checkered people: Rahab, the prostitute, Ruth, that brazen Moabite, and King David himself, father of a son with another man's wife. Brokenness abounded!

If we are honest, many of our families are much like Jesus' family. Sprinkled throughout our bloodline are scandals, betrayal, addictions, and moral failure. My paternal grandmother was an alcoholic, who lost her marriage due to her addiction, my father, as a teenager, attempted suicide as a result of a mother who couldn't raise him and a stepmother, who wouldn't, and, eventually, was raised by a grandmother. My mother's father abandoned a wife and children to begin another family that she would become part of and mental health issues—including a struggle with depression—etched their mark upon both her and her brother. For most of my life, I have struggled with depression. Brokenness is an unwelcomed guest that many of our families are familiar with. The common challenge is to overcome our embarrassment and to look for God's wondrous power to transform each one of us.

Joseph struggled as we do. He is engaged to Mary and had reason to believe that the wedding would proceed according to the tradition and custom of his Jewish faith tradition. Then, Mary is pregnant with a child that is not his. Soon, Mary would be showing. Careful wedding plans have now gone awry. Joseph must have felt betrayal, embarrassment, and anger. What is he to do? On one hand, Joseph, being a righteous man, could not tolerate his fiancée's apparent infidelity. The law and personal honor demanded that he break off the engagement. There seemed to be no other option. On the other hand, Joseph loved Mary and could not imagine her suffering the indignity and ridicule that would be hers by a public separation on the charge of infidelity. So what does Joseph do? A quiet separation would protect both Mary's welfare and Joseph's honor.

Then, God gives Joseph a new commandment, "a new and higher law," writes Thomas Long, that required "a new and higher righteousness": "Joseph son of David, don't be afraid to take Mary as your wife, because the child she carries was conceived by the Holy Spirit."[1] Here was an invitation to shatter the confines of a law absent of grace and become a genuinely righteous man that moves toward others, including his fiancée, with embracing love. Rigid obedience to the law cannot and should not stand in the way of God's mercy. In the chancel of First Presbyterian Church of Delray Beach is a beautiful stained-glass window. Someone in worship once commented to me that the beauty of that window provided comfort each week. Yet, one must not overlook that the beauty of that window is created from shards of broken glass painstakingly reassembled by the hand of a master artist.

Forgive me, O Lord, when my failures and the failures of others prevent me from loving myself and others as you love in the person of Jesus. With the hand of a Master Artist, work beauty from the brokenness in my life. Amen.

---

1. Long, *Matthew*, 13.

102

Instant Family

> *"In the same way, when we were minors, we were also enslaved by this world's system. But when the fulfillment of the time came, God sent his Son, born through a woman, and born under the Law. This was so he could redeem those under the Law so that we could be adopted."*
>
> GALATIANS 4:3–5

INSTANT FAMILY, A 2018 American comedy film starring Mark Wahlberg and Rose Byrne, weaves a story of a married couple considering the option of adopting a child. The hopeful parents are brought to an adoption fair where they have the opportunity to meet children they may consider adopting. As the story unfolds, the couple becomes foster parents to three siblings, one a teenager—foster care a requirement on the journey towards adoption. As foster parents, there are laws that govern the dynamics of the relationship they will have with the children. One such law is that children's cell phones cannot be taken away. Although this "new" family initially experiences joy, it doesn't take long for things to get hectic. Though the movie is a heart-warming comedy, it does grapple honestly with the struggles and difficulties that are a part of any family, particularly with an "instant" family like this one.

We were very much like the three children in the movie. The three children were in a foster system with its own regulations and rules and we were in "this world's system" with laws that made claims upon us. The Apostle Paul writes that we were "enslaved" to the world's way of looking at things. We are no stranger to how the world sees things; to the values that shape a world's outlook on life. The worship of money, the passionate pursuit of success and position, and the desire for comforts found in ease, food, and drink form the tapestry of a world outlook. Initially, that outlook may not appear to be enslavement. It all seems to be quite attractive, particularly to those who are still striving for them. Yet, with all the promises of happiness with this outlook, those who are honest will confess to a deep-seated dissatisfaction with life. What remains is a hope for something more.

In the movie, *Instant Family*, the three children desire something more than foster care with all of its rules, restrictions, and uncertainty. Realizing how much they love and care for the three children, the couple also longs for something more, something deeper. Eventually, they all gather for a court hearing to decide on the question of adoption. It has been a long, broken road to the court hearing but the three children and the couple all want to become a legal family. Love has gripped each of their hearts. The old system of foster care no longer brought deep satisfaction and joy. The adoption is finalized and the laws that governed foster care fall away. The relationship of the children to their adoptive parents will now be governed by a more generous and gracious dynamic. Each of the five begins the joyous discovery together of what it means to belong to each other.

In the person of Jesus Christ, our own enslavement to the world and its values has ended. We have been adopted as God's very own children. It is an adoption that has been secured by a God that desires something more for us, something less restrictive, and more gracious, something less uncertain, and more shaped by family ties. This adoption brings with it a new outlook on life, a new way of seeing things. Creation is the work of a purposeful God. It is not something to be exploited for personal gain but something that is to be managed well so that it may be a blessing for all people. The possibilities of human life are no longer limited by our own ingenuity and strength but are expanded by God's own creative purposes. Adoption releases us from the pursuit of meaning and happiness in material things and invites us to experience these things in relationships with others and with God. Those things that are valued by the world cannot satisfy and ultimately lead to brokenness and death. Attention to a relationship with loved ones and God is life and peace.

Help me, O God, to confront the values of this world that deny life and peace. Amen.

103

The Struggle to Doubt

"I know, Lord, that our lives are not our own, that we're not able to direct our paths."

JEREMIAH 10:23

MY EARLIEST MEMORY OF doubting God was as a young child. I received as a birthday gift a beautiful, leather-bound Bible. I had graduated from a children's Bible to a "real" Bible that was a joy to hold in my hand—the rich, supple, black leather with a genuine silk bookmark attached to the binding. The elegant pages were gilded with gold and the absence of pictures was, for me, the mark of a mature Bible. Continually, my brother, Wayne, and I heard from our parents that God's strength was their strength for daily living. Accepting my parents' faith as my own did not require any intentional decision from me. My belief in God was more organic, as I believe is true for most children living in a Christian home. Belief was a natural part of life—a life wrapped in demonstrations of trust in a loving God by parents who, for the most part, were happy. God was spoken of as a powerful force that has, in Jesus Christ, intruded on our lives with powerful love and care.

Then, one evening my parents came home with a puppy—a collie. Until he was housebroken, the puppy would be kept in a large cardboard box during the night. Even now I wonder if portable, home kennels were available in the late sixties. If they were available, why did we settle for a *cardboard* box? Nonetheless, the cardboard box proved to be a poor choice on the first night. The new addition to our family tipped over the box and had a delightful romp of the house. And, as any dog owner knows, puppies love to chew. That night, the chew toy of choice was my new, leather-bound Bible. I was devastated. More, I experienced doubt about the existence of an all-powerful God. Certainly, if God was real, God would have protected God's Holy Word to us from being consumed by a puppy! Everything my parents had built their life on seemed to be crumbling.

Yet, my first round with the experience of doubt in God quickly became a struggle. My parents' faith remained unshaken. More, my father—a layperson—began taking me with him as he visited members of the church, members experiencing a devastating loss of one kind or another, to read Scripture to them, pray with them, and love them. Even as a child—or because I was a child—I could clearly see hope returning in their eyes. Something greater than my father's presence and spoken words were happening in each home we visited. I had no answer to why God would allow a mere puppy to feast on God's beautifully bound word. But God kept showing up in my parents' life and the lives of those they loved in the name of Jesus Christ. I remained angry for longer than I should have about that chewed Bible. But doubting God became a burdensome struggle.

Thoughtful people today are pondering the significance of what is happening across the world. Time-honored political alliances are crumbling, terrorist organizations are multiplying, and the threat of nuclear war is once again disturbing our hopes for peace. Faith in God is now being asked to do some heavy lifting. An increasing number of people now look at the appalling amount of evil in the world and question how such things can be reconciled with the existence of a loving God. Perhaps the prophet Jeremiah has something of value to add to this conundrum: "I know, Lord, that our lives are not our own, that we're not able to direct our paths." Simply, we are not in charge. We may have certain expectations of how God should be at work in the world, like preventing puppies from making a chew-toy out of a leather Bible, but that is not ours to direct. God was God before us, is God now, and will be God tomorrow. So, it becomes a matter of where we direct our focus. Direct your gaze toward all the evil, hurt, and destruction in the world, and doubt wells up. Direct your gaze upon the eyes of those who are loved by Christ, in the midst of difficulties, and doubt struggles.

Holy God, I am not capable of understanding your work in the world. But you have demonstrated your love for me in the cross of Jesus Christ. May this be enough for me. Amen.

104

Sandcastles

"But everybody who hears these words of mine and doesn't put them into practice will be like a fool who built a house on sand. The rain fell, the floods came, and the wind blew and beat against that house. It fell and was completely destroyed."

MATTHEW 7:26, 27

HE IS KNOWN AS Mr. Sandman. Mark Mason traded his high-paying career in sales to make sandcastles. From every indication, he is doing very well with his new vocation. A recent issue of *Islands* magazine reports that companies like Disney and Coca-Cola hire Mark and his crew—Team Sandcastle—to build custom sand sculptures, some going for more than $100,000 a pop. Additionally, Mark's team builds sculptures for major personal events like wedding proposals. People are surprised when they learn that "building sandcastles" is Mark's profession. Mark understands. He told Sarah Sekula, writer for *Islands* magazine that he thinks the same thing. "It's just crazy cool!"[1]

Mark understands, of course, that everything he builds today has a very short life. Sandcastles crumble. High tide, rain, wind, and multiple other factors quickly and effectively remove all traces of Mark's skillful creations. Regardless of the size of the sculpture or its complexity, each one is

---

1. Sekula, "Mr. Sandman," 47.

temporary. It is simply the nature of the building material of choice. Some sand has greater firmness than other sand. Mark's preference is for the sand of the Bahamas with Grand Cayman a close second. But sand is sand. Eventually, it all washes away.

Matthew asks that we consider carefully the material we select when we build our life. Specifically, Matthew asks that we look closely at our foundation of choice when we build. Sand is a poor choice. Rain will fall, floods will appear and the wind will blow and beat against our lives. These things are inevitable, says Matthew. So consider carefully how you will build. We may build a life every bit as spectacular as the sculptures of Mr. Sandman. But if they are built on a foundation of sand, that life is only temporary. Such a life cannot stand in the storms of life.

There is a place for sandcastles. They are sometimes extraordinary and cause delight to beachgoers. But a sandy lot is no place to build a life. A life of greed is one built on a sandy lot. A life of immediate gratification and self-indulgence is one built on a sandy lot. A life of power and position or arrogance is a life built on a sandy lot. Rigid adherence to one political position without appreciating another viewpoint can be a sandy lot. Any of these may seem lovely for a moment. But torrential downpours will wipe it all away. The wise not only pay attention to God's Word, each day they secure the foundation of their lives by that word. And theirs will be a dwelling that even the greatest storms of life cannot shake.

Sandy lots are so appealing, O God. Forgive me when I seek to build my life upon wealth, arrogance, or anything else but your holy word in the Bible. Amen.

105

Ambition

"Whoever wants to be first among you will be the slave of all, for the human One didn't come to be served but rather to serve and to give his life to liberate many people."

MARK 10:44, 45

AMBITION—THAT RESTLESS IMPULSE THAT continually sets our eyes on more opportunity, more status, and more position—has been common from generation to generation. The love of self and the desire that others notice us is deep-seated in human nature. It may be one of the most elemental and voracious of all human appetites. Even among Jesus' disciples, we see the tightening grip of ambition upon the human psyche, James and John asking Jesus that he grant that they are allowed to sit, one on his right hand and the other on his left. It is careful choreography, competing for prestige and honor as though someone silently requests another for a nomination for the Nobel Peace Prize. It would be difficult to find a man or woman who hasn't given yield to the desire for more.

The impulse itself is neither good nor bad. The question is one of intention; is personal ambition driven by the desire for greater contribution or self-elevation? The young woman who works hard on a law degree so she may be useful to under-resourced people in the community has channeled her heart, energy, and intellect for the sake of others. *Doctors Without Borders* is staffed with medical doctors who are driven to respond quickly to medical humanitarian emergencies without any thought of personal enrichment. Jesus speaks to a wider and deeper motive of positive contribution in the parable of the talents: those who sought to increase the value of what they have for the sake of someone else pleases God. Those who are handicapped by concern for their own welfare will lose everything.

The disciples James and John were ambitious for the wrong reason. They were caught in the primitive craving to be seen, respected, and revered regardless of their fitness for the role they requested. They sought to look around and ask, "Who is bigger?" "Who is honored?" "Who has more?" Contribution seems to be absent in their desire to sit on either side of Jesus in God's Kingdom. There is a convulsive struggle that their personal hunger for importance is satisfied. The problem is a moral one. The pursuit of it corrupts character. The Bible grapples with it on nearly every page. And Jesus had a great deal to say about it.

Observe Jesus' reply to the disciples, "Whoever wants to be first among you will be slave of all." What a reversal of how ambition is understood! Here is a philosophy of life that has personal stature built upon the foundation of humility and contribution. For Jesus, nobody can be great until his or her life is driven by service to another. The highest ambition is not in jockeying for a position in the social sphere; the highest ambition is achieved through saying "no" to self for the sake of someone else. Jesus wants the disciples to understand that what ultimately redeems life and provides the deepest meaning is not located in being recognized, served, and honored but in contributing to the common good. It is a way of life that redeems from pettiness and offers something more enduring than selfish power.

Forgive my silly ambitions and equip me for greater service to others. In Jesus' name, I ask. Amen.

106

Not Waiting for Happiness

"I'm not saying this because I need anything, for I have learned how to be content in any circumstance. I know the experience of being in need and of having more than enough; I have learned the secret to being content in any and every circumstance, whether full or hungry or whether having plenty or being poor. I can endure all these things through the power of the one who gives me strength."

PHILIPPIANS 4:11–13

HAVE YOU NOTICED HOW many people have delayed their happiness? They seem to believe that if they can achieve a little more success, acquire a little more wealth, or marry the right person then they will possess happiness. Happiness, they believe, is what follows effort, time, and, perhaps, a little luck. It is as though happiness is somewhere out in front of everyone who is industrious enough to pursue it. Happiness is something to grasp, they believe, and their minds remain fixed upon it until they have taken ownership of it. Striving day upon day toward the possession of happiness, what they miss is that the secret of happiness is already present in the lives of those who long for it.

Paul's letter to the Philippian Church provides the secret of happiness—as God's people, we are to live in humility, looking out for others more than for ourselves. That is a great reversal of the commonly accepted formula for happiness. Essentially, Paul teaches that if we are always chasing after happiness, happiness always remains beyond our grasp. On the other hand, if we occupy ourselves with looking out for others, adding value to other people, and promoting their welfare, happiness quietly joins God's people and takes-up residence in them. Paul is urging God's people to break free of the tiny little world of themselves and join the great enterprise of God's work in the world.

Here, in the fourth chapter of Paul's letter to the Philippian Church, Paul further develops the secret to happiness. Having shared the secret of happiness, disclosed in the activity of Jesus who accepted humility to become like us, for the purposes of restoring us to God, Paul points to a mysterious strength that converges in our service to one another. That strength comes not from any person—or from the community of God's people—but from the outside. It is God's strength. There is far more going on when God's people join with one another for the promotion of the welfare of others. The same Christ who became human to serve now empowers and enables God's people in their service to one another.

Shortly following the death of his wife, J. R. Carmichael entered a nursing home. Yet, if you inquired about him, you learned that he is never in his room. It seems that each morning Mr. Carmichael would shower, dress, eat breakfast, and then move from one residential room to another. In each room, Mr. Carmichael spoke with the resident about their family, read the Bible to them, prayed with them, and told them that he loved them. Then it was off to the next room to do the same thing. Mr. Carmichael missed his wife every day but he never waited for happiness. Happiness found him, as he loved others deeply.

Dear God, guide my thoughts and behaviors today so that I may recognize opportunities for service to others. Amen.

107

A Multitude of Anna's (Nathanael Hood)

"There was also a prophet, Anna the daughter of Phanuel, who belonged to the tribe of Asher. She was very old. After she married, she lived with her husband for seven years. She was now an 84-year-old widow. She never left the temple area but worshipped God with fasting and prayer night and day. She approached at that very moment and began to praise God and to speak about Jesus to everyone who was looking forward to the redemption of Jerusalem."

Luke 2:36–38

OF ALL THE THINGS in the Bible that puzzle and frustrate historians and theologians, perhaps the greatest is the nearly thirty-year gap in the story of Jesus' life between his birth and the start of his ministry. What happened during these lost years? The Bible only gives us a few details. One of the most significant happens in the second chapter of Luke when Mary and Joseph take the infant Jesus to the Temple in Jerusalem for the first time. During this presentation, the Holy Family meets a man named Simeon. The text doesn't tell us much about Simeon—all we know for certain is that he was a "righteous and devout" man who had received a promise from the Holy Spirit that he would not die before he laid eyes on the Messiah. And indeed, on that day, that promise was fulfilled. The text tells us that the Holy Spirit itself came to Simeon and guided him to the Temple whereupon he took the infant Jesus in his arms and praised God, proclaiming him a revelation to the Gentiles and a glory for Israel.

Although he may have fallen a little out of importance in our Protestant tradition, Simeon is a very important figure in both Catholic and Orthodox Christianity. In addition to being canonized as a saint in both traditions with multiple feast days, he is also venerated as a prophet. He has been immortalized in paintings, stained glass, and altarpieces all over Christendom, and he has been the subject of music from some of the greatest composers in history, such as Johann Sebastian Bach. Not just that, but the aforementioned blessing Simeon gave while holding the Infant Jesus—known as the Nunc Dimittis—has been used by the Catholic Church as a prayer since the fourth century. Truly, Simeon is a model for steadfast faith being richly rewarded.

But I suspect Simeon's story provides small comfort for most people looking for evidence of God's presence in the world. Most of us will never witness a miracle like Simeon. Most of us will live lives like Anna. For you see, Simeon wasn't the only one who recognized the infant Jesus when he was first brought to the Temple. There was another—there was an old woman named Anna who lived in the Temple courtyard. She was unique in her familiarity with loss and heartbreak. According to the text, she was widowed only seven years after getting married. According to Luke, she never remarried, and depending on how you translate the original text, she spent either the next sixty-odd or eighty-four years living in the temple courtyard without means or family which, in the time of ancient Israel, made her a non-person. She was a prophet, yes, but a prophet on the margins, well familiar with all the pains, and disappointments, and injustices of life.

And yet! Anna recognized the Messiah. Unlike Simeon, Anna recognized the Christ all by herself. Then she did something even more extraordinary: she spread the Word! Shortly after his blessings, Simeon disappears from the biblical record. But not Anna. She stayed. She witnessed. Indeed, most of us will not live lives like Simeon. Most of us will live quiet, unseen, under-appreciated lives. Most of us will wonder if the world ever will get any better if our prayers truly mean anything if our lives are being used by God at all. One can't help but wonder if Anna, in her loneliness, ever felt the same. But again, it was Anna who recognized the Messiah and witnessed to the world. Perhaps it was because of her difficult life, not despite it, that she was so capable. We cannot all be Simeon. But we can all strive to be Anna. And in that striving, by touching others with our quiet Christian compassion and love, we can create a chain of healing greater than anything any of us will ever be able to comprehend. It takes a Simeon to shock the world. But only a multitude of Anna's can save it.

Almighty Father who sees all, knows all, and loves all, please grant us the fortitude, faithfulness, and conviction of Anna so that we might not be discouraged as we eagerly await the day when you make all things right once more. Amen.

108

The Spirit of Christmas

"Glory to God in heaven, and on earth peace among those whom he favors."

LUKE 2:14

THERE IS A CHRISTMAS song that ponders in a rather wistful manner, why the world is unable to embrace the spirit of Christmas all year long. At Christmas, we crawl out from our hard shell of self-concern, our eyes sparkle with wonder, and we behave with an uncharacteristic charity toward all people. We slog through eleven months of drudging effort, eyes squarely focused upon survival in a competitive marketplace with little attention to others, and then Christmas comes. We throw off the heavy coat of selfishness for a time. Kindness permeates the places of our souls made callous by fear of scarcity and generosity flows from hidden springs in our hearts. We play, we laugh, and we are amiable to strangers and friends equally. That Christmas song is on to something. Why can't we have the spirit of Christmas all year long?

Bethlehem is a divine interruption. The world today is a little different from the world that welcomed the birth of Jesus. Enemies are everywhere and national security continues to be a pressing concern. The inequity of wealth among people of every nation conveniently ignores the apostle Paul's call that those who have much shouldn't have too much and those who have little shouldn't have too little (2 Corinthians 8:13–15). But Bethlehem invites the world to a fresh imagination; to imagine a world where instruments of war are repurposed into farming instruments and people impulsively and joyfully share from their abundance so that others may simply have enough. Bethlehem asks that we look at the world differently, and asks that we live differently.

The spirit of Christmas is a deep and persistent call to pay attention to God. It is a call to see and participate in the creation of a new world where peace and goodwill abound. Bethlehem is not an occasional indulgence—an occasion where we lay aside for a moment careful attention to our health and consume copious quantities of Christmas cookies and eggnog. Bethlehem asks that we care about the world of which we are a part. Bethlehem invites us to join the angels in announcing that God has unleashed upon the world a new order where all people may find carefree rest in God. Bethlehem is not a charming dream. It is not an aspirational goal. Bethlehem is a confident and certain reality. God has come into this world and nothing is going to be the same.

Go to Bethlehem this year. Go and bow down before this magnificent birth of a new world order. Discover in Bethlehem God's divine intention for each of us; discover that peace and goodwill are not for one month of the year but God's gift to be embraced and shared all year. But if you go to Bethlehem, recognize that Bethlehem makes demands upon all who visit. Bethlehem asks that you dedicate your life to speeding up the tempo of goodwill in all your relationships. Bethlehem will ask you to guard your speech and exercise restraint in the use of acrimony, harsh, and mean criticism. Bethlehem will demand civility, humility, and respect for others, particularly for those you disagree with. And Bethlehem will ask of you uncommon generosity toward others. Bethlehem asks a good deal from all who visit. But Bethlehem gives in return God's peace. That is the spirit of Christmas.

Lord Jesus, mold me and shape me this holiday season so that I am useful to you in building disciples and transforming lives through your power. Amen.

109

How to be Miserable

"Love is patient, love is kind, it isn't jealous, it doesn't brag, it isn't arrogant, it isn't rude, it doesn't seek its own advantage, it isn't irritable, it doesn't keep a record of complaints, it isn't happy with injustice, but it is happy with the truth. Love puts up with all things, trust in all things, hopes for all things, endures all things."

1 CORINTHIANS 13:4–7

THE OTHER DAY I came across a piece written by Earl Nightingale that he titled, *How to Be Miserable*. He provided remarkable clarity about some of the things I have been wrestling with recently, clarity about self-inflicted misery. Nightingale writes, "The first step to real, professional-type, solid, unremitting misery is to get all wrapped up in yourself and your problems—real or imagined. Become a kind of island, surrounded on every side by yourself. By turning all of your thoughts inward upon yourself, naturally, you cannot spend much or any time thinking about others and other things. And so, finally, the outside world—the real world—will disappear into a kind of Hitchcock-type fog."[1]

Nightingale continues with a stinging observation that the type of person who chooses misery, who turns inward upon himself or herself doesn't have much in the wisdom department. Otherwise, they simply wouldn't

---

1. Nightingale, *Success Starts Here*, 104.

do it. In the absence of wisdom, they turn inward and discover that there is not much there. There is a kind of vacuum, and they have to embellish perceived, or real, hurts and slights from others or invent things entirely. Negative—and harmful—behavior is then directed outward toward those who have caused them harm. This behavior may simply be for punishment, to cause pain equal to what they are experiencing, or to manipulate others to meet some relational expectation.

Where Nightingale provides an unpleasant portrait of a miserable person, the apostle Paul provides divine knowledge—or wisdom—for fleeing from misery: love others, particularly when that love is difficult. Paul beautifully expresses the very nature of love by its positive attributes—"love is patient, love is kind." Paul provides additional wisdom by sharing what love isn't and doesn't do—"it isn't jealous, it doesn't brag, it isn't arrogant, it isn't rude, it doesn't seek its own advantage, it isn't irritable, it doesn't keep a record of complaints." What Paul provides is a different portrait from Nightingale, a portrait of a person who actively participates in the unity and well-being of relationships with another.

It is widely embraced that the Christian faith is less to do with the right beliefs and more to do with the right behavior. A person may have a grasp of the Holy Scriptures that is unparalleled, able to articulate a particular theological position with uncommon clarity, and yet remain untouched by God's transforming power—the transformation that deepens love for God and love for others. Such a faith is a lazy faith because it requires no effort. Love requires effort. Love demands that we struggle against an impulse to turn inward and compile a record of complaints against another. Such love "puts up with all things, trust in all things, hopes for all things, endures all things." It is a love that knows no misery.

Forgive my petty grievances, hurts, and complaints, O God. Forgive my lazy faith that fails to love you and others deeply. Fill my whole being with the desire and power to tear up my list of complaints and demonstrate patience and kindness to all. Amen.

110

Once Upon a Time in Denmark... (Nathanael Hood)

> *"Yet whatever gains I had, these I have come to regard as loss because of Christ. More than that, I regard everything as loss because of the surpassing value of knowing Christ Jesus my Lord. For his sake I have suffered the loss of all things, and I regard them as rubbish, in order that I may gain Christ."*
>
> PHILIPPIANS 3:7, 8 (NRSV)

THERE ONCE WAS A man from Denmark who told a story about a mighty king. The king, said the Dane, was the mightiest in the world. No other prince or leader, knight or peasant dared oppose his will. He clothed his body with rich jewels and lavish robes, and whenever he toured his kingdom he rode in a royal carriage with an armed escort. The king wanted for nothing—no earthly good or luxury escaped him. Yet the king, the Dane explained, was lonely. Then one day, he fell in love. But not with a queen or princess of a faraway kingdom. Not a rich merchant or skilled artist. The king fell in love with a poor maiden from an even poorer village.

Now, the king knew he could have anything he wanted. There were none with his wealth, none with his power, none with his strength in battle or conflict. Yet his love left him paralyzed with uncertainty. If he arrived in her village with his rich jewels, his lavish robes, his royal carriage, and armed escort, the maiden would surely accept his hand. But would it be for love or fear? Would she spend her life resenting or hating him for giving her no choice? What if she only agreed to marry him because she wanted his wealth, his power, his palace? Yes, the Dane sighed, he could never truly know her love if he came to her as a king. So this threw off his finery and abandoned his entourage. He clothed himself in rags and went to her village alone. It was there, as a powerless, penniless beggar, that he managed to woo the maiden and win her heart.

This story was told hundreds of years ago by Danish philosopher Søren Kierkegaard, a man whose name tends to glaze over the eyes of lay people who know nothing about him other than his notoriety as a Philosopher with a capital "P." But Kierkegaard was one of the oddest philosophers of his age, a gloomy, death-obsessed man who juxtaposed the increasing secularization of Europe's intelligentsia with a fervent yet unusual faith. He passionately loved Jesus yet passionately detested organized religion, particularly the Danish church of his day and age. In the above parable of "The King and the Maiden," he provides a bold explanation for one of the central scandals of Christianity: God's choosing to be born human and live and die as one. For Kierkegaard, it was only by approaching humanity as a "beggar" that God could truly win its love and devotion. If God had demanded fealty of all creation—not just God's covenant people the Jews—as a conquering king, it would require fearful surrender instead of joyful acceptance. Only by exercising free will could humanity establish a relationship with God that truly mattered.

But there's a different reading to this story, one that Kierkegaard perhaps didn't intend. What if humanity—with all its egotism and excess, selfishness and pride—is the king and Christ the maiden? We certainly see this idea reflected in the story of Paul, a dogmatic Pharisee who abandoned his fundamentalist insistence on rules and regulations after an encounter with Jesus. After finding Christ, he cast off all his wealth and love of legalism for a closer, truer relationship with God. Everything he once held dear in his life he "regarded as rubbish" after his conversion, casting them off as Kierkegaard's king did his wealth and finery to court his beloved maiden. So too must we all reassess and reevaluate what we cherish in our own lives. Is our quest for wealth and power keeping us from loving our neighbors as we do ourselves? Is our desire for material luxuries or sex preventing us from living the kind of simple, righteous lives Jesus called us to? Are we too busy living as kings to remember that we've been called to live as beloved children of the Almighty?

Lord, help us abandon our greed and shallow desire for riches and possessions that threatens to make us forget about you and your all-consuming, all-redeeming love. Help us come not as kings but as paupers to your feet. In your Son's name, we pray. Amen.

111

Dissatisfaction with the Ordinary

> *"Therefore prepare your minds for action; discipline yourselves; set all your hope on the grace that Jesus Christ will bring you when he is revealed. Like obedient children, do not be conformed to the desires that you formerly had in ignorance. Instead, as he who called you is holy, be holy yourselves in all your conduct; for it is written, 'You shall be holy, for I am holy.'"*
>
> 1 PETER 1:13–16 (NRSV)

RALPH WALDO EMERSON SHARED in a lecture, "We plant trees, we build stone houses, we redeem the waste, we make prospective laws, we found colleges and hospitals, for remote generations. We should be mortified to learn that the little benefit we chanced in our own person to receive was the utmost they would yield."[1] Emerson decried the tendency of people to live below their true capacity—to chance little of their enormous potential. The life they make for themselves is not what it could be, not what it should be. Living below the capacity available to them, they should not experience a surprise that what they receive in return is little. In fact, such people should be "mortified."

This is Peter's concern for the one who follows Christ: "Therefore prepare your minds for action; discipline yourselves." The encouragement from

---

1. Emerson, *Emerson: Essays and Lectures*, 219.

Peter is that the Christian strive forward, stretching personal ability and gifts for maximum benefit. The "hope" Peter speaks of is not wishful thinking. Rather, it is a certain expectation, which follows personal effort—an expectation lodged firmly in the promises of Jesus. Careful preparation of the mind, that is, clear and focused thought, is demanded followed by intentional participation in God's work in the world. Discipline will be required less the Christian once again is conformed to former ways that are largely unproductive.

Success in any organization is determined by the quality of organization and effort. Similarly, the success or failure of a person depends on the way he or she manages himself or herself. We all produce things, behaviors, and attitudes that reflect our management, or lack of discipline and personal management. As such, we should gauge the quality and the importance of who we are becoming in each area of our lives—our personal growth, relational growth with family, friends, and colleagues, professional contribution, and spiritual growth. Without determined, intentional action, we ease back into ordinariness.

Peter asks that we claim our identity as God's chosen people. Accordingly, God's people are to live "holy" lives—that is, we are to separate ourselves from ordinariness and live distinctly as those who follow Jesus Christ. "Holy" does not presume that will live perfectly, without stumbles, difficulty, and occasional rebellion and disobedience to God. It does suggest that when we stumble, it matters to us, that we expect more from ourselves, and rise and struggle forward in obedience once again. It is the intention of the heart that leads believers to behave in ways that seem strange to those who have not answered the call to be "holy"—to live into an extraordinary life as God desires for us.

Forgive my willingness to live an ordinary life, without disciple or resolve. Remind me of who I am and to whom I belong. Stir my heart by your Holy Spirit that I may be dissatisfied with the ordinary and strive for the extraordinary so that my life may bring honor and glory to your Son, Jesus. Amen.

112

Maintaining Calm in the Tumult

"Most important, live together in a manner worthy of Christ's gospel. Do this, whether I come and see you or I'm absent and hear about you. Do this so that you stand firm, united in one spirit and mind as you struggle together to remain faithful to the gospel. That way, you won't be afraid of anything your enemies do."

PHILIPPIANS 1:27, 28A

SOME YEARS AGO, A young man shared with me that years earlier he made a profession of faith in Jesus Christ. However, in the time that followed, he never sought to grow in his relationship with Jesus. Now his life was moving through a crisis, and not moving through it very well. This brought uncommon insight to him. He said, "I never did anything with my faith so now my faith is not doing anything for me." Apparently, this young man reduced the Christian faith to right beliefs. He confessed before a church that Jesus Christ is his Lord. He believed in Jesus Christ and that was that. Nothing more is required. What he was now learning—in the midst of a personal crisis—is that the Christian faith is not merely right beliefs. The Christian faith is something that we do, and optimally, in a community with others.

In his present tumult, what this man desired is calm. Some years ago, William George Jordan wrote, "Calmness is the rarest quality in human life. It is the poise of a great nature, in harmony with itself and its ideals. It is the moral atmosphere of a life self-reliant and self-controlled. Calmness is singleness of purpose, absolute confidence, and conscious power ready to be focused in an instant to meet any crisis."[1] Simply, the person who is calm identifies a singleness of purpose and pursues that purpose with both sturdy confidence and an intentional strength of resolve. This is precisely the point Paul makes in his letter to the Church in Philippi: "live together in a manner worthy of Christ's gospel." That is our purpose. Further, Paul asks for a steady resolve toward this regardless of external circumstances—whether Paul comes to see them or is absent from them.

A familiar song during the Christmas season has this refrain, "I'll be home for Christmas, you can count on me. I'll be home for Christmas, if only in my dreams." Initially, the response is a chest that swells with anticipation and joy. A loved one is coming home for Christmas! However, the chest deflates when the refrain continues, "if only in my dreams." Notice here that joy, or its absence, is dependent on something from outside of the individual—something that is beyond the grasp of the individual to control. Will a loved one be home for Christmas or not? Paul is saying that joy and a life of obedience to Jesus Christ are not dependent upon some external circumstance; not dependent upon whether Paul comes to be with them or is absent from them. Calm is available either way once a mind is focused on a great purpose.

These few sentences of Paul conclude with the promise that fear and uncertainty will not fill the heart if the mind is set upon the single purpose of living for Christ's gospel. If we hand authority to external circumstances for our well-being, we confess our inferiority to them. We grant them the power to dominate us. It is then that worries of every measure stir us to unease, wears upon us, and eventually, we wear down to surrender. Calm dissipates. Paul announces it does not have to come to that. "Live together in a manner worthy of Christ's gospel." Do that and the natural result is that you will not be afraid of anything your enemies do. Malice and slander, difficulties and hardships, disappointments and failures may assail you. Calmness will remain.

Grant to me, Oh God, that in the midst of uncertainties, I may cling to the certainty of your power and love for me. Amen.

---

1. Nightingale, *Transformational Living*, 39.

113

Where Joy Is Found

"Know this, my dear brothers and sisters: everyone should be quick to listen, slow to speak, and slow to grow angry. This is because an angry person doesn't produce God's righteousness."

JAMES 1:19, 20

SYDNEY HARRIS SHARES AN occasion when he was walking with a friend home from the office. On the way, his friend stopped at a newsstand to purchase the evening paper. Completing the transaction, Harris' friend thanked the vendor politely. The vendor didn't even acknowledge it. "A sullen fellow, isn't he?" Harris commented. "Oh, he's that way every night," shrugged his friend. "Then why do you continue being so polite to him?" Sydney Harris asked. "Why not?" inquired his friend. "Why should I let him decide how I'm going to act?" Notice that the operative word is "act." His friend *acts* toward people. Many of us react toward them.[1]

This is the guidance James provides—"quick to listen, slow to speak, and slow to grow angry." In addition to conforming to the format of a letter, James belongs to the literary genre of Wisdom literature. Such literature was widespread throughout the Middle East during the first century CE. Advancing understanding of wise instructions for life in general, sacred Wisdom literature communicates to readers how to live happily as a disciple of Jesus Christ. Various values and actions consistent with discipleship are

---

1. Nightingale, *Transformational Living*, 37.

examined and urged as faithful expressions of fidelity to God. Here, James implores Christians to "act" toward one another rather than "react."

James knows who he is. He is a disciple of Jesus Christ. This knowledge provides James with an understanding of the behavior that is now expected of him—the understanding that refuses to return anger with anger, incivility with incivility. Each one of us has natural impulses and internal responses to the behavior of others. Yet, failure to harness those impulses, when they would be hurtful to another, is to surrender the command of our conduct. That is slavery to impulses, which make us mere responders to others. That is when our discipleship stumbles—those occasions when we pour out invective after it has been poured out over us.

Throughout the teachings of Jesus, we are enjoined to return good for evil, to turn the other cheek when the hand of another strikes us. That requires uncommon strength, and uncommon control of sinful impulses to defend our honor. That requires that we "act" as Jesus demonstrates in his own life and ministry, rather than "respond" as Peter did with the sword the night Jesus was arrested in the garden. Nobody is unhappier than the one who has surrendered command of his or her inner impulses and strikes back when injured—physically or emotionally. Yet, God's righteousness expands when we return anger with love. That is where joy is found.

God, don't let me surrender to my impulse to respond when I am in disagreement with another. Deepen my capacity to listen and widen my love for others. Amen.

114

Telling the Story Again

"As Paul and Barnabas were leaving the synagogue, the people urged them to speak about these things again on the next Sabbath."

Acts 13:42

Tom Tewell shared with me that some years ago, the pastor of First Presbyterian Church of Pittsburgh, Pennsylvania, preached a sermon that so captured the hearts and minds of the congregation that the governing board passed a resolution that on the anniversary of that sermon each year, the pastor was to preach it again. Some time ago I heard an interview with Robin Roberts, a host of the morning show, Good Morning America. She spoke candidly of her Christian faith and her morning time with God before going to work. She mentioned a favorite devotional guide that she used each morning—one that provided a meditation for each day of the year. On January 1 of the following year, she started through the same devotional again.

During my ministry in Bucks County, Pennsylvania, I was asked in one week to preach a Christian message of hope for two different families who were burying a loved one. Neither family had a church home or a pastor. Each service was in a different funeral home. A dear friend of mine, Bill, was close to both families and attended both services. In each service, I preached the same sermon. Though both families expressed gratitude to me for my message, each saying that the message was precisely what they needed to hear, Bill shared his disappointment with me following the second service.

Bill's complaint was that he had already heard that sermon earlier in the week. I simply reminded him that I was not preaching for him.

It has never been my practice to preach the same Sunday morning message twice in the same congregation. Yet, often I will reuse an illustration in other sermons. This is for two reasons: I believe that no other illustration has the same force to advance the message I wish to convey, and, the illustration embodies such truth within itself that I wish to impact more lives with its use. Worshipping communities are like streams—you never step into the same stream twice. The water from the first experience has now moved on. The second experience is always in new water. Likewise, the second telling of the illustration nearly always reaches persons not in attendance during the earlier usage. I'm not preaching to those who have already heard the illustration.

It is natural to grow tired of hearing most stories over and over again. But stories that capture some truth; stories that instruct and inspire do not grow old. That is because they stir something in us each time. Much like some who read Dickens' *A Christmas Carol* each Christmas, the Bible and illustrations that open the truths of the Bible clearly and powerfully are not ones we grow tired of. Inspiration for living in difficult times leaks and must be refreshed. Reading a strong book of meditations that strengthens in one year can do the same the next year, just as Robin Roberts has experienced. So, as Paul and Barnabas were leaving the synagogue, the people urged them to speak about these things again on the next Sabbath.

Jesus, I am grateful your story is told over and over again and, at times, provides fresh insights and experiences of your presence. Amen.

115

Determining Your Own Outcome

"From now on, brothers and sisters, if anything is excellent and if anything is admirable, focus your thoughts on these things: all that is true, all that is holy, all that is just, all that is pure, all that is lovely, and all that is worthy of praise. Practice these things: whatever you learned, received, heard, or saw in us. The God of peace will be with you."

PHILIPPIANS 4:8, 9

TWO MEN OF SIMILAR age were hospitalized following a heart attack. Both were treated by the same doctor and both were placed on the same hospital floor. Most importantly, both men received a similar prognosis from the doctor—the damage each suffered was about the same and both received the same guidance from the doctor, change their diet, reduce stress, and exercise regularly. That is where the similarities stopped. The responses of the two men were strikingly different from each other. One took a mental and emotional journey to a dark place, saying to his family and friends that his body was shot and nothing could now be done. The other told his wife that he would immediately change his diet, modify his workload, and hire a personal trainer. What was cause for despair for one was filled with challenge and opportunity for the other.

The life lesson here is that it is not what happens that matters. What matters is how you respond. How each one of us responds to unexpected—and unpleasant—challenges of life determines the outcome. Every person who faces a similar circumstance has a choice to make. Either they accept defeat by the circumstance or they will see the possibility of adapting and moving forward creatively. We all struggle with challenges, changes in health, broken career paths, and disruptions that surprise us such as this pandemic, Covid-19. Often such forces move toward us without our consent. Nor can we stop them. Yet each person has the capacity to make a decision in the direction his or her life will now move. Optimism may remain out of reach for a season. However, giving up does not have to be a choice.

This is precisely the lesson that the apostle Paul teaches the Christians in Philippi—that what we put into our minds determines what the outcome will be. Paul uses two powerful words, "focus" and "practice." As we turn our minds toward something, the "focus," and follow that with "practice," what we do is program our minds with positive thoughts and behaviors that result in an optimal outcome. Both are important. It is not enough to turn our eyes toward all that is true, holy, just, pure, lovely, and worthy of praise. We must also put each of these into practice in our life. They must be a stimulant that propels us in a new direction. Exposure alone is simply insufficient. Paul wants us to understand that as we intentionally direct our lives according to God's word, we choose the outcome of our lives and we experience God's peace.

Armed with Paul's guidance, any of us can greatly improve our response to stressful and, potentially, debilitating situations. What seems to be a cruel and devastating situation to one person is an opportunity for reexamining priorities and life direction for another. As someone once observed, a virus may be all around and yet cause no infection until the virus finds access into our body. Which causes the illness—the virus or that it got inside of us? Naturally, the virus outside our body is powerless over us. It is only inside the body that the virus can wreak havoc. No one chooses for the virus to enter our bodies. That is what makes a virus so terrifying. Nevertheless, we can choose our response to every difficulty—choose whether, or not, we will "let it inside" our heads to do it's worse. What we choose makes all the difference.

God, you have infused the world with your care and love. Remind me that I have the capacity to choose my response to every circumstance and that your power remains close by to carry me through every difficulty. Amen.

116

God's Hope for Us in the New Year

"Jesus Christ is the same yesterday, today, and forever! Don't be misled by the many strange teachings out there. It's a good thing for the heart to be strengthened by grace rather than by food. Food doesn't help those who live in this context."

HEBREWS 13:8, 9

GOD'S AIM FOR ALL people is that our hearts be strengthened. Not hardened, unyielding, and unwilling to settle differences. This past year has produced many such hearts; hearts that are embittered by unkind political rhetoric, economic uncertainty, and fear of a virus that seems unstoppable. That is a heart that is incapable of civil, respectful discussion—only monologues, bouncing off others as though they were a hard surface. And oftentimes they are! Hard surfaces that lack the humility to listen deeply to others, which lack the capacity or willingness to harness disagreement for the advancement of personal thought. What God desires are hearts that are strengthened in a personal relationship with Jesus Christ.

Hearts strengthened by God's grace, strengthen by a daily decision to learn of Jesus Christ and allow that instruction to direct the course of our thoughts and behavior result in a milder, more temperate, more compassionate nature! As someone once wrote, in Jesus Christ, we have, "Before each of us an image of what we ought to be."[1] In a very practical course, what this means is that the image of Jesus Christ should become a living reality within each person. That is not a person who clings to rules or some interpretation of moral conduct that is foisted upon another. It is a person that recognizes that fallibility marks each one of us and moves toward another with compassion and acceptance.

Often resolutions are made at the beginning of a New Year. Many times they are broken—and broken early—and some are kept, even if feebly. Yet, according to our lesson this morning from Hebrews, there is one desire that God has for everyone. That is the desire that we are not led in the wrong direction this New Year by any other voice or authority than what is found in the Bible, "Don't be misled by the many strange teachings out there." A heart that is centered, and continually strengthened, in Jesus Christ is God's aim, God's hope for each of us. After all, any other desire or hope we may have will end in disillusionment if not deeply rooted in a relationship with our creator.

God's hope for us does not depend upon our own strength of resolve, our ability to exercise absolute discipline in the course of our daily lives. We are not strong enough. This is precisely why so many resolutions in the New Year fail. Our intention is sincere and strong. Our discipline stumbles. What God promises is an uncommon strength that comes from God that helps us make Jesus Christ the pillar of our thoughts and actions. Only one thing is needed—that we say to Jesus Christ today, and each day this year, "Here I am, do with me according to your will!" God's promise is that our hearts will be strengthened. It is then that our lives will exhibit God's commandment—the commandment of love.

God, I find it difficult to look to others for strength. Many times I find it difficult to acknowledge that I need anything. Yet, my faith falters, and I become impatient with those who disagree with me. Forgive me, fill me with a hunger to know Christ more fully and the humility to follow Christ more deeply. Amen.

---

1. Source unknown

117

Disillusionment With God

"The burning sand will become a pool, and the thirsty ground, fountains of water."

Isaiah 35:7

There is, perhaps, no greater disappointment in life than to experience disappointment with God. Missed opportunities, unrealized dreams, and friends who fail us are no small matter. They can be debilitating at times. Yet, most people also recognize that such disappointments are the stuff of life. With a strong network of family and friends, many find that they are able to push through such disappointments. But what are we to do with our disappointment with God? This is the most shattering of disappointments. "No longer is there a wide, comfortable margin between peace and the edge of doom," writes that great Scottish preacher, James S. Steward.[1] Disillusionment with God is startling, surprising, and overwhelming. In a deep spiritual sense, such disillusionment is taking-up residence in the desert.

Isaiah has a word for those desert moments—or days. In dramatic fashion, Isaiah speaks of a grand reversal, "The burning sand will become a pool, and the thirsty ground, fountains of water." With incredible verve, he takes the most frightening and cynical judgment of the world that says that this life is nothing more than "burning sand" and reverses it. God is not absent nor will God remain silent. The word from the Lord is that the desert

1. Stewart, *The Wind of the Spirit*, 70.

places of life will become an oasis; living water that quenches our fears and dispels the darkness.

What does this mean? In effect, Isaiah acknowledges his common experience with ours that life is full of disappointments, broken dreams, and dashed hopes. More, Isaiah is no stranger to fears that come like a bolt of lightning, unnerving our sense of comfort and security. But he also wants to remind us of history; Israel's history of a God that is never far off, a God that appears in the midst of struggle and uncertainty with the hand of a shepherd, confidently leading us forward into God's future for us. In every situation, even when the darkness of the hour seems to have the upper hand, grace reigns.

Understand, of course, that the very struggle with disillusionment dispels any notion that faith is always experienced without struggle. Any spiritual journey occasionally moves through desert places, where the ground is hot and parched. But, Isaiah asks that we steadily move forward, particularly when our steps are labored and weak, for a wonderful discovery lies ahead of us, the same discovery that Isaiah made. Present circumstances that seem like burning sand will, by God's promises, become a pool of cool water. Additionally, you will find yourself in the company of those who have discovered that they would rather travel the most difficult road with God than any other road without him.

Forgive my disillusionment, O Lord, and restore my heart to the certain knowledge that, in the midst of difficulty, you are present. Amen.

118

How To Live by Faith

"Faith is the reality of what we hope for, the proof of what we don't see."
HEBREWS 11:1

HAROLD BLAKE WALKER WRITES, "We live by faith or we do not live at all. Either we venture or we vegetate. If we venture, we do so by faith, simply because we cannot know the end of anything at its beginning."[1] Walker applies this principle to marriage, the pursuit of a career, and the challenge of overcoming any of life's difficulties. There is little certainty in life. Either we risk obtaining what we desire or we remain single, fail to realize what our potential may be, and are stopped by any resistance that places itself between us and what we want. Once we accept the veracity of Walker's premise, the question becomes, "How do we proceed with an act of imaginative faith?"

We begin by paying attention—paying attention to the object of our desire. I first noticed the woman that I would eventually marry in Hebrew Language Class. She was attractive, clearly intelligent, and engaging with other students. As many men have said before me, any notion of a romantic relationship with her would be a reach. Yet, I refused to simply dismiss the possibility. I paid attention to her. I looked for opportunities to engage in conversation with her. Then I looked for clues that she may be responsive to a friendship, moving to a deeper engagement, and finally, the most terrifying

---

1. Nightingale, *Transformational Living*, 77.

risk of all, asking her out on a date. She could have politely refused. Clearly admired by both students and faculty, this was a risk.

This same dynamic is at play in any arena of life. If we desire anything, we begin by paying attention to the small things, gathering clues here and there for the next step that we will take. We make a mental picture of taking possession of what we want and strive forward toward it. That is what this passage from Hebrews means by "Faith is the reality of what we hope for"—we strive forward as though what we desire is now a reality—that we have already taken possession of it. Yes, moving forward may meet with failure. That woman in Hebrew Class may have said "no" to my request for a shared dinner. But the answer was located on the other side of faith; on the other side of taking the risk to ask.

The Book of Hebrews does not minimize the difficulty of faith. An easy faith is a contradiction of terms. Faith, as we have acknowledged, carries an element of risk. And great faith has always had to reckon with great doubt. We possess faith only as we fight for it each day—keeping our eye on the object of desire and recapturing its allure each day. Then we must doubt our doubts and move steadily forward in the direction we wish to go. Yes, the burden of doubt occasionally presents struggle and strain. All great ventures of our lives require struggle and strain. But triumphs are not won without an unquenchable belief that we can achieve what we desire. It all begins with one step forward. That is living by faith

Great God, strengthen me when weaken by doubt. Kindle, again and again, a strong belief that you are an ever-present strength in times of difficulty. Help me recognize your transformative grace that surrounds me. Amen.

119

How Can I Find God?

"It's impossible to please God without faith because the one who draws near to God must believe that he exists and that he rewards people who try to find him."

Hebrews 11:6

The beginning of the matter is faith. Faith does not mean the absence of doubt. As Jesus spoke to his disciples for the last time, the Bible tells us that some of them doubted. Their doubt did not bother Jesus. What Jesus did was to command them how they were to live after he left them. Here, faith is the determination to live "as though it is true." When two people make marriage vows to remain together "until death do they part" they are aware of the staggering divorce rates. They are aware of the possibility that their marriage may fail. Yet, they begin their life together on faith, the determination that they will remain together until death. Hebrews instructs that we begin the search for God "as though God does exist."

Faith is not putting aside all doubt. It is determining to believe that God is there, just as we are present in the world. Faith is not putting aside all arguments against the existence of God but, rather, choosing to "accept as true" that God loves and understands and is interested in the smallest details of our life. A serious quest for God will put away all excuses for not beginning to seek God, excuses such as not having sufficient time to be alone with God each day, and sincerely strive to be in a personal relationship with someone as real and present as a spouse or dear friend. Faith is an acknowledgment that God is someone who is worth our worship, our love, our striving to learn from, and a decision to follow.

Let the one looking for God then turn each day to a quiet place, a place free of the possibility of interruption and distraction. In silence, think of God as present. Perhaps make a mental picture of God standing directly in front of you or seated right beside you. If it helps, picture God as Jesus groomed as your favorite picture of Jesus, wearing the traditional dress of the Hebrew people of Jesus' day. Some find sitting in a church before a stained-glass window of Jesus helpful, as do I. Imaginatively, look into tender eyes and see arms outstretched to embrace you. At that moment, confess how you have wronged others and God. Pour out your hurts, disappointments, and longings. Share with God your unmet needs.

Then, after the silence, accept the forgiveness of God, the forgiveness you have heard proclaimed from the pulpit, read in the Bible, or shared with you by those who believe in Jesus. Accept the forgiveness even if you find it difficult to believe that anyone can forgive you, even God. By faith, trust the promise that you are forgiven. Trust that God has taken all that you are ashamed of and removed it from you. As God has placed all of it behind you, now make a mental picture that your back is turned to it and you face forward with no guilt. In that new freedom—and in gratitude—resolve to learn from Jesus and to live as Jesus teaches us to live. Hebrews promises that God will reward you—promises that you will find God.

I turn toward you now, God. Diminish the grip of doubt on me. In faith, I claim the truth that you are present, present in the world, and present in my life. Hear the agonies of my heart, forgive my sins, and open my mind to learn of Jesus. Amen.

120

Memory and God

"But Zion says, 'The Lord has abandoned me; my Lord has forgotten me.' Can a woman forget her nursing child, fail to pity the child of her womb? Even these may forget, but I won't forget you."

Isaiah 49:14, 15

I was once told of a college professor who had been married for nearly thirty-five years when his wife became ill with dementia. Anyone who is familiar with this cognitive disease knows that eventually all memory is stolen from the individual. The professor did his best to juggle his teaching responsibilities and caring for his wife until he could no longer do both. As he put it, he faced one of the most difficult decisions of his life when he placed his wife in a memory care center located nearly two hours from their home. Each day, following his last class, he would drive the two hours to share dinner with his wife. After some time with her, he drove the two hours back home to teach the next day.

Four hours of drive time each day eventually caught up with the professor. The emotional and physical toll was unmistakable as he realized that such drive time each day was not sustainable. Only one option presented itself—one option as the professor saw it. He would resign his teaching position at the college, sell his home, and move closer to his wife. When this decision was shared with the administration of the college and his students, they urged him to reconsider. With love and compassion, the administration and students told the professor that his wife no longer knew who he was and that she has now forgotten him. Perhaps make the drive less often—maybe on the weekends. Stay, they all asked. Stay with us.

With equal love and compassion, the professor refused. "Yes, my wife no longer knows who I am. She has forgotten everything. But I know who I am. I am her husband. Thirty-five years ago I made a promise to her. I intend to keep that promise." That day the professor did more than demonstrate the worth of a promise made and a promise kept. Most powerfully, the professor taught his greatest lesson of all—that a loss of memory does not make any of us less a person. As long as his wife had breath, she was a person of value, a person to be cherished. Those who can no longer remember our names or stories shared in the journey of life continue to hold a special place in our hearts and mind.

Isaiah asks, "Can a woman forget her nursing child, fail to pity the child of her womb?" Tragically, answers Isaiah, "Yes, sometimes yes." Yet, Isaiah quickly moves the conversation forward and adds these words, "Even these may forget, but I won't forget you." Isaiah announces to us that, in the end, what ensures our worth—our value—is not what we can remember or fail to remember. What ensures our personhood is that God remembers us. Often our memories are so much a part of who we are that we cannot imagine an identity without them. What the professor teaches us—and Isaiah affirms—is that we are more than our memories. When our memories fail us they are held on our behalf by those who love us.

Thank you, God, that you don't forget me, even though I may forget you. Amen.

121

A Very Strange Town (Nathanael Hood)

> *"So then, if anyone is in Christ, that person is part of the new creation. The old things have gone away, and look, new things have arrived! All of these new things are from God, who reconciled us to himself through Christ and who gave us the ministry of reconciliation."*
>
> 2 Corinthians 5:17, 18

EARLIER THIS MONTH I spent a few days vacationing in St. Augustine with my family. This may seem an odd choice for a vacation, but the older I get the more I feel myself drawn toward ancient things. It doesn't get more ancient—at least in North America—than St. Augustine. Founded in the sixteenth century by the Spanish, it's the oldest continuously-inhabited European city in America. Walking its streets was like traveling backward and forwards in time through different eras and cultures. Of all its magnificent sites and attractions, none captivated me quite like the Plaza de la Constitución. When it was first built as the town center by the Spanish, royal decrees mandated that it be the literal center of the community's religious, government, and commercial functions. As such, it's bordered by the stately Governor's House, the nearly two-hundred-year-old Trinity Episcopal Church, and the breathtaking Cathedral Basilica of St. Augustine, home to the oldest Christian congregation in the contiguous United States. And then, in the center of the plaza, there's a small open-air pavilion. It's easy to miss, particularly in the shadow of the churches. But none should. For this is the old slave market.

The city and people of St. Augustine don't like to talk about the slave market. In a place where every other manhole cover seems to have a historical marker, it's conspicuously missing one. None of the travel brochures we read mentioned it, and neither did any of our tour guides. It is, perhaps understandably, absent from the city's official tourism website. Of all the historical sites we visited there, it was the only one I didn't walk through. I was afraid it would scorch my feet. I remember not feeling sadness at the sight of it, but anger. Not just the righteous anger one would expect at such a site, but indignant anger towards the two churches—one Catholic, one Protestant—who for centuries looked upon it without blinking. I was reminded of the story of Saint Telemachus, a fourth-century monk who was martyred after literally throwing himself between two gladiators in a Roman amphitheater to stop their fighting. Every day the members of those churches didn't do likewise and throw themselves at the slave market to destroy it, they failed in their sacred duties as Christians.

It makes one wonder how they as churches—and we as a larger nation of Americans—are supposed to move forward with the egalitarian promises and demands of our Christian faith after so many years of racial injustice and with so much left to be done. The Apostle Paul was likewise confronted with a congregation with generations of violent racial baggage in his Second Epistle to the Corinthians. Corinth was a Greek city that over a century earlier had been sacked, destroyed, and rebuilt by the Romans. In the time of Paul, its fledgling Christian community would've contained Roman colonizers, Greek descendants of the conquest, and local Jews who had likewise been subjugated by Rome. Crucially, Paul doesn't ignore the strife. Instead, he labels them "old things" that have been replaced by "new things" as part of God's "ministry of reconciliation." What was this reconciliation? We're not sure. Frustratingly, the biblical narrative of the Corinthian church ends with this epistle.

But St. Augustine's narrative—indeed, our country's narrative—continues. I have no doubt that in the years since the end of slavery both the Basilica and Trinity Episcopal have confessed and repented of their church's inactivity while the market was active. But that reconciliation takes more than just forgiveness, it takes rebirth. I mentioned earlier that there is no historical marker for the slave market in the Plaza. But there is one celebrating a very different moment in the city's history: the St. Augustine movement in the 1960s when Christian Civil Rights leaders like Martin Luther King Jr. marched and fought there for their people's freedom. King and his fellow "Foot Soldiers"—some black, some white—re-sanctified that Plaza with blood and bravery, and it was more powerful a witness of God's ministry of reconciliation in this world than any church apology ever could be. So must we all struggle, together as one, towards God's final reconciliation.

Gracious Jesus, help us to never lose sight of our duty as Christians to fight for justice for all peoples in all places at all times. Guide us in this work of reconciliation. Amen.

122

A Prescription for Living

"Love is patient, love is kind, it isn't jealous, it doesn't brag, it isn't arrogant, it isn't rude, it doesn't seek its own advantage, it isn't irritable, it doesn't keep a record of complaints, it isn't happy with injustice, but is happy with the truth."

1 Corinthians 13:4–6

EARL NIGHTINGALE SHARES SOME wisdom for living he learned from Dr. Frederick Loomis who published an essay in 1949, "The Best Medicine."[1] Dr. Loomis wrote, "It's but little good you'll do, watering last year's crops. Yet that is exactly what I have seen hundreds of my patients doing in the past twenty-five years—watering with freely flowing tears things of the irrevocable past. Not the bittersweet memories of loved ones, which I could understand, but things done which should not have been done, and things left undone which should have been done." Dr. Loomis went on to write that one cannot live adequately in the present, nor effectively face the future, when one's thoughts are buried in the past. What must be done, insists Dr. Loomis, is to stop thinking about yourself—and how you have been hurt—and start thinking about other people.

This is precisely the teaching of the apostle Paul in these words he shares with the Christian community in Corinth, "(love) doesn't keep a

---

1. Nightingale, *Insight: A Time-Saving Source*, 5.

record of complaints." We habitually think of love as a feeling or as an emotion. Yet, Paul shows no indication in 1 Corinthians 13 that love is to be understood in this fashion. For Paul, love is cognitive; it is a decision that produces behavior. Love—indeed the love demonstrated by Christ—always moves toward other people positively, seeking their welfare. Such love takes no notice of wrongs received by another. Rather, love sees the possibilities of changing people and moving all humanity toward the Kingdom that Christ embodied in himself.

Dr. Loomis writes that by the simple device of doing an outward, unselfish act today, each person can make the past recede; "The present and future will again take on their true challenge and perspective." He concludes his essay by noting that, as a doctor, he has seen this approach being far more effective in changing lives than any prescription he could have ordered from the drugstore. As Earl Nightingale observes, those were the last words written by Dr. Loomis but they have kept him alive in the minds and actions of thousands, perhaps millions, of people who have chosen to test for themselves their practical value.

We all know people who nurse an injury, a slight or unkindness, perceived or real, they have received from another. Or, perhaps, they have suffered a tragedy in the past and simply cannot move past the hurt. They mull the memory over and over, keeping it fresh. What is done is done, and there is no remedy; no returning to the past to undo what was unpleasant. It is here that Dr. Loomis is very wise. The past cannot be changed but the present can. The course that is available, if one chooses, is to cease thinking about oneself and start thinking about others. Indeed, if we wish to destroy the envy, the anger, and the evil that lurks in the world—and in our hearts—we refuse to react emotionally to the slights or harm done to us by others and respond with love. It is a prescription for living that we learn at the foot of the cross.

Turn my eyes from my own past to opportunities to be of service to others today. Amen.

123

Happy People

"'Happy are people who are hopeless, because the kingdom of heaven is theirs.'"

MATTHEW 5:3

CROWDS AGAIN GATHERED NEAR Jesus. Wherever Jesus seemed to travel, word would quickly move among the community and people would drop whatever activity that engaged them to listen for a word from Jesus—any word. Such was the power of the spoken word that fell from the lips of Jesus. That day was no different than today. As the old maxim goes, "Time is money." If people stopped whatever they were doing to hear a word from Jesus, there was perceived value in that word. The value was simply that Jesus addressed life—life, as we have to live it. Jesus' words were never dissociated from life. They were deliberate, vital, and life-giving. Jesus never spoke to simply capture an ear. Jesus came to solve problems with living.

On this particular day, the first word spoken by Jesus was, "Happy." It is not possible to overestimate the significance of that beginning. This was not a chance word—a word chosen at random. Jesus could not begin his sermon that day with any other word. It was an inevitable word. The whole point of God coming to God's people in flesh and blood, to live life as we lived life, was to experience life as we experienced life. Life is difficult. Daily, the determination to be happy, to experience life as God intends, meets with disappointment, inequity, and struggle. Our experience is Jesus' experience.

In the final analysis, Jesus sought to lessen the struggle. So, Jesus chooses this day to offer practical guidance for a happy life.

It is a welcomed word. The world is captive to an instinctive desire for happiness. Many may struggle for happiness day following day on what seems an endless journey. We might imagine that to be the story for many who gathered that day to listen to Jesus. Yet, the desire remains undiminished. However painful life may become, people cling to the hope—the possibility—that happiness might be claimed. Each of us believes in it, we seek it, the thought of happiness possessing us, demanding to be possessed. It is as though the great verdict of the world is that God intends that we are happy and Jesus has come to do what is necessary to deliver on God's intention.

As the people listened that day to Jesus, they heard God's manifesto—they heard God's singular concern for the well-being of all people. This would be the driving purpose, the driving force at the center of Jesus' ministry. The absence of happiness was the cause of the world's misery. The broken, the listless, and the weary gathered at the foot of a mountain that day to be encouraged that hope remained in their grasp. Lives scorched by sin; lives on the cusp of despair nevertheless hoped against hope that there might be another day with beauty available to them. Matthew tells us that such a number gathered that they were a crowd. Looking at them, Jesus sat down and taught them. He began with one word, "Happy."

Thank you, O God, for your concern for me. Encourage me with Christ's words when I grow discouraged. Remind me that your desire for me is that I know happiness. Amen.

124

Don't Complain

"The whole Israelite community complained against Moses and Aaron in the desert. 'Who are we? Your complaints aren't against us but against the Lord.'"

Exodus 16:2, 8b

Lowell Russell, formerly Executive Secretary and Director of the National Presbyterian Church and Center, Washington, D.C., once shared a lesson he learned from an attorney—a series of propositions that the attorney had written down on paper and kept with him at all times. There were three: "Never tell anyone how much you have to do. Never speak of your problems, your difficulties. Never talk about your disappointments." In other words, he was saying to himself, "Don't complain!"[1]

My friend and mentor, Arthur Caliandro, who followed Norman Vincent Peale as the senior pastor of Marble Collegiate Church in New York City, once shared with me his conviction that every pastor would be wise to preach on forgiveness at least three times a year. Caliandro believed that the single greatest obstacle to obtaining full Christian maturity was our difficulty with forgiveness. Any failure to forgive results in a weight that must be carried—by both the injured and the one who caused the injury. For Caliandro, the greatest burden was carried by the one who failed to forgive. Over time, the accumulation of "transgressions" that remain unforgiven

---

1. Russell, *Best Sermons*, 79.

results in stagnation of our spiritual growth. Christian growth isn't possible without the extravagant practice of forgiveness as Christ forgives us.

Perhaps my friend is correct. Yet, I contend that another hindrance to our growth as Christians is our propensity to complain. Here, in the Book of Exodus, the whole Israelite community complained against Moses and Aaron in the desert. Food was scarce, the days in the desert were hot and the journey through the desert seemed as though it would never end. Life back in Egypt as slaves seemed to present a better quality of life than a trek through the desert! So, the whole Israelite community complained.

Moses and Aaron's response seems to suggest the uselessness of negative thinking and speaking. Yes, the days in the desert were difficult. Discouragement is to be expected. But time and energy "moaning and groaning" provided no relief. So Moses and Aaron deflected the complaints; redirected the complaints made against them to God. It was the exercise of extraordinary leadership. That is because it forced upon the Israelite people the absolute necessity to pay attention to God, to "make their complaint" before God, and then "to listen" for how God would respond. It is then that Moses and Aaron fulfilled their primary call to spiritual leadership—beginning the conversation between God's people and God. That is where spiritual growth occurs.

Thank you, O Lord, for your abiding presence in my life. Strengthen and support me in those moments I become discouraged and the way becomes difficult. Amen.

125

The Deepest Form of Prayer

"Come to me, all you who are struggling hard and carrying heavy loads, and I will give you rest. Put on my yoke, and learn from me. I'm gentle and humble. And you will find rest for yourselves."

MATTHEW 11:28, 29

IN THE DEEPEST DISQUIET of the day I am reminded of Ernest Hemingway's words in *The Old Man And The Sea*, "'But man is not made for defeat,' he said. 'A man can be destroyed but not defeated.'"[1] We live in an anxious time. Trouble and tumultuous trials capture the larger narrative of the present day. Jesus is correct that there seems to always be present some war or rumor of war—both wars of combat and wars of poverty, illness, disillusionment, and failure. A thousand-antagonist line-up to squash any optimism we once may have had about life. As I have written elsewhere, we may profess faith but that faith is hesitant, uncertain, and unsatisfactory. If Hemingway is correct, if men and women are not made for defeat, then some resource must be available to combat the destructive forces that rage all around us—something more sound and sturdy than the temporary escape various addictions provide.

The Russian novelist, Fyodor Dostoyevsky captures the psychological and spiritual impact such anxiety, despair, and disillusionment can imprint

---

1. Hemingway, *The Old Man*, 96.

upon our consciousness in his short story, *The Dream of a Ridiculous Man*.[2] The protagonist despairs of life, fails to find any meaning in life, and is convinced nothing in the whole world made any difference. One evening, a little girl desperate for help suddenly grasps him by the elbow. But he did not help her. On the contrary, something made him drive her away. If life is meaningless, if nothing really mattered anyway, then this little girl is nothing more than a distraction. Arriving at his small apartment he is resolved to take his own life. Before the decision is executed, he falls asleep. Through a startling and poignant dream, he is made to realize that as long as he is alive, life was not meaningless and that the world—in some way or other—now depended on him.

This invitation from Matthew's Gospel is set in a larger teaching where we learn that God has chosen to reveal the same truth to the world. Life is not without meaning and each one of us is called—in one way or another—to make a difference. When life's storms rage and swirl and we are disheartened and disillusioned Jesus offers himself—"come to me, all of you who are struggling hard and carrying heavy loads, and I will give you rest" (Matthew 11:28). Jesus becomes for each of us that inner resource that guarantees that we are not defeated. Here, Jesus is immensely practical, "Put on my yoke, and learn from me" (Matthew 29). In that culture, the yoke was a symbol of obedience to the wisdom of God. Similarly, Jesus' yoke is obedience to all Jesus teaches and Jesus' call to serve others, to recognize that the world is dependent upon us. To come to Jesus is to learn from Jesus and to join Jesus himself in serving the world in a manner that God's Kingdom flourishes.

Each one of us is under a divine compulsion. We must go out and try to take a world that is upside down and set it right. That requires that we lay down our arms of rebellion and turn from seeking our own desires and ambitions and begin to be concerned with God's own purposes in the world. It is accomplished by living in obedience to God's will. It is God who can accomplish the inexplicable. God can bring to pass in our turbulent, confused, and frantic day a peace that is transformative—a peace that recognizes beauty where once we only saw brokenness and hears the cry of a little girl and realize that we cannot drive her away. Does that mean a life now lived with ease? Not at all! But it does mean that in those moments when we grow weary from life's strains, moments when disillusionment seems as close as the next breath we take, we can find rest in prayerful communion with Jesus. This is the deepest form of prayer that the disciples knew.

In the uncertainties of life, O God, make me certain of your presence, care, and love. Amen.

---

2. Dostoyevsky, "The Dream of a Ridiculous Man," 214–322.

About the Authors

W. Douglas Hood, Jr. has been the Senior Pastor of the First Presbyterian Church of Delray Beach, Florida since 2012. He holds a Master of Divinity from Columbia Theological Seminary and a Doctor of Ministry from Fuller Theological Seminary. Doug was the 2015 Moderator of the Presbytery of Tropical Florida and was a commissioner to his denomination's General Assembly in 2014 and 2016. His sermons and articles have appeared in *Lectionary Homiletics, Preaching Great Texts, Biblical Preaching Journal,* and *Preaching Word & Witness*. Doug is married to Grace, has two children, Nathanael and Rachael, and resides in Boynton Beach, Florida.

Nathanael Cameron Hood is completing his Master of Divinity degree at Princeton Theological Seminary. He holds a Bachelor's degree from Ursinus College and a Master's degree from New York University—Tisch. His writings have appeared in Christianity Today and RogerEbert.com.

Bibliography

Bartlett, Gene E., "Some Things We Know Without Proof." In *The News in Religion and Other Sermons,* New York: Abingdon-Cokesbury, 1947.
Bouknight, William R., *The Authoritative Word: Preaching Truth In A Skeptical Age,* Nashville: Abingdon, 2001.
Brooks, Phillips, *Twenty Sermons,* New York: E.P. Dutton, 1890.
Brueggemann, Walter, *Isaiah 40–66,* Louisville: Westminster John Knox, 1988.
Brueggemann, Walter, and William H. Bellinger, Jr., *Psalms: New Cambridge Bible Commentary,* New York: Cambridge University Press, 2018.
Cobb, James G., "Real Love, Real People . . . What an Idea!" In *Preaching 1 Corinthians 13.* St. Louis: Chalice, 2001.
Coffin, Henry Sloane, *Joy in Believing,* New York: Charles Scribner's Sons, 1956.
Cribb, Betsy, "Vintage Sand Pails: The throwback beach toys carry summertime nostalgia in spades." *Coastal Living,* July/August, 2017.
De Pree, Max, *Leadership Is an Art,* New York: Crown Business, 2004.
Dostoyevsky, Fyodor, *The Best Short Stories of Fyodor Dostoyevsky,* London: Folio Society, 2021.
Durant, Will, "Fosdick Calls Wise 'Best Christian.'" *New York Times* (February 4, 1925). https://www.nytimes.com/1925/02/04/archives/fosdick-calls-wise-best-christian-the-rabbi-in-turn-describes.html.
Emerson, Ralph Waldo, *The Complete Works of Ralph Waldo Emerson: Society and Solitude, Twelve Chapters,* Boston: Houghton, Mifflin & Co., 1904.
———. *Emerson: Essays and Lectures,* New York: Literary Classics of the United States, Inc., 1983.
Fischetti, Mark, "Fact or Fiction?: Feed a Cold, Starve a Fever, *Scientific American* (January 3, 2014). https://www.scientificamerican.com/article/fact-or-fiction-feed-a-cold.
Fosdick, Harry Emerson, *The Hope of the World,* New York: Harper & Brothers, 1933.
———. *The Power to See It Through: Sermons on Christianity Today,* New York: Harper & Brothers, 1935.
———. *Riverside Sermons,* New York: Harper & Brothers, 1958.
———. *What is Vital in Religion: Sermons on Contemporary Christian Problems,* New York: Harper & Brothers, 1955.
Foster, Richard J., *Freedom of Simplicity,* New York: Harper Collins, 1981.
Frank, Madeline, "Persistence Is the Key," (August 23, 2021). https://ezinearticles.com/?Persistence-Is-the-Key&id=10503510.
Fretheim, Terence E., *First and Second Kings,* Louisville: Westminster John Knox, 1999.

Gambuto, Julio Vincent, "Prepare For The Ultimate Gaslighting," *Cognocenti*, (April 14, 2020), https://www.wbur.org/cognoscenti/2020/04/14/gaslighting-coronavirus-julio-vincent-gambuto.

Goodwin, Doris Kearns, *Leadership in Turbulent Times*. New York: Simon & Schuster, 2018.

Hemingway, Ernest, *A Farewell to Arms*. London: Folio Society, 2015.

———. *The Old Man and the Sea*, Norwalk: Easton, 1952.

———. *The Sun Also Rises*, New York: Scribner Classics, 1954.

Jowett, J.H., *Thirsting for the Springs: Twenty-Six Weeknight Meditations*, London: H.R. Allension, Limited, 1907.

Lamont, Anne, *Small Victories: Spotting Improbable Moments of Grace*, New York: Riverhead, 2014.

Long, Thomas G., *Belief: A Theological Commentary of the Bible, 1 & 2 Timothy and Titus*, Louisville: Westminster John Knox, 2016.

———. *Matthew*, Louisville: Westminster John Knox, 1997.

McCracken, Robert J., "The Peril of Conformity," *Best Sermons: 1951–1952 Edition*, New York: McMillan Company, 1952.

Morin, Amy, *13 Things Mentally Strong People Don't Do*. New York: Harper-Collins, 2014.

Morris, Edmund, *The Rise of Theodore Roosevelt*, New York: Random House, 1979.

Nightingale, Earl, *Insight: A Time-Saving Source of New Ideas for Busy People*, Chicago: Nightingale-Conant Corporation, 1988.

———. *Your Success Starts Here: Purpose and Personal Initiative*, Shippensburg, Sound Wisdom, 2019.

———. *Transformational Living: Positivity, Mindset, and Persistence*, Shippensburg, Sound Wisdom, 2019.

Pascal, Blaise, *Pensees*, London: Folio Society, MMXI.

Redding, David A., *The Miracles of Christ*, Westwood: Revell, 1964.

Rosa, Nelly, "I Want My Legacy to Live On," *Caribbean Beat*, January/February, 2020.

Russell, Lowell, *Best Sermons, Volume X*, New York: Trident, 1968.

Sekula, Sarah, "Mr. Sandman: This is his livelihood," *Islands*, May, 2015.

Stewart, James S., *The Wind of the Spirit*, Nashville: Abingdon, 1968.

Taylor, Barbara Brown, *The Preaching of Life*, London: Cowley, 1993.

Thoreau, Henry David, *Walden*, Norwalk: Easton, 1981.

Walls, Laura Dassow, *Henry David Thoreau: A Life*, Chicago: University of Chicago Press, 2017.

Williams, Clayton E., "Living Today Forever," *Best Sermons: 1955 Edition*, New York: McGraw-Hill, 1955.

Wright, Tom, *Matthew for Everyone: Part One*, Louisville: John Knox, 2004.

Young, Nic, "Secrets of Noah's Ark," *Nova 42*, no. 15, Arlington: Public Broadcasting Service, October 7, 2015.

www.ingramcontent.com/pod-product-compliance
Lightning Source LLC
Chambersburg PA
CBHW050840230426
43667CB00012B/2083